Freddie Williams
Double World Speedway Champion

Peter Lush

**"Hide not your talents. They for use were made.
What's a sundial in the shade?"
Benjamin Franklin**

Freddie and Pat's philosophy of life. It was on display in their
kitchen at home, and is on Freddie's gravestone.

London League Publications Ltd

Freddie Williams
Double World Speedway Champion
© Peter Lush.
Foreword © John Chaplin.

The moral right of Peter Lush to be identified as the author has been asserted.

Front & back cover design @ Stephen McCarthy.

A CIP catalogue record for this book is available from the British Library.

Published in March 2019 by London League Publications Ltd, PO Box 65784, London NW2 9NS

ISBN: 978-1-909885-21-9

Cover design by Stephen McCarthy Graphic Design
46, Clarence Road, London N15 5BB

Editing and layout by Peter Lush

Printed and bound in Great Britain by Ashford Colour Press Ltd, Gosport, Hants PO13 0FW

Foreword

Anyone will tell you Freddie Williams was the quintessential Mr Nice Guy of speedway – though he did have his on-track mean streak, as every man who ever reached the summit of the sport did. And that's why I called him 'The Jekyll and Hyde' World Champion. Freddie, who reached that summit not once but twice, died on 20 January 2013, after suffering a stroke.

Freddie was unique, of course. Not only was he the only Welshman to win the world title, he was the first British rider to become a double World Champion, something that was not beaten until Tai Woffinden's third title win in 2018.

I wrote his obituary for the *Speedway Star*, and it was the saddest and most emotional obituary I have ever had to write. Because Freddie Williams was a friend. He was also a warm, modest, fun-loving gentleman – in the finest sense of the word – off the track, with a perpetual twinkle in his eye. He rode for the most famous team in the world, Wembley – and only for Wembley – for 10 years, and in all that time, he confessed, he found it irksome to sign autographs for fans, bow to the inevitable demands of the media and accept all the other trappings of fame.

He spent the rest of his life trying to pay back to the sport what he came to realise had been an attitude he very much regretted. He said many times: "I went about things the wrong way. I know that now as I have got older." He had considered all that celebrity, and the hero worship that went with it, something of a nuisance. He always insisted: "I never understood why people would think me marvellous. I never considered myself a great World Champion. A fortunate one, yes. There were better riders than me in those World Finals that I won."

Be that as it may, Freddie Williams went about ascending to the top of the speedway world in as dedicated, determined, meticulous and comprehensively prepared a way as any World Champion, either before or since his two successes in 1950 and 1953. But in the rough, tough, relentlessly demanding – often cruel – speedway world, you don't win two World Championships unless you also have a high degree of motorcycling talent. And Freddie certainly had that. He also possessed the required amount of ruthlessness on a bike. "You had to be ruthless to be a winner", he said.

After becoming established in the Wembley team in 1948, Freddie volunteered with Howdy Byford, Cyril Roger and Dent Oliver to tour Australia with Jack Parker's England team in the winter of 1949–50. "I grew up a lot on that tour", he said, "Parker taught us a lot about life." That he also learned a lot about speedway on that tour there is no doubt. He came back to England and Wembley and won the World Championship. It had been a mere four year apprenticeship.

I first met Freddie, and experienced his modesty, unselfishness and desire to put something back into the sport, at a special *Speedway Star* magazine fan-festival weekend. It was an all-star question-and-answer session and a full house turned up to see the line-up of former World Champion Tommy Price, Birmingham captain Phil 'Tiger' Hart, Belle Vue and England captain Jack Parker and Freddie. He had driven a considerable distance early on a Sunday morning, and would not even accept a breakfast, let alone any travelling expenses.

More than half a century after hanging up his leathers, Freddie was always available to do his PR thing for the sport. I never knew him to turn down a request to do a personal appearance to further the cause of speedway racing.

The last time I saw him was on the Grand Prix day in 2012 in Cardiff. He had come to support me at a book signing session in the town. He stayed for two hours and then, with a protective arm around his wife Pat, they disappeared unrecognised into the crowds. That night he presented the winner's trophy in the Millennium Stadium to Chris Holder, who went on to win the World title that year. I had urged the Grand Prix organisers to involve Freddie in the event, and many members of his extended family were there to see him do the presentation.

It saddens me greatly that, though other speedway personalities with a far lesser pedigree than Freddie have MBE and more attached to their names, I was unable to get his name onto a Royal Honours list despite having the backing of Freddie's home town MP, Lords Coe and Montagu and even a direct appeal to the Prince of Wales himself.

Freddie had received recognition in Wales when he was inducted into the Welsh Sports Hall of Fame. Geoff Bray, the then Hall of Fame Secretary, supported the honours nomination. I had told Freddie what I was doing, and he said: "Oh, I don't know, there are people who deserve an honour more than me." I replied that "even the lollipop ladies helping children across the road receive an honour – you really deserve one." But it was not to be. Freddie died before I could organise a further nomination.

I'm fairly sure that Freddie, a humble World Champion, would have considered doing the presentation at the Speedway Grand Prix in 2012 enough of an honour.

John Chaplin

John Chaplin, a career Fleet Street journalist, is generally acknowledged throughout the speedway world to be the leading authority on the history of the sport. An author and broadcaster, his pedigree goes back 60 years to when he first saw speedway racing at Perry Barr, Birmingham in 1946 and he claims to be a lifelong Birmingham fan. He founded and edited his own hugely successful *Vintage Speedway Magazine* and is a regular contributor to *Speedway Star* magazine and *Classic Speedway*.

John's previous publications include: *Wings and Space: A History of Aviation, Speedway: The Story of the World Championship, John Chaplin's Speedway Special: The Classic Legends, Ove Fundin – Speedway Superstar, Tom Farndon: The Greatest Speedway Rider of Them All* (with Norman Jacobs), *Ivan Mauger: The Man Behind the Myth, Speedway Superheroes* (with John Somerville), *Speedway: The Greatest Moments* (with John Somerville), *Main Dane: My Story* by Hans Neilsen (Edit, production, design), *History of the Speedway Hoskins* by Ian Hoskins (Edit, production, design), *A Fistful of Twistgrip* and *Speedway Legends* (with John Somerville).

Introduction

I never met Freddie Williams. I first watched speedway at Wembley in the early summer of 1970. I had never heard of the sport before a friend took me there on a Saturday night. I was a football fan, and watched cricket in the summer. But I soon became a 'regular' at the speedway meetings, and a Wembley Lions supporter, which I still am! I remember Freddie being the team manager, but unlike football, where the manager is very often the spokesman for the team and their club, in speedway that role is usually fulfilled by the promoter, in this case Freddie's long-time friend Trevor Redmond.

The idea for this book came after I had completed our book on the Wembley Lions. Through that book I met Bert Harkins, the 1970 to 1971 Wembley Lions captain, and ended up publishing his autobiography as well. Bert had put me in touch with Freddie's daughter Jayne. I sent her a copy of the Wembley book and she ordered another six! In the spring of 2017 I went to meet her to discuss doing this book. She was enthusiastic, and I started work.

Some people say that a biographer should not meet the subject of their work. I disagree. To be able to sit down with someone, usually after they have retired from the sport where they made their name, and reflect on their career, is a privilege and – to me – the ultimate primary source. Yes, you have to check everything they say, stories change over time and memories fade, but it is still their memories, opinions and views that you are being given.

With the passing of time – Freddie retired from speedway over 60 years ago – there were very few of his teammates still around. It was a privilege to spend time with Ian and Jen Williams, although of course Freddie and Ian only rode together for a limited time in South Africa. But his memories were very valuable, as were his sister Kate's, who at the end of my interview simply said "He was our big brother."

It was also great to meet Brian Crutcher, another Wembley Lions legend, who could also give me his recollections of what life as a speedway rider was like in the early to mid-1950s.

However, some of the most interesting interviews were with Freddie and Pat's three children, the results of which can be found in Chapter 17, *A Sporting Family*. None of them had seen Freddie ride, because he retired four months before Jayne, the oldest, was born. But their memories of their parents were an important part of the book.

Bert and Edith Harkins also were very supportive; maybe not surprising given how they met. Edith suspects that Pat was doing a bit of 'matchmaking'. If she was it was very successful, because they have now been married for over 40 years.

The speedway part of this book was relatively straightforward to write. Although I would not describe myself as a real speedway historian compared to some other writers, my work on the Wembley Lions gave me a good background to do this book. I have tried to write a book about Freddie and his family, and to avoid repeating too much from the Wembley Lions book. To find out about the Lions' magnificent achievements, that book is still in print! Similarly for Eric and Ian, I have concentrated on their achievements, not their teams.

Maybe from a general sports history viewpoint, the most interesting part of this book is Freddie and Pat's sporting legacy, which was more complicated to write, as I have little knowledge of the sports involved. It is not unusual for children to follow their parents into the same sport. Sons and daughters follow in their parents' footsteps. When I started watching speedway, John Louis was becoming a star at Ipswich. After Wembley closed, I became an Ipswich supporter. John's son Chris followed his father into the sport, and following his retirement as a rider became the promoter at Foxhall Heath.

But what is unusual about the Williams family, if not unique, is the different sports that Freddie and Pat's children excelled at, which has continued to the next generation. Two international equestrians, two professional golfers, an ice skater and now a young footballer. One of them, half-jokingly, said to me 'Its in the genes'. Other family sayings – 'In it to win it' and 'Second is the first loser' were also put forward. When we first met, Jayne told me that Freddie 'enjoyed winning' rather than enjoyed riding. Sarah told me about the quotation from Benjamin Franklin which is on the title page of this book, and how it reflected her parents' approach to sport and clearly influenced their family.

Freddie Williams senior comes across as a determined, austere man. He clearly had a major influence on Freddie and Eric, whose determination to succeed he encouraged. Ian comes across as more laid-back, although it should not be forgotten that he had a very successful speedway career in his own right. Pat also showed determination to succeed in her sport; the anti-social hours required for ice skating training, of being at a rink in the early morning before it opened to the public, and moving to London to have a better chance of succeeding in her sport are both testimony to that.

But to me, Freddie was a different character from his father. He achieved great popularity in speedway, as John Chaplin outlines in his foreword to this book. His family remember many people turning up at Freddie's funeral who they did not know. It was past teammates and opponents who came to pay a tribute to a former World Champion who they liked and respected. In a sport as combative as speedway, that is not always the case.

His passing also saw the publication of obituaries in many different newspapers, including some which rarely cover speedway, as well as in motorcycling and motorsport magazines.

What also comes across is how important their family was to Freddie and Pat. The support given to their children and grandchildren, of not just turning up to watch, but very practical – for example – Freddie getting an HGV licence so he could drive the horsebox to shows or Pat going out early with Joanna when she was training as a skater.

Finally, thank you to everyone who helped with this book. Any mistakes are my responsibility. Meanwhile, just enjoy finding out about the first British speedway rider to become World Champion twice, a record that was not beaten until 2018, when Tai Woffinden won his third Speedway Grand Prix series.

Peter Lush
January 2019

Thank You

Thanks to various members of the Williams family, including Linda and Mandy in New Zealand; Bert and Edith Harkins; Brian Crutcher; Matt Jackson for statistical records; John Somerville for providing photos; John Chaplin for writing the foreword and his advice and support; Hayley Redmond; Peri Horne; Steve Hone; Trevor Meeks; Steve McCarthy for designing the cover, the staff at Ashford Colour Press for printing the book and the staff at the British Library and the Brent archives at Willesden Library for their help with supplying materials for the research.

The Speedway press: To save space and to make the text easier to read, the *Speedway News* is referred to as the *News*, the *Speedway Gazette* as the *Gazette,* the *Speedway Star* (or *Star & News*) as the *Star* and the *Speedway World* as the *World*.

Tributes to Freddie Williams

Freddie's funeral was at St Gregory's Church in Welford in Berkshire on 30 January 2013, 10 days after he died. It was very much a speedway occasion, and a celebration of Freddie's life and achievements. Freddie's coffin was brought into the Church to the sound of *Entry of the Gladiators*, the Wembley Lions anthem. On his coffin was a Number 1 Wembley Lions body colour, loaned for the occasion by Bert Harkins. Bert also gave the eulogy, and all Freddie's children and adult grandchildren read tributes. His granddaughter Harriet sang the Welsh hymn *There is a Green Hill*. At the end of the service, the coffin was carried out of the Church to the sound of the *Pathe News* audio commentary of Freddie's 1950 World Championship victory. Outside the church, a Rotrax JAP speedway bike, also with a Wembley body colour, was on display.

Over 150 mourners attended the service. Obituaries appeared in many different publications. Tributes were made to Freddie from people throughout the sport. Bert Harkins said in the *Speedway Star* that "Speedway lost one of its true legends ... and his wife Pat and family lost a truly wonderful father, grandfather, mentor and husband." Bert said that he had a friendship with Freddie "that lasted many years". He also spoke about Freddie's support for the WSRA and said that he was "a true gentleman."

Classic Speedway had featured the last interview that Freddie did in edition 19. In the following edition, the magazine included several tributes to him. Ove Fundin recalled how when he first met Freddie, he was a "big star" while Ove was a young foreign rider, and said how kind Freddie was to him. He outlined "For over 25 years, my wife Iona and I always sat at the same table at the WSRA dinner as Freddie and Pat;" and how the couples had swapped houses for a holiday, and how Freddie had "filled the fridge with my favourite ice cream."

Another Swedish star, Olly Nygren spoke of how he felt "very sad" when he heard the news that Freddie had passed away. He recalled how they raced against each other, and rode together in South Africa in 1954–55. He said that he had invited Freddie to his 75th birthday party and that "I could listen to him for hours." And, of course, he mentioned his part in Freddie's 1953 Championship win, when he "fixed Split" in the crucial race.

Barry Briggs said that Freddie was a "clever tough rider". He said that Freddie "remained competitive" even after he stopped racing, always "had his kids' sporting interest at heart" and that Freddie wanted David to have the best golf clubs and Joanna the best skates.

Brian Crutcher remembered how he had met Freddie at Wembley in 1953, when he joined the Lions, and going with him and Pat to South Africa the same year along with Trevor Redmond. He said that Freddie "always came down to Bournemouth for the veterans' dinners, where he'd meet another good friend of his, Ken Middleditch."

Reg Fearman said that they had been "pals for many years since we rode speedway", while Danny Dunton said that Freddie was "a very good sportsman, a hard but fair rider, and a really good team member." He regretted that Freddie rode for Wembley and not his Harringay team. From Swindon, both Alun Rossiter and Terry Russell said how they would miss Freddie, who attended their meetings with his brother Ian. Terry said how Freddie always thanked him for the hospitality he was shown, and commented that "it is always a pleasure and an honour to have people like Freddie coming along."

Finally, *Classic Speedway* Editor Tony McDonald said how Freddie had sent him a hand-written note thanking him for the article Tony had written. Tony said he would "treasure the note forever".

About the author

Peter Lush grew up in London, where he still lives, a bus ride from Wembley Stadium. When the Wembley Lions closed in 1971, not wanting to support one of their London rivals, he became an Ipswich Witches fan. He watched them on-and-off until he drifted away from the sport in the mid-1980s. He rediscovered speedway about 20 years later and started watching again on television. He finally decided to go to a live meeting at Rye House, only to find it was rained off when he got there. He now watches regularly on television, goes to the Cardiff Grand Prix each year and two or three other meetings. He has a great interest in the sport's history, and reads *Backtrack* and *Classic Speedway* regularly. He wrote, with John Chaplin, *When the Lions Roared – The story of the famous Wembley Speedway team*. He contributed to the *British Speedway Memories* book produced by Retro Speedway, writing mainly about how wonderful the Wembley Lions were.

He started watching rugby league at Fulham in October 1980 with Dave Farrar. In 1995, with Michael O'Hare, they wrote *Touch and Go – A history of professional rugby league in London*, and Peter and Dave set up London League Publications Ltd. The company has now published around 90 books, mainly on rugby league. Peter often has to work on book development and design, but has written or edited 12 books on rugby league and two cricket grounds guides. He was also joint editor of the national rugby league magazine *Our Game*, and has written for various magazines, journals and newspapers on the game and other sports. In real life he is the director of Training Link, a charity providing basic skills training to help people find work, in central London and co-ordinator of Kilburn Older Voices Exchange, an older people's community group in north west London.

About speedway

One of the interesting points about speedway is that it is both an individual and a team sport. In some sports, such as cricket or baseball, the individual records are very important, but they are achieved as part of a team. In speedway, there are individual events, such as the World Championship in Freddie's time and today the Speedway Grand Prix, and team competitions.

For almost all speedway meetings, the scoring is very simple – three points for a win, two for second, one for third, none for last. But in a team match, the two riders from each team are encouraged to ride together, to try to beat the two from the other team. To stop teammates racing against each other, and because riders are paid based on the points they score, in league and cup meetings, if two riders from the same team finish first and second or second and third, the one who follows his teammate home is given a bonus point. This counts toward their average and in their pay, but not the match score. There is no bonus point for a rider finishing last. In the text, the bonus points are shown (+1) after the rider's score.

The CMA (calculated match average) for a rider is based on four riders per meeting. A rider who averages two points a ride has a CMA of 8 (4 x 2). Not all the riders have the same number of rides in a match, and this provides a way of comparing their performances.

Contents

Wembley veterans: Bill Gilbert, Charlie May, Tommy Price, Freddie, Trevor Redmond, Brian Crutcher, Bill Kitchen; front: Jimmy Gooch, Roy Craighead and Den Cosby. (Courtesy John Sommerville)

Freddie and Max, Charlie and Harriet's son and his great grandson.
This photo was taken a few days before Freddie died. (Photo: Joanna Anthony)

1. Growing up in Port Talbot

Port Talbot lies roughly halfway between Cardiff and Swansea on the South Wales coast. It is famous for three things – steel, rugby union and – maybe surprisingly for what is a predominantly industrial working class town – actors. Apart from the three Williams brothers, it has no apparent connections with speedway.

Steel was established as the town's main industry in the 1830s. It was where Freddie's father spent much of his working life, as a skilled crane operator. It is still an important employer today.

Rugby union is the town's main sport. The current Aberavon Wizards have their roots in the tin workers in the town in the 1870s. The club was one of the great Welsh teams of the amateur era in rugby union. Since the game first introduced leagues in the 1990–91 season and then went 'open' in 1995 and allowed professionalism, it is not the force it was, and now plays in the second tier of the Welsh semi-professional game. Forty eight of its players have represented Wales, but the last one was in 1988. Some of its players in the amateur era switched to rugby league, and had successful careers in that code of rugby football.

Richard Burton CBE, who was at school with Freddie, Sir Anthony Hopkins CBE and Michael Sheen OBE all went on from Port Talbot to have internationally recognised careers in the theatre and film. A new generation has come to the fore, with Rob Brydon one of the most prominent. Angela V. John in her book *The Actors' Crucible*, lists 50 actors from Port Talbot who found success on the stage or screen. She quotes a young actor, Matthew Aubrey, as saying "It's fascinating – for such a macho town, it's alright to be an actor."

Freddie was born on 12 March 1926. The 1920s and 1930s were often tough times in South Wales. In his history of Wales from 1880 to 1980, Kenneth O. Morgan says that "From the start of the 1920s and emphatically so after 1923, right down to the latter years of the 1930s ... Wales, especially the coalfield, was paralysed by a collapse in its industrial, manufacturing and commercial life. It experienced mass unemployment and poverty without parallel in the British Isles ... South Wales plunged unprepared into a depression and despair which crushed its society for almost 20 years." He continues: "South Wales suffered probably more acutely than any other industrial region from this prolonged stagnation of trade and industry. It had a uniquely high proportion of its working population engaged in extractive industry, mining, metal manufacture, quarrying and the like. It suffered from being an area of primary production rather than of manufacture of finished products."

The high levels of unemployment saw many people leave the region to find work in other parts of Great Britain. Freddie recalls his dad working in the parks at one time, and the family having a lodger in their already crowded house. When interviewed by Brian Burford, Ian remembers his father working as a steamroller driver. But the family's situation stabilised when Freddie senior got work at the steelworks. He had a skilled job as a charger crane driver, and worked in the steel industry until he retired.

Freddie senior married Hetty Griffiths, who came from a middle class family who owned shops in Port Talbot. The *Port Talbot Guardian*, in its coverage of Freddie's 1950 World Championship win, reported the Mayor as saying that the Williams family "had long been important members of the town. [Freddie's] maternal grandfather, the late Mr Owen Griffiths, had been a great musician. His paternal grandfather had come within winning distance of securing the Bisley rifle shooting championship." Ian recalls his paternal grandparents working at the 'big house' in Margam.

Councillor Richard Evans said that "What the late Mr Griffiths did in the world of music, the Williams boys have been doing for speedway." The newspaper reported that "Alderman Graham Griffiths said that the boys' father was also a keen sportsman, and was respected in the Ward on that account. 'I am sure that he has been taught all the tricks of speedway by his father, and that he will agree that many of the tricks of the trade have been taught him by Margam Mountain.'" He recalled seeing the Williams brothers and Freddie senior riding on the mountain side.

Freddie senior with Freddie (right) & Eric
(Courtesy Sarah Williams)

Freddie was the first of the Freddie senior and Hetty's four children. Eric and Ian both became speedway riders; Kate – who was taught by her father to ride a motorcycle – married and stayed in Port Talbot where she still lives. The family home was 180, Margam Road in the Margam area.

The school system in Wales when Freddie went to school was attending an infant school, Groes School in his case, then an elementary one, Eastern School. At the age of 11, students could do an exam, the scholarship – equivalent to the English 11 Plus – to go to Secondary School. Freddie did so, was successful and went to Port Talbot Secondary School, where one of his classmates was Richard Burton.

In a biography of Richard Burton, *And God Created Richard,* Tom Rubython writes: "The scholarship exam was the be-all and end-all of academic life at Eastern [Burton's Elementary school]. Being entered in it was itself an achievement, and passing it was exceptional. Passing the exam enabled pupils to attend the Welsh equivalent of an English grammar school – in Burton's case this was Port Talbot Secondary School. Securing a place was the modern-day equivalent of graduating on to university but, back then, it meant an even more certain future. These boys were guaranteed a position amongst Wales' elite, with the promise of a well-paid and reputable job when they finally left school." Burton took the Scholarship exam in March 1937 and went to Port Talbot Secondary School in the autumn of 1937. Freddie was a few months younger than Burton, but would have been in the same school year.

The school became Dyffryn Comprehensive. Freddie and Richard Burton were in class 5M. Freddie was interviewed by Mike Jones of the *Western Mail* on 25 June 2011 before being a guest of honour at the Speedway Grand Prix in Cardiff. Jones said that they were "linked by a powerful shared experience: a childhood in 1930s Depression South Wales".

Freddie said in the article: "We were competitive in whatever we did. That could have been rugby, riding motorcycles, acting, anything." There is a school photo of a rugby team with Burton and Freddie – aged 12 or 13. Freddie recalled about playing rugby union: "I was

2

such a little fellow in a team of really robust boys but I had a reputation for being fearless. It stood me in great stead. I worked out very quickly that, no matter how big a rugby player was, if he was tearing down the field at you and you tackled low he couldn't go anywhere without his legs. I could work out things like that and it's an ability I took onto the speedway track. It served me well over the years and I suppose I've got Port Talbot to thank for that." Mike Jones commented that both of them loved playing rugby at school and both went on to reach the pinnacle of their chosen fields. Rugby union was a tough sport then, and was important at school and in the community.

Freddie remembered them being in a school play together. Burton was King Arthur, Freddie was a 'soldier' and just had to say 'Qui va la' (who goes there). "They may only have been a few small words but, I tell you, I sweated so much over them," he said. He went on: "It's amazing to think that somebody who went on to such global fame was in the same class as me. Richard was quite obviously a different type of character to the rest of us; he was always a little aloof." He concluded: "It remains one of my claims to fame that I went to school with the great Richard Burton".

When Freddie finished school, the Second World War had started. He left school at the age of 14 and became an apprentice in the Naval Dockyards in Portsmouth in 1941.

Interviewed by Tony McDonald, he explained that: "When I was 16 we were members of the Air Training Corps (RAF cadets) and spent time at our local aerodrome. We had access and took flights in all sorts of planes, even though the war was on." It was his ambition to be a fighter pilot. However, his parents were against this idea. He recalled: "Mum had lost three brothers during the First World War, so she didn't want me to follow them into the Air Force. My Uncle Reg was a fighter pilot who was shot down and awarded the Military Cross for valour.'"

So he undertook a five year apprenticeship as an engineer fitter in the Naval dockyards. He also joined the Home Guard as a Despatch Rider, developing his love of motorcycles that had come from his father.

Ian says that Freddie senior had "one of first chain driven motorcycles around streets of Margam." There were motorcycle clubs in each town and he was a member of the Neath club, who organised scrambles and trials events.

During the War and after peace was declared in 1945, Freddie would return home at weekends to ride in grass track meetings. He would use the 1938 350cc AJS bike for the trip, and then, in Freddie senior's workshop, strip it down to make it suitable for grass track racing. At the end of the weekend, when Freddie had often been up against the more powerful 500cc JAP speedway bikes, they would reassemble the bike as a road machine and Freddie would return to Portsmouth.

Photo: Kate Drew (right) with her daughter Erica.
(Courtesy Sarah Williams)

Eric said that their house did not have electricity until after the War, and that the cooking and lighting were from gas. Freddie senior's workshop was a corrugated iron 'lean-to' at the back of the house. It had Freddie senior's father's former carpentry bench with a carpentry vice and some spanners. The lighting was by gas, fed through a rubber tube from the house supply. It was not very safe when mixed with petrol fumes. A torch was used to provide extra light for more intricate repairs.

Eric joined the Neath motorcycle club where his father and Freddie were members. He remembered a trip with Freddie in 1946 to watch the Manx Grand Prix races on the Isle of Man. Freddie senior gave them permission to go as long as they stayed with the other club members. However, there were only six other members on the trip. Eric recalls being embarrassed because their father had insisted that they wear "war-time anti-mustard gas balloon type garments over the top of our army surplus greatcoats, jodhpurs and knee boots." The other members had Barbour brand waterproof jackets. However, Eric did say that they did not wear the anti-mustard gas garments once the trip started. However, they put them back on when they reached the Brecon Beacons in pouring rain, and appreciated their father's foresight.

Meanwhile, Eric said that Freddie was "literally drooling" over a 1939 four-valve 500cc Rudge Ulster that one of the 'older' club members was riding. He asked for first refusal if the man ever wanted to sell it. Eric said that Freddie "wasn't short of money" as he won four or five weeks' wages through wins at grass track meetings, with Freddie senior tuning his bikes.

In the Brecon Beacons, the owner of the Rudge that Freddie had his eye on crashed as he slid on a bend. Freddie approached him and asked him if he found the bike too fast, and wanted to sell it. The Rudge owner had to go to hospital, where Freddie convinced him to sell the bike, by offering Eric's AJS in part-exchange. The owner of the Rudge was not so badly injured that he would take Freddie's bike, which had been ridden to and from Portsmouth many times.

By the time they reached Liverpool to get the ferry, Freddie and Eric were the only ones to complete the trip. Eric does not say why the others dropped out, but it had been very wet on the way to Liverpool, and maybe they did not have the waterproof gear that the Williams brothers used. They used a cabin that had been booked for the whole group in a holiday camp, and rode round the Island the next day. They survived the perilous roads that made up the course, and watched the racing. Eric recalls that they were overawed by road racing, and watching Eric Lyons on his Triumph Tiger 100 in the 500cc class. Then they returned home, thinking about how to explain to Freddie senior that they had continued the trip despite the lack of the older club members who were meant to look after them.

When they arrived back home, Freddie went to complete his deal to buy the 1939 Rudge Ulster. Eric remembers the bike being very noisy, which must have annoyed the neighbours. But he was also happy with the bike he got from the deal, which was more suitable for the trials riding he enjoyed.

Some speedway riders discovered the sport when they went to meetings as children. This was not the case for Freddie. Speedway has a limited tradition and history in Wales. From 1928 to 1930, there were both team and individual meetings in Cardiff. There was also a track at Pontypridd. In 1929, a Wales team beat the Wembley Lions at the Empire Stadium, and lost 40–23 to England at Wimbledon.

In 1935, there was a short season of meetings intended to pave the way for a league team in 1936. Cardiff joined the Provincial League, but the team did not attract enough support to last and withdrew from the league in June. A further meeting was held in 1937.

There is no record of Freddie ever having attended a meeting. There were other short-lived teams or venues that staged speedway in the sport's early days.

Speedway returned to Cardiff in 1951, but only completed two seasons in the league before withdrawing in 1953. Freddie did run winter training sessions in South Wales in the early 1950s, when he was not riding abroad. Subsequently, there have been teams in Neath in 1962, and Newport, who ran for 14 seasons from 1964 to 1977 at Newport County's Somerton Park football ground. A new promotion started in 1997 and continued until 2011 at the Hayley Stadium. There was also a team in Carmarthen from 2002 to 2004.

Apart from the Williams brothers, and the early pioneers such as Ivor Hill and 'Pip' Price, there have been very few Welsh speedway riders. Leo McCauliffe captained Wimbledon and reached the World Final in 1963, scoring seven points. In the 1940s and 1950s, Les and Ray Beaumont rode for Cradley Health, Tamworth and Leicester. In 1951, The Gazette mentioned Chris Boss (Bristol), Trevor Davies (Norwich), Jack Dawson (Halifax) and Harry Hughes (Cardiff) as possible members of a Welsh team along with the Williams brothers. In more recent times, Phil Morris had a successful career with various clubs, including the Newport Wasps, from 1991 until he retired in 2009. He is now the Race Director for the Speedway Grand Prix.

One event that does give speedway a high profile in Wales – albeit for a weekend – is the Speedway Grand Prix meeting at the Principality (formerly Millennium) Stadium in Cardiff. "Are you going to Cardiff this year?" is a common question among British speedway fans. The city centre is taken over by the speedway supporters, with people enjoying the fanzone and the city's attractions, pubs and restaurants. Between 40,000 and 45,000 attend each year. For some, it is their annual outing to the sport, and many tee-shirts and other regalia are seen from teams who have not raced for many years.

Freddie presented the prizes to the successful riders in 2012. Over the same weekend, his son David was the tournament director for the Johnnie Walker Golf Championship at Gleneagles, and the following day announced the winner at the end of play.

Freddie senior, Freddie and Ian at a grass track meeting.
(Courtesy Ian Williams)

Freddie riding at a grass track meeting. (Courtesy David Williams)

6

2. Starting out: 1946 to 1948

During the War years, speedway had survived through weekly meetings held at Belle Vue. After the end of the war in Europe in May 1945, some tracks resumed holding meetings. But there was to be no league competition until 1946.

There was a huge demand for entertainment at the end of the War. Huge crowds attended football and rugby league matches, and cricket in the summer. But in the evenings, apart from greyhound racing, speedway was one of the few sports that people could watch. The sport entered an enormous growth period that lasted until the early 1950s.

Speedway was reorganised into two divisions, both of six teams. The National League had five pre-war teams: Wembley, West Ham, Wimbledon, New Cross — all from London — and Belle Vue. They were joined by Odsal, based at the massive rugby league ground in Bradford. The Northern League was effectively the Second Division.

Each National League team could choose one 'grade one' rider from the pre-war riders available in 1946. Belle Vue had chosen Jack Parker, so the Lions chose Bill Kitchen, who had been a pre-war star with Belle Vue. Most teams chose six or seven pre-war riders. Wembley only chose three others apart from Kitchen — Tommy Price and George Wilks who had ridden for the team before the War, and Bob Wells. Arthur Elvin — soon to be knighted — decided on a different policy. He told his speedway manager, Alec Jackson, to find young British riders to fill the rest of the team places.

Wembley advertised for riders in a motorcycle magazine, inviting them to write for a trial to the Lions at Wembley Stadium. Freddie had never even watched speedway, but had considerable experience in grass track racing, and was offered a trial at Rye House. The Lions had hired the Hertfordshire track to stage the trials, and then train the best prospects.

In Alec Jackson, Wembley had the ideal man to build a team. He had pre-war experience as a rider and manager, and during the war had been a Major in the Army's Signals Corps. Many of the aspiring speedway riders were former Army dispatch riders, and Jackson knew the best of them. Some, like Split Waterman who came on the scene later in 1946, had ridden in the forces speedway meetings staged at army camps in Europe and other areas during the latter part of the war. In all, around 300 riders were given trials by Wembley at Rye House.

Freddie had been a dispatch rider with the Home Guard in Portsmouth and recalled when interviewed in 2012 that he had to borrow leathers the first time he rode at Rye House. Freddie also recalled that Rye House was "carnage" with horrific accidents by the young or inexperienced riders. Bill Kitchen was the main instructor at Rye House, and went on to become Freddie's mentor as he established himself with the Lions.

But Freddie's hopes of establishing himself in the rebuilt Wembley team suffered a major setback when he injured his ankle in a grass track meeting and missed the 1946 season. Eric explained how the accident happened. For grass track meetings, Freddie used a motorcycle they called 'The Rat', a 1938 AJS. Freddie had a grass track meeting near Southampton, so Eric and Freddie senior took the bike to Southampton, attaching it to the sidecar of Freddie senior's 500cc Matchless bike. Eric was surprised to be told by his dad that he was also going to have a go at grass track racing. The brothers would use the same bike, but only had one steel shoe between them. Freddie came back to the pits, and gave the steel shoe to Eric to use in the novices race. After the race, trying to hastily take the steel shoe off to give to Freddie, Eric broke the leather strap that held it in place. Freddie senior produced a piece of clothes line that he had used to tie the bike to the sidecar to use for the steel shoe. He tied it on, but did not have time to cut back the loose ends. They got pulled into the primary chain during the race, which pulled Freddie's foot into the sprocket. Freddie's ankle was a mess, and Eric rode the Matchless bike to the hospital, following the ambulance. Freddie and his dad did not blame Eric for the accident, but Eric was, understandably, very upset by it.

The Lions must have seen his potential, and said that they wanted him back when he recovered from his injury. He was in hospital in Southampton, and had severed tendons. His career may never have taken off had it not been for a Czechoslovak surgeon who was working at the hospital, and used Freddie as a 'guinea pig' for a new technique of stitching the tendons back together.

Freddie was also relatively young compared to some of the aspirant Wembley novices. At the start of the season Alf Bottoms was 27 years old, Roy Craighead 29, Bill Gilbert – who had some pre-war racing experience – 29, Stan Hodson 24, Charlie May 28, Split Waterman – who made his Wembley debut in 1947 – was 22 and Bronco Wilson was 25. Freddie was just 20 at the start of the 1946 season.

Wembley won the League in 1946, in front of massive crowds home and away. Bottoms, Craighead, Gilbert, May and Wilson all rode regularly for the Lions, so Freddie would face fierce competition for a team place when he returned to action in 1947.

1947

Fit for action, Freddie resumed training at Rye House. In 2012, he recalled being invited to stay with Bill Kitchen after one of the training sessions at Rye House, rather than return to Portsmouth straight away. (It is unclear if this was in 1946 or 1947). He was very impressed with Kitchen's comfortable home. He had a room of his own to stay in and there was after shave lotion available in the bathroom. Very different from sharing a room with Eric and Ian in Port Talbot. He saw the possibilities of what success in speedway could bring.

He made his debut for the Lions in a reserves match in the second half of Harringay's first meeting of the season on Friday 4 April, at Green Lanes. The main attraction had been a Best Pairs meeting. Harringay had declined a place in the First Division in 1946, but were now returning to the sport. Bronco Wilson, Split Waterman and Charlie May were Freddie's team mates in a six-heat match. The Racers won 20–16, with Freddie, on a track he had never ridden or probably seen before, scoring two points when Norman Lindsay had an engine failure in heat four. He finished last in his other two rides.

Alec Jackson clearly saw the potential in Freddie, but realised that his new protégé needed more experience through races in the second halves of home meetings. *The Broadsider* commented in early April that Wembley "will have last season's League winning side to call on plus a 19-year-old newcomer who threatens to make a name for himself. He's Freddie (Taffy) Williams from Wales. Manager Alec Jackson is proud of his 'cub' who will quickly develop a full Lion's roar."

Freddie recalled his first meeting at Wembley, on Thursday 8 May, when the Lions faced Wimbledon. He had to walk from one end of the stadium to the pits. He walked with Bill Kitchen, and remembered the huge roar from the 50,000 to 60,000 crowd when they saw their hero.

Records from the second half scratch races are not always complete. Freddie recalls looping at the gate in his first ride. He learnt a good lesson from this – to concentrate at the start – and never did it again. The records do show that he came last in the Junior Scratch

Race that evening. Freddie and Charlie May would ride against the two Wembley reserves – presumably to give the two reserves an extra ride, as they often only had two in the main meeting. On other occasions, they would ride against youngsters from the opposition. In his third meeting, he was third in a Wembley Scratch Race heat, but only because Charlie May fell off.

Wembley was never an easy track to ride for a newcomer, let alone learning in front of thousands of enthusiastic Wembley fans. Unlike some tracks, who just ran a few scratch races after the league or cup match, Wembley put resources into the second halves of their meetings, inviting star riders from other teams, or promising riders from the Second Division. Part of the reason for this was that the matches were often one sided because Wembley were so strong at home, and Sir Arthur Elvin recognised that the second halves could help retain the supporters' interest after a succession of 5–1s in the main match.

In his fourth meeting, Freddie fared a bit better, beating Bronco Wilson and Charlie May in the Wembley Scratch Race to reach the final, where he finished second to Bob Wells. These races were for the second string and reserve riders, the heat leaders rode in the Stadium Scratch Race.

Freddie continued to gain experience in the second half races. Split Waterman, who had built up considerable experience in the army speedway meetings during the War, had become established in the team. So the competition for even a reserve spot was as intense as ever.

On Monday 4 August, Freddie won his first trophy in speedway, the August Trophy scratch race. It followed a London Cup match against West Ham. The London Cup ties were over 18 heats, rather than the usual 14 in the league, so most of the first team riders did not ride in the second half. Freddie won his heat, and then won the final, beating Wilf Plant, Bill Gilbert and Bob Wells. Plant had been invited just for the second half of the meeting, maybe so the Wembley management could have a look at him. Another of the riders who took part was Wally Green, who would later become a World Championship Final opponent of Freddie's.

On 21 August, Freddie made his first team debut in a British Speedway Cup match against Wimbledon at Wembley. But he made his debut in tragic circumstances. Bronco Wilson, who had been one of the Rye House trainees in 1946, and had won a regular team place with the Lions, was killed in a track accident at Harringay the previous Friday. He was the only Wembley rider to die in a track accident while riding for the Lions in the post-war era.

The Broadsider's headline for the match report was "Freddie Williams wins Wembley team place". The match reporter commented that "Freddie Williams, riding as reserve for the Lions, had his first taste of team riding, and had to fight hard to gain his two points. Freddie is as yet in need of a little more experience." His debut was in heat eight. His partner, George Wilks, won the race. Freddie finished third, beating the Dons' George Saunders. Freddie had an engine failure in his second ride, and finished third in his final race, when Archie Windmill's bike packed up.

The more experienced Charlie May replaced Freddie in the Lions' next match. Freddie's next first team rides came on Thursday 11 September. While the British Riders Championship Final was being staged at the Stadium, Freddie was part of a Lions team that faced a North of England team at Middlesbrough's Cleveland Park Stadium. Bill Kitchen, Tommy Price and George Wilks were all in the big meeting at Wembley, so it was an unfamiliar looking Lions outfit that won 44–39. Two local riders were at reserve for Wembley, so Freddie had four rides in the main team. Three last places were followed by a win in heat 12, beating Joe Crowther.

9

An early shot of Freddie riding for Wembley. The body jacket is the one used in the 1946 season.
(Courtesy JSC)

10

Freddie continued to build up experience in the second halves at Wembley. On 2 October in the Wembley Scratch Race, he won his heat and was second in the final, beating Bob Wells and future Wembley team-mate Eric French. Similar results in the next two second-halves showed that he was competitive with both the opponents' reserves and his colleagues challenging for the same spots in the Lions set-up.

Freddie's debut in the National League First Division – won once again by the Lions – came in the last match of the season on 23 October, when the Lions comfortably beat the Bradford Boomerangs at Wembley 60–24. Freddie had two rides, finishing last in heat eight and third in heat 12, beating Bradford's Bill Baird.

Freddie had done enough to get an entry in the *Speedway Who's Who* section of the *The People's Speedway Guide*. It said that his favourite track was West Ham, although it is hard to see when he had ridden there, he 'liked to be drawn number one', was single, worked as an engine fitter, and his hobbies were motorcycling and shooting.

It had been an important season for Freddie. He had ridden regularly, and built up some experience. However, the challenge now for him was to try to win a regular place in the Lions team. Looking at the record of his competitors for a place in the Lions line-up, Roy Craighead and Bill Gilbert, with averages in the National League and National Trophy matches of 6.18 and 5.46 respectively, had done all that was expected of them. Split Waterman, a newcomer at the start of the season, had averaged 7.60 in his National League matches, building on his experience in Army speedway, and was rightly seen as one of the sport's rising stars. In many teams that average would have made him a heat leader.

Bob Wells had averaged 4.88 in the National League fixtures. However, Alf Bottoms only rode in two meetings due to ill health, and for the 1948 campaign moved into the Second Division, joining Southampton. Charlie May had struggled, averaging 3.88 in 16 National League fixtures. And, of course, the sad loss of Bronco Wilson also meant that Wembley had one second-string less for the 1948 campaign.

1948

After dominating the sport for two seasons since the War, the Lions faced a multitude of problems in 1948. The staging of the Olympic Games meant that the Empire Stadium was not available for speedway until the beginning of September. So the Lions home fixtures were staged at Wimbledon. There was considerable correspondence and concern about how the huge Lions following would fit into the 30,000 capacity Wimbledon Stadium. It soon became clear that the concern had been unnecessary. Faced with a difficult journey, the attendances at Plough Lane were not large.

If this wasn't enough, on Tuesday 13 April, Bill Kitchen had a bad fall at West Ham and broke his arm. Six weeks later, George Wilks broke his thigh in the home match with Harringay. The Lions had lost two of their three heat leaders. The speedway authorities allowed the Lions to sign a replacement, and American star Wilbur Lamoreaux arrived in early June, and stayed with the team until the end of the season.

Freddie faced two new rivals for a team place in the reserve slots: Peter Robinson and Bill Kemp. The former never settled as a Lion, and soon returned to Third Division racing. Bill Kemp had joined the Lions on leaving the forces, but only rode a handful of meetings before joining Third Division Cradley Heath on loan. The *News* commented after the team's first two challenge matches: "Freddie Williams, Wembley's new dynamic reserve, whose performances so far this year have set the experts wondering just where Alec [Jackson] finds 'em."

Left: Freddie in action at Wembley.
(Courtesy Hayley Redmond)

Below: 1948 Wembley team at Belle Vue: Tommy Price, Wilbur Lamoreaux, Freddie, Alec Jackson (Manager), George Saunders, Bill Gilbert, Bob Wells, Split Waterman, Bill Kitchen (on bike)
(Courtesy JSC – Wright Wood)

The Broadsider said after the Lions' defeat at West Ham: "Wembley have made a useful discovery in Freddie Williams who rode with the skill of a veteran." After only four meetings, partly due to Kitchen's injury, Freddie became a full team member in a 56–27 defeat at New Cross. He "showed up well" according to The *Broadsider*, scoring 3+1 from 4 rides. The Lions' fortunes improved three days later at Bradford, with an eight point win; Freddie contributing 4+1. It must be remembered that he was riding on most of these tracks for the first time.

The Lions 'home' season at Plough Lane started on 29 April; earlier than usual. Freddie turned in his best performance so far, with 8+1 points. The *News* said that he "combined skill with speed to add one win, a second and two thirds." But the report in *The Broadsider* estimated the crowd at a paltry 6,000. The Lions soon relaxed the restrictions they had made on admission at Plough Lane, but whether the crowds increased much is unclear. They did flock back when the Lions returned to Wembley in September.

The *News* said that Freddie was "turning out to be such a 'find' for Wembley." The Lions hit some form in the league in May, with a 30 point win away to Wimbledon, and a draw at Belle Vue. But losing George Wilks for the rest of the season against Harringay finished any chance they had of another league title. The Lions lost to the Racers by 19 points, but for Freddie, with eight points from four rides, the match was notable for being the first time he had topped the scorers for Wembley. The *News* reported that "Brilliant riding by Steve Ison and Freddie Williams was the feature of the match in which Harringay were always on top... For Wembley, Freddie Williams showed great promise, winning the tenth race after being placed third to Ison and Grant."

Three weeks later, the *News* noted "...the determined effort of Freddie Williams, who rode with the skill of a veteran to win the opening race after a ding-dong struggle with [Cliff] Watson." The Lions lost by two points at West Ham in an Anniversary Cup match.

The sport was not yet in a position to run a World Championship, so the British Riders Championship was staged as an alternative, although foreign riders based in Britain were included. Freddie was drawn in the Second Division qualifying round meetings at Birmingham, Bristol and Norwich. He scored seven at Birmingham in front of a 26,000 crowd, 11 at Bristol and then eight at Norwich, so did not qualify for the next round. He was 16th with 26 points. Only the top three qualified for the next round, and Wembley team-mate Bill Gilbert was the lowest qualifier with 39. Gilbert managed to reach the Final, and finished joint fourth with 10 points.

However, Freddie did ride as a replacement for the injured Tommy Price in Wembley's home meeting in the final qualifying rounds, after three riders pulled out. He won heat one and scored 10 points, tying with four other riders for second place and showing the progress he had made. This was his first double figure score in top-flight racing, albeit from five rides. He bettered it with 11+1 in the Lions' first meeting back at the Empire Stadium, at 67–40 win over West Ham in the London Cup semi-final. Also at Wembley, He also scored 11 from four rides in a 60–24 massacre of the Lions' former landlords, Wimbledon, on 30 September.

Freddie was gradually attracting more attention. In July, John Britten wrote in *The Broadsider* that speedway was nearing its pre-War standard "thanks to post-war unknowns", and said that "Wembley's 22-year-old Freddie Williams is another who rapidly approaches stardom."

The same month, *The Broadsider* reported on a match between Second Division Bristol and a combined Wembley, Harringay and Wimbledon team with the unlikely name of the Gayledons. Freddie scored seven points and "was dynamite itself in some of his races ... the crowd yelled with delight as he won the sixth heat ..." In Wembley's win at Wimbledon, he "followed up his performance in the British Riders Championship round with a well-earned nine points." In a win at West Ham near the end of the season, *The Broadsider* commented that "... Some of the racing was good, thanks to exhilarating Tommy Croombs, Split Waterman and the up-and-coming Williams."

For a new team member, Freddie was remarkably consistent. He did not score a zero throughout the season, and after April, only scored one point once from his four or five rides. The Lions did not have a chance of winning the league, but found success in the National Trophy and the London Cup. In all their post-war success, the National Trophy often proved elusive. But after a narrow two point aggregate win over Belle Vue, they demolished Harringay by 46 points on aggregate in the semi-final, and then faced New Cross in the final. The south east London team won the league, but Wembley won both legs of the National Trophy Final, by 20 points at home and four away.

In the London Cup, Wembley also faced New Cross in the final. This tie was a little more even, but Wembley won comfortably enough by 17 points on aggregate.

So Freddie could reflect on winning two of the sport's four trophies available to a London team in his first season as a regular team member. He rode 46 official matches for the Lions, scoring 231 points and 53 bonus points. In the League and National Trophy, his CMA was 6.16, 5.42 in the Anniversary Cup and 5.60 in the London Cup. He was the only Wembley rider to ride in every league match. *The People Speedway Guide* commented that he "established himself as one of the year's discoveries".

Another success for Freddie was winning the Southern Centre Grasstrack championship. He was successful in the 500cc class, the only time he won this event.

Stenner's Speedway Journal (Autumn [September] 1948) published an article by John Marston on Freddie and Eric. It noted the influence of their father in developing them as speedway riders. It concluded that after the 1947 season, where he was "gaining experience fast", Freddie "never looked back" after gaining a permanent place in the team after Bill Kitchen's accident at West Ham.

Looking at the Wembley team averages in the National League and National Trophy matches, Freddie finished seventh. But George Wilks only rode 12 matches, Bill Kitchen 14 and Wilbur Lamoreaux 17. The American was unlikely to stay with the Lions in 1949 – there had been controversy that they were allowed to keep him once Bill Kitchen had returned to action. But, back at the Empire Stadium, Sir Arthur Elvin would expect the Lions to win the league again, and competition for places would be as fierce as ever.

3. 1949: An established Lion

Back at the Empire Stadium, the Lions team saw some changes from their 1948 line up. Not surprisingly, Wilbur Lamoreaux had to be released, and Wembley also allowed George Wilks to go on loan to West Ham, who were seen as being under-strength due to Eric Chitty breaking his leg while riding in Australia. Three new youngsters were recruited from Rye House, and Freddie's brother Eric was sent on loan to Second Division Cradley Heath to get more experience. Bill Kemp moved permanently to the midlands side. Roy Craighead moved to Southampton, but Alf Bottoms returned to Wembley from the south coast side, his health fully recovered. Another new recruit was New Zealander Bruce Abernethy, a flamboyant and popular rider who was another challenger to Freddie for a regular team place.

Freddie's impact in 1948 had brought him to the attention of the speedway journalists. In the *Gazette*, Basil Storey said that the younger riders would be challenging the established stars in 1949. At Wembley, he highlighted Freddie, Split Waterman and Bill Gilbert. He also made Freddie one of his riders to follow in 1949.

Coming Speedway Stars, published by the *Speedway World*, included Freddie among the riders featured. The booklet said that he "started his career as a junior rider in the Lions' team. He made gradual progress and Alec Jackson nursed him along slowly until last season, when injuries badly hit the team. Here was Freddie's chance, and he did not let his manager down. The careful nursing and instruction he had received in the past proved a great success, and he quickly settled down into the hard riding of first division racing. With the return of the Wembley invalids, Freddie could not be dropped and kept his place in the side. Alec Jackson considers him to be one of the most promising riders in the division."

As usual, Wembley started the season 'on the road' before the Stadium was available for home meetings, because the track could not be laid before the FA Cup and Rugby League Challenge Cup Finals were played. No challenge matches were arranged, and of seven league meetings away from home, the Lions won two, drew one and lost four. Freddie started the season well. In the Lions 53–31 win at Harringay, the *News* reported that "Vic [Duggan] was outstripped from pillar to post by Williams and Gilbert in a clever team ride by the Wembley pair" in winning heat 14. *The Broadsider* commented that Freddie "will soon be in the running for test honours. Fifteen days later, the Lions went down by 25 points at Birmingham. *The Broadsider* reported that "Once the home team had established a long lead the Lions appeared dispirited and only Williams and Bottoms kept up the fight."

On 12 May, Reg Theobald named his 12 'most improved riders' in *The Broadsider*. Freddie was at number six, with Theobald outlining that: "Early season form suggests that Freddie will gain international recognition. Partnered by Bill Kitchen, Williams is fulfilling his promise of Rye House training days. More than once he has headed the Wembley scorers." The other riders listed were Mike Erskine, George Newton, Billy Bales, Cyril Roger, Malcolm Craven, Jack Biggs, Dent Oliver, Ken Le Breton, Nobby Stock, Jock Grierson and Bruce Semmens.

Back at the Empire Stadium, things improved for the Lions. A crowd of 63,000 saw New Cross beaten by 22 points in the opening night meeting on 12 May. *The Broadsider* reported that "Freddie Williams, though in trouble with his cornering, went fast enough to only drop one point."

The first test in a five match series against Australia was at the Empire Stadium on 26 May. For England, only Bill Gilbert was named in the team, but Freddie and Split Waterman were named as the reserves. Vic Duggan and Graham Warren dominated the meeting, both scoring 18 point maximums. Peter Foster in his *Speedway Ashes* book, says that the match was a 'debacle' for England, and that "only the reserves came out with any credit." Norman Parker was withdrawn after three scoreless rides, and Freddie took his place as Jack Parker's partner. The report in *Stenners' 1950 Annual* says that he "struck up a happy understanding with Jack Parker which continued in the second and third tests." Foster says that "In an attempt to stem the tide, the English reserves were called upon frequently in the second half and both Waterman, and especially Freddie Williams showed a tenacity that was sadly lacking in their team mates." *The Broadsider* agreed, saying that the two riders "saved the first test… from being the biggest and gloomiest rout of an international speedway team since the series … began in 1930". The *News* said that the two riders "went in, heads down, and did a very creditable job." The England team provided only two heat winners, Freddie and Bill Gilbert with one apiece. Freddie ended up with a creditable 9+2 from five rides, and was England's joint top scorer.

Freddie moved into the team along with Split Waterman for the second test at Birmingham. The Australians won again, but this time only by two points, although had Graham Warren been fit to ride on his home track, the margin undoubtedly would have been much wider. Freddie scored 7+1, including two heat wins. The *News* commented that "Williams was a trier, won a couple of heats in good style, but still lacks experience for the big occasion." Given that he had not yet completed two full seasons as a Wembley team member, that was maybe not surprising.

In the *News's* preview of the third test, their writer said that "Freddie Williams seems to be the ideal partner for Jack [Parker]. He is young; is blessed with the experience of a much more seasoned rider and is an obvious replacement to the missing half of this famous brotherhood." England turned things round at New Cross, with the Australians clearly missing Vic Duggan, and won 62–46. Freddie scored 6+2 again partnered with Jack Parker. Freddie missed the last two matches through injury, but there was already speculation about whether he would be chosen to tour Australia with the Lions in the winter.

In *The Broadsider*, John Britten wrote: "My bouquet for modesty goes to new test star Freddie Williams: 'I had all the breaks, even in the first test' he says. When I asked him whether he expected to be nominated by the Control Board for the England team to tour Australia, he replied: 'I may be lucky if two or three of the top liners drop out.' Freddie, incidentally, likes the New Cross circuit: 'Not much work' he says. 'Almost before you know where you are you're back in the pits again.'"

In the same magazine, in July, Ray Reardon reported: "One of my happiest recollections of the third test is of the earnest coaching given by Jack Parker, the England skipper, to Freddie Williams, his partner and babe of the side. Freddie did well. And, apart from his own skill and great courage, the fans would have understood had they seen them, veteran and youth, crouching on their heels in the pits, analysing every feature of the track conditions."

Freddie was chosen for the fourth test, although the selectors paired him with Wembley colleague Tommy Price. However, he sustained a knee injury and could not ride.

The Lions recovered form after returning to the Empire Stadium, and with an occasional lapse, dominated the National League, winning it by nine points ahead of Belle Vue. Freddie was scoring consistently, with most of his paid scores in double figures. He secured his first paid maximum against New Cross at the Empire Stadium on 23 June, and then a full maximum against Harringay, also at home, in a 65–19 slaughter on 21 July.

16

Wembley 1949: Tommy Barnett (trainer), Freddie, Jackie Gates, Alec Jackson (manager), Bruce Abernethy, Den Cosby, Alf Bottoms, Bob Wells, Bill Gilbert, Tommy Price, Buster Brown, Split Waterman, Bill Kitchen (on bike). (Courtesy JSC)

Freddie around this time.
(Courtesy Peter Lush)

Also in July, Freddie rode in the World Championship in his own right for the first time. The previous season he had ridden as a reserve. This time he was in the third round, a ruthless stage of the competition. There were five meetings, with the top two from each round going through. One bad race or engine failure could mean the end of a rider's chances for another year. Freddie was drawn at Ashfield in Glasgow, and finished with 14 points, one behind local hero Ken Le Breton. The *News* reported that: "Freddie Williams is riding so well for Wembley – and England – that it is only due to him that he should reach the championship round."

Incredibly, Tommy Price had to compete in this round, poor early season form had seen him not seeded through to the next round. He duly won the meeting at Newcastle, and went on to take the title, and become the first British World Champion in September. Sadly for Freddie, a second half knee injury at West Ham in early August saw him miss the rest of the month, which included the World Championship qualifying rounds. He was drawn at Wimbledon and Birmingham, and in the *Broadsider*, Ray Reardon was tipping him as a possible finalist.

While he was injured, the Lions went out of the National Trophy to West Ham. Freddie also missed the semi-final of the London Cup, but returned to action for the Final, also against the Hammers, which the Lions won comfortably. A new experience was a trip to Brno in Czechoslovakia with Split Waterman. He won two races in the elimination rounds, but lost in the final to Fritz Dirtl, the Austrian star.

Freddie's scores in the last six weeks of the season were clearly affected by his knee injury, and a subsequent injury to his leg in September. His CMA in National League meetings was 7.40, which would have made him a heat leader in most teams. For the Lions, he was only the fifth highest scorer. However, it had been an important season for him. Ray Reardon wrote that he was "getting better and better". Once again, he had been part of a team winning two domestic trophies: The National League and the London Cup.

In October, Freddie was preparing for his trip to Australia. He was looking forward to resting his knee on the trip. *The Broadsider* commissioned him to be their reporter on the trip, and said that the tests "will be the biggest thrill of Freddie's young life. Those thrills will be passed onto us just as Freddie writes his impressions of them ... Everything he sees in Australia will be new and fresh to him and probably to us." The magazine also said that Freddie was "one of the greatest riders discovered since the sport resumed after the War." Certainly, facing the Australians on their own tracks, in unfamiliar surroundings, would be a new challenge for Freddie.

4. Touring down under

After his successful 1949 season, Freddie had a great opportunity to get international experience when he was chosen for the England squad to tour Australia. However, how much competition for places there was is unclear. In an interview with *Vintage Speedway Magazine* (issue 2), he recalled how "We were at an SRA meeting and Jack Parker ... said no one wanted to go to Australia for the winter. Howdy Byford of West Ham was sitting next to me and we shouted 'We'll bloody go!' And then Cyril Roger of New Cross said he'd go as well. The next thing I knew, we were on the boat."

Interviewed in *Classic Speedway* in 2012, Freddie recalled that "Jack was a lovely man. I remember when he was chairman of the SRA [Speedway Riders Association] and got a group of riders together at Birmingham in 1949 and told us he couldn't find a team of top British riders to tour Australia ... the likes of Howdy Byford, Cyril Roger, Dent Oliver and myself all stood up and said 'we'll go'. Jack may not have taught us much about speedway racing on that tour but he taught us a lot about life. I grew up a lot in that era."

In 1948, England had been beaten 5–0 in the test series. The Australian tracks were larger than those found in Great Britain, and the tourists also faced an enormous travelling commitment. The first two meetings had been close, but in the fourth test, at Newcastle, England lost by 50 points. However, Peter Foster says that the 1949–50 England squad was the strongest ever to go to Australia. The squad was Jack Parker, Bill Kitchen, Dent Oliver, Ron Clarke, Cyril Roger, Oliver Hart, Howdy Byford and Freddie. Six had World Final experience, but only four had ridden in Australia before: Parker, Kitchen, Oliver and Hart.

The *Broadsider* reported that each rider was given £250 in Australian currency to cover the return fare. They were guaranteed earnings of £10 a week in Australia, and for the test matches were paid £2 per start and £2 per point. For other meetings, they were paid £1/10 (£1.50) per start and point. Average earnings at this time were around £6 per week, which puts these figures in context.

The trip by sea to Australia took around six weeks. By 24 November, having been inoculated against Cholera and vaccinated against Small Pox, the party had passed through the Bay of Biscay, been through the Suez Canal, visited Aden and spent four hours in Bombay, where they went round the city in a taxi. Writing many years later, Freddie recalled "The Bay of Biscay when the whole team was sick for days. The reason given was that speedway riders were so fit with a supreme sense of balance (I didn't think we had any sense) so we were allergic to the ship's motion."

He said that when the ship arrived in Tangiers "Passengers were allowed ashore for 24 hours with a list of places not to visit. One such place with a no go was the Black Cat so the speedway boys were soon in taxis with instructions to the drivers 'The Black Cat'. It was soon obvious why it was off limits. But we were young, inexperienced and what the hell! Before the 'exhibitions', which I will not tell you about, we were grouped together in this enormous bar when suddenly [one of the riders] started to shout 'Hey, less of that, less of that'. 'What's the matter?' 'This bird keeps touching me up, stop her.' This, of course, bought loads of laughter from the boys.

After a memorable night we returned to the ship, but one of our lads was missing ... he only just got back in time. The main gang plank was up and they got him on board up the special entrance used by the customs officers. We, of course, wanted to know where he had been and what he'd been up to. 'I'm saying nowt' he said. Then he mumbled 'Cooking's in its infancy in Bradford' (I think he said cooking). Then he fell asleep." Freddie also said that passing through the Suez Canal was the 'memory of a lifetime'.

The tourists had a couple of warm up races, then the next day faced a strong New South Wales team, who won 77–31. Bill Kitchen top scored for the visitors, whose only heat winner was Jack Parker. Freddie scored three points, and local reporter Frank Assenza said that "the younger [British] riders are just 'dazed' by the faster and bigger Aussie tracks."

Freddie's report said that New South Wales "really wiped us up. But don't get the mistaken notion that we were outclassed. Far from it. Looking on from the pits when it wasn't my turn to ride it was really a grand meeting to watch … You'll hear of more disasters before we get settled in as a team. But, believe me, the boys are really putting their backs into the job. They are determined to prove that the pessimistic forecasts of dismal failure of the England team were unwarranted."

Freddie felt that it was not slow motors that were responsible for the defeat, but that "we were not riding the big Aussie tracks the right way." He explained that the line needed to ride a third-of-a-mile circuit was very different from British "saucer bowl circuits". He believed that he could keep up with the Australians if he rode wider on the bends, and stayed away from the white line. He also said that the track was very slick. Another issue facing the British riders was having to use silencers on their bikes. The riders had not been able to adjust their bikes before the meeting to take account of riding with silencers.

A week later, the British riders took part, along with nine Australians, in the New South Wales Championship. Aub Lawson won the meeting, but the British riders showed some improvement. Freddie finished with six points, one behind Cyril Roger who was the top British rider. Freddie reported that Oliver Hart and Ron Clarke had bought a car between them, which immediately developed various faults. "They laughed at Dent Oliver and me" he wrote. "We had to buy push bikes to get around Sydney. Now the laugh's on them." He also said that the food was wonderful and he was enjoying five milkshakes a day. But he also said that there was a shortage of transport, and that the riders were having to use horse-boxes as garages at the Sydney Showground. They were working hard on their bikes, and were "staggered and puzzled and frantically seeking lost compression, so far unsuccessfully."

On 16 December, the riders rode in a Sports Ground versus Royale meeting, with Freddie scoring 1.5 points. The next day, the Royale track staged the first test match, and – maybe not surprisingly – the Australians won 76–32. Only Freddie's Wembley colleague Bill Kitchen reached double figures. England did not provide a heat winner. Even without Vic Duggan, the Australians were far too strong for the visitors. Jack Biggs scored a six ride maximum, and Aub Lawson was also unbeaten by an opponent. Frank Assenza said that the British riders seemed more at home on the smaller Showground track than the huge Royale one. Freddie scored five points, and followed this with 11 in the two-lap title meeting at the Sports Ground. But at the Royale track, he struggled again with just five points riding for Royale against Maitland, and then three points in the return at Maitland.

Most of the riders had a three day break after the first test, and Freddie reported on their trip out into the country. They stayed on Frank Arthur's farm, and went out hunting rabbits for three days. Freddie again noted the quantity of food, saying that it looked like enough for a month, not three days.

The Broadsider also reported that he had been moved into a heat leader slot for the second test, at the Sydney Sports Ground. The England team improved, but still went down 67–41. Freddie was third highest scorer with six points. However, a serious accident to Bill Kitchen, who was concussed as well as breaking ribs and a bone in his foot, saw him ruled out of the rest of the series. Eight days later, the English riders restored a little pride when Jack Parker won the four lap Australian title. Freddie finished with five points. He reported in *The Broadsider* that the big tracks were playing "the merry dickers with engines. New barrels, pistons and valves are needed after every second meeting." He said that the riders were spending so much time repairing their bikes that they were thinking about moving their beds from their hotel into the workshops.

The next week the whole sport was shocked by a triple crash at the Sydney Sports Ground that saw Ray Duggan and Norman Clay killed. Freddie wrote that "The deaths of Ray Duggan and Norman Clay have knocked all the joy out of racing, not only for the Australians but for the English riders as well." Freddie attended the funeral, along with some of the other English riders.

The third test was in Brisbane, the day after the terrible accident in Sydney. Once again, the British riders struggled on a large track, and lost 72–36. Freddie was partnering Jack Parker, and managed three paid five in his rides. A week later, the series returned to Sydney, and the Australians went 4–0 up with a 68–40 win. Freddie again scored three points. A week later, the Australians won the fifth test, again 68–40, with Freddie just scoring two points paid four, again partnering Jack Parker.

The sixth test, in Melbourne, saw a change in the England team's fortunes as they avoided a whitewash. However, the Australians rested Graham Warren, Jack Biggs and Ken Le Breton. Despite this, the 6,000 crowd was the season's best. With the scores level after 16 heats at 48–48, Jack Bibby broke his leg and was excluded. England won the heat 5–1, and another maximum win in the final heat secured the test for the visitors. Freddie failed to score in the tourists' 70–38 defeat. Again the home team rested some of their stars. Their top scorer was Jack Young, with 17 points, a sign of things to come. Freddie was having dental trouble at this time, and after a dentist broke a tooth while it was being extracted, had to go to have an operation in a nursing home to solve the problem. Different reports and records show that Freddie rode in one of the last two tests, but not both, due to his dental problems. There is a record showing he scored two points at Melbourne, which gives more detail than other accounts.

Cyril Roger wrote in the *Gazette* on 21 January: "Freddie Williams, who has shown really fine form out here, is now tootling round on an engine called 'The Bomb'. It's a fast motor and has a reputation for having pulled many real star riders out of bad patches. Not that Freddie has struck a bad patch, but if this motor justifies all the good things said about it, we can expect some real fireworks from the popular young Wembley Lion."

Freddie's final report for *The Broadsider* said that the series win for the Australians was "the best thing that could have happened for speedway in Australia. As defeat followed defeat the crowds increased. If we had been the winning side I feel sure that attendances would have dropped as quickly as a thermometer tossed into a refrigerator." Writing in the *1950 Stenners Annual*, Russ Thomas says that "interest waned" after the third test, but the attendance figures do not bear that out. The crowd in Adelaide was 20,000. Freddie noted: "The stadium was packed although it lies five miles outside of the city. Work out the cost, travel on top of five shillings admission and one shilling for a programme ... There are no stands, only mounds of earth as vantage points."

He said that the riders "had a grand time in Adelaide. I was a passenger in the winning craft in a speedboat race. The spectators were delighted when I told them that this was one of the first races in which I had been first over the line since coming to Australia."

Left: Freddie and some of the Australian riders in Brisbane: Oliver Hart, Freddie, Alan Gerrard, Graham Warren, Ken LeBreton, Jack Biggs, Ron Clarke (Courtesy JSC).

On the test series, he concluded: "We took a terrific beating. Try as hard as we really did in workshop and on the track, we just couldn't match the Aussies for sheer speed of motor. The accident to Bill Kitchen made all the difference to the England team. Remember that Bill ... was going as well as most of the Australians until his smash up. This overwhelming defeat should make the likely England riders of the coming summer all the more eager to wipe it out with a sweeping reverse."

However, interviewed by John Chaplin in 1993 in *Vintage Speedway Magazine*, Freddie said that "We learned a lot in Australia. The Aussies fiddled, there's no doubt about it ... I'd be going round the Sydney Showground as fast as I could on a good JAP engine, when one of the Aussies would go round the outside of me. He'd be on a 'big one' – a motor with a little more than 500cc. They weren't the top-liners and they would never appear in a test match. They knew that there was always the chance of their engines being measured at an international. The way they did so well in ordinary meetings, and never any good in tests, was always proof to me that they cheated."

In his report of the tour in *Stenners*, Russ Thomas said that the riders never stopped trying: "They plugged away however hopeless the task and by the end of the tour were going a great deal faster than at the beginning." He also said that their engines prepared for British conditions were not suitable for the larger Australian tracks, and that future touring teams should be given proper workshops. However, given that some of the riders had ridden in Australia before, it seems strange that knowledge of what was required to set up their bikes for Australian tracks was not shared. Also, Jack Parker and his nephew Dennis, who joined the squad to cover for Bill Kitchen, used a separate workshop facility from the rest of the team. Freddie wrote many years later that "Perhaps Dennis was using Aussie tuning like his uncle Jack." Thomas did say that the riders worked hard and that the tour manager, Harry Tovey, said that their conduct "was beyond reproach on and off the tracks."

Basil Storey said in the *Gazette* after the tour that Dent Oliver, Cyril Roger, Freddie and Howdy Byford "apparently never struck anything like their National League form [in Australia]." While Freddie had not found great success on the track, the experience he gained was invaluable. It gave him the confidence to arrange future overseas trips, and contributed to his all-round development as a speedway rider. But no one would have predicted the tumultuous events of the season to come.

5. 1950: A memorable season

Freddie arrived home from Australia in time for the start of the new domestic season. John Wick reported in the *World* that his brother Eric would replace Split Waterman in the Wembley team. Waterman had left the Lions to join north London rivals Harringay for a £3,000 transfer fee. Eric had ridden for Cradley Heath in the Second Division in 1949, but despite his relative inexperience started well. Wick also said that it was hoped that Bill Kitchen and Freddie would be 100 per cent fit when they returned from Australia.

Even with the loss of Split Waterman, the Lions still looked very strong. Tommy Price, George Wilks, Bill Kitchen and Bill Gilbert were all still at 'heat leader' standard. Young New Zealander Bruce Abernethy was in his second season as a Lions regular team member and was expected to improve. Alf Bottoms was still there, and competing for reserve places were Jimmy Gooch, Den Cosby, Bob Wells and Jack Gates. One more rider was recruited during the season – Bob Oakley ed from Southampton in July – and he made an immediate impact.

As usual, the Lions started with a series of away matches before opening night at Wembley on 11 May. There were six challenge matches, including a rare trip to Edinburgh, and two league matches, at West Ham and Bristol. In the challenge match at West Ham, the *World* reported that Freddie was in "sparkling form". Reporting on the league win at the same venue, they reported that "The Lions ... rode well as a team, and showed powers to fight back and ride through the dirt when behind, Bill Gilbert and Freddie Williams excelling at this particular style." In a challenge match win at Birmingham, they reported that "The brothers Williams were particularly impressive."

After opening at home with a narrow win against New Cross, and then a more comfortable one over Wimbledon, the Lions faced Belle Vue. Tony Fowler reported in the *World*: "Wembley gained a second heat success in heat seven when Freddie Williams rode what must have been the race of his career. Starting well, Jack Parker tailed him by inches for the whole of the race, trying every method of track craft to pass the Welshman but Williams held the lead and to the delight of the roaring crowd crossed the finishing line half a length ahead of Parker." He also said that "For Wembley, Freddie Williams, improving with every match, rode in great style to gain 10 points ...". *The Gazette* reported on the same meeting: "Freddie Williams ended up highest scorer for the Lions against Belle Vue in the all-important League match at Wembley. Freddie, gating splendidly from the outside, gained a terrific advantage on the first bend which made him almost impossible to catch. The most exciting race of the night was the final heat. Williams and Price beat Louis Lawson and spoilt the Belle Vue boy's maximum."

Although Eric had made a good start for the Lions, he recalled in *The Eric Williams Story* (part 11) that he was not made welcome by the established Wembley riders. Maybe there was resentment that he was immediately given a team place, rather than a reserve slot, or maybe speculation that he would take someone's place. He recalls riding with Tommy Price, and then Price asking Freddie to ask Eric to leave room for Price on the track! He says that in his early days with the team it was only Freddie who spoke to him, which undermines the image the Lions had of good team spirit.

Freddie always worried about having either of his brothers – more usually Eric, he only rode regularly with Ian in South Africa – as his partner. This was borne out when Freddie and Eric rode together in the last heat of the Lions' 55–29 win at Harringay the day after the New Cross meeting. It was reported that Eric fell in the race, when they were up against

Split Waterman and Vic Duggan. Eric said in *The Eric Williams story* that Waterman cut across from the outside gate after the start, and tried to come past him on the inside, where Eric believed there was no room. The result was Eric being pushed into Freddie, and his footrest ripping the spokes out of Freddie's back wheel. Freddie and Split both crashed, while Vic Duggan ended up on the dog track. Eric was still on his bike, but the wheel sprocket of Freddie's bike had gone through Eric's boot, badly cutting his foot.

Eric was taken to hospital, and missed the Lions' next four meetings. Apart from concern about his brother, Freddie was annoyed that he was excluded for being the cause of the race being stopped. Duggan and Waterman got a 5–1 against Bob Wells in the rerun race, but fortunately for the Lions they had the match comfortably won. In *Vintage Speedway Magazine* (Vol 2 No.1) in 1994, Freddie recalled that "The best moments I had in speedway were the world championship wins, of course. The worst were riding with my brother Eric. We had some bad accidents together and he always came off badly. Eventually I had to refuse to ride with him. When you go into those corners, you really don't care about anybody – and Eric was always the unlucky one."

The *News* reported that Freddie had ridden in a grass track meeting at Ashton Combine staged by the Southampton and Bishop's Waltham Motorcycle Clubs. He scored a maximum nine points in the Star Riders Match Race, followed by Bob Oakley with eight. Freddie also got the best time of the day in the eliminating heat of the under 1000cc (open) solo event. He did four laps of the 528 yard tack in 1 minutes, 34.2 seconds.

Freddie was chosen for the first test against the Australians at West Ham on 6 June. He was partnering Tommy Price, and scored 5 (+2) in a 60–47 defeat. He was dropped, along with Cyril Roger, Malcolm Craven and Split Waterman for the next test at Belle Vue. Despite his consistent scoring for Wembley, he was only recalled for the last match of the series, at the Empire Stadium, as reserve. England had won the series, but pride was still at stake. In fact, Freddie rode six times, scored 8 (+2), but finished last in the final race of the evening, which meant the Australians won 55–53. Freddie chased Jack Young in the last heat in "treacherous conditions" but could not catch him to give England a draw.

On 15 June, after the first test, the editorial in the *News* said that "Two men were included who did not seem to me to merit their selection on present form (please remember those three words). I refer to Freddie Williams and Cyril Roger. Both are fine riders, but I cannot recall either of them being particularly brilliant on a big occasion such as a test." Freddie was to prove the writer wrong before the end of the season.

A couple of weeks after the test match, Freddie scored his first maximum of the season in a 60–24 rout of West Ham. The *Gazette* said that he "was Wembley's outstanding rider, and he came right back to form with a maximum." He followed that with three paid maximums and another maximum in the next six home Wembley meetings. In the clash with New Cross, the Gazette reported that "Freddie Williams was in brilliant form for the Lions, being unbeaten." Against Wimbledon on 13 July he scored nine from four rides in a 48–33 defeat, and then against Belle Vue on 20 July, scored 10 from four rides, but this was not enough to prevent the Lions going down to their second home defeat of the season. His only other maximum or paid maximum for the Lions came in the last meeting of the season, a 54–30 win over Harringay. Although Freddie was not as consistent away from home, when the Lions won 52–31 at Harringay in June, the *News* said that he was "easily Wembley's outstanding rider". In July, the Lions went down 51–32 at West Ham. The *World* said that "Only Wilks, Freddie Williams and Price were able to make some grand attempts to stem the tide, but a lack of strong second strings spoiled their efforts."

Freddie leading West Ham's Aub Lawson at Custom House on 2 May 1950 (Courtesy David Williams)

Wembley Lions 1950: Tommy Price, Jimmy Gooch, Alf Bottoms, George Wilks, Bob Wells, Duncan King (manager), Bruce Abernethy, Eric, Jackie Gates, Freddie, Den Cosby, Bill Gilbert, Tommy Barnett (trainer), Bill Kitchen (on bike). (Courtesy JSC)

Eleven days later, the Lions were beaten by 20 points at Odsal. The *World* commented that newcomer Bob Oakley "and the Williams brothers were the only impressive Wembley riders."

Once again, the Lions dominated the National League, eventually heading the table by 10 points from Belle Vue. But the National Trophy was a different story. On 5 August, the Lions went down 79–29 at Birmingham. Freddie scored just four points from five rides. According to the *World*, along with George Wilks and youngster Den Cosby, he was one of the "mainstays" of their narrow win in the second leg at Wembley, but the Lions lost heavily on aggregate. Wembley did retain the London Cup for the third season running. Harringay were beaten by three points on aggregate in the semi-final, and then Wimbledon by just a point in the final. So Freddie had two winner's medals as part of the Wembley team.

For the Lions, Freddie finished the season second in the Wembley riders National League and National Trophy averages, on 8.49. Tommy Price was top with 9.41, and George Wilks took the third heat leader spot with 8.23. But Wembley's strength in depth was shown with four other riders averaging seven points, Eric Williams on 7.43, a remarkable figure for a debut season in the top flight, Bill Kitchen on 7.59, Bill Gilbert on 7.36 and Bob Oakley was on 7.27.

Stenners 1951 Annual, reviewing the Lions' performance, said that "Wembley won the League Championship … on their merits. Nevertheless, they failed to produce real championship form. Had there been one really strong challenger in the field, Wembley might not have been champions." However, the article did say that "There's a new backbone forming to the Wembley line-up – the Williams brothers, Fred and Eric, and Bob Oakley."

Of course, the World Championship had been a big part in the last three months of Freddie's season, and that is covered in the next chapter.

Left: 1950 Wembley programme signed by Freddie.
Right: Team line-ups from the programme of the England versus Australia test at West Ham on 6 June 1950. England lost 60–47 in front of a 50,000 crowd.

6. The 1950 World Championship

Freddie's 1949 World Championship campaign had been scuppered by injury. He had qualified from the third round, but never got the chance to compete in the final Championship round that could have taken him to the first World Championship Final since the War. The previous year he had ridden in one meeting as a reserve, so his experience in the sport's premier competition was very limited.

The first World Championship Final had been held in 1936. A complicated system using bonus points from the previous rounds saw the Australian Lionel Van Praag take the title, despite Bluey Wilkinson being undefeated on the night of the final. Van Praag beat Eric Langton in a run-off after they had tied on points. The bonus points system continued the next year, but this time American star Jack Milne won his five rides on the night to take the crown. The meeting was dominated by the Americans, with Wilbur Lamoreaux, who rode for Wembley in 1948, being runner-up, and Cordy Milne, Jack's brother, finishing third.

In 1938, the last final before the War, saw another Australian, Bluey Wilkinson, take the crown. He tied with Jack Milne on the night on 14 points, but this time the bonus point system worked in his favour and he won the title by one point. Wilbur Lamoreaux was third. The 1939 Final, scheduled for 7 September, was cancelled because War had been declared four days earlier.

After the War, speedway resumed a full programme in 1946. However, very few overseas riders were available, so a British Riders Championship replaced the World Championship. A handful of overseas riders riding in British speedway did enter. Wembley dominated the event; Tommy Price won the title with a maximum and Bill Kitchen was runner-up on 13 points. The competition grew in 1947, with the launch of the Third Division. Jack Parker won the title, with Bill Kitchen again finishing as runner-up, this time after a run-off. He had tied with Parker on 14 points.

In 1948, there was more of an international presence. Eleven of the riders in the final were English, there were three Australians, an American – Wilbur Lamoreaux – and a Canadian, Eric Chitty. Australian star Vic Duggan won the title, with compatriot Ron Johnson as runner-up. Alec Statham was third, providing an English presence on the rostrum. From Wembley, Tommy Price had failed to qualify, but Bill Gilbert rode well to finish fourth with 10 points. Split Waterman had qualified as reserve, but took the place of Aub Lawson who was injured. Waterman also finished with a very credible 10 points.

By 1949, with the sport more established again internationally, the authorities decided to run a World Championship again. Tommy Price won the meeting with a maximum, and thus became the first British World Champion. Jack Parker was runner-up on 14 points, with Belle Vue's Louis Lawson third on 13. For Wembley, Bill Kitchen finished sixth with nine points, and Bill Gilbert eleventh with six.

In March 1950, the *World* reported that 252 riders were going to enter the World Championship that year. This included riders from Norway, Austria, Sweden, Holland and other European countries. Thirty eight First Division riders would enter at the third round stage, along with 74 from the second round. The two highest scores from each of seven meetings would go into the Championship round, to make a total of 48 riders at that stage. The 16 highest scorers on aggregate would qualify for the World Final.

The competition started in June, with meetings at Poole, Liverpool, St Austell, Oxford, Leicester, Exeter, Rayleigh and Swindon. Seventy three riders qualified for the second round, 55 were eliminated. Each rider only rode in one meeting In July, the second round meetings followed the same formula. There were meetings at Glasgow White City, Fleetwood, Plymouth, Sheffield, Halifax, Norwich, Coventry and Edinburgh. Again, 128 riders entered, and 73 qualified for the third round. Rising Australian rider Jack Young was one of five riders to qualify for the third round with a maximum 15 points. The third round took place at the end of July, with 112 riders involved, but only 14 qualified for the Championship round. The top two in each meeting went through, and only nine Second Division riders made it through. A young Swede, Olly Nygren, who went on to have a long career in British speedway, rode at Southampton but could only muster five points.

The Championship round took place from 19 August to 5 September. There were nine meetings, with each rider taking part in three. This gave a rider who had one poor meeting a chance to qualify for the final, although this could still be very tough, as Freddie found later in his career. This time he started poorly, with six points at Belle Vue, which was never one of his favourite tracks. Five days later he scored 13 in the meeting at Wembley. *Speedway World* reported that he was "joint runner-up with Danny Dunton. Williams slipped badly in trailing Dunton and [Aub] Lawson in his second ride conceding his only defeat of the evening." Lawson won the meeting with a 15 point maximum. Bill Kitchen had three engine failures which effectively eliminated him from the competition.

Freddie was in the final qualifying meeting at West Ham. He won the meeting with 14 points, and comfortably qualified for the final in seventh place. The *Speedway World* reported that he did not start well and that in heat seven Louis Lawson's engine failed, and Freddie overtook Rigg and Hart to win the heat. In heat 20 he gated well to win the meeting and the £50 prize money.

Jack Young, with 39 points, headed the qualifiers. Tommy Price was the only other Wembley rider to qualify, although former team mate Split Waterman would also be there, having qualified with 32 points.

The composition of the 18 riders (including the two reserves) who qualified for the final was very significant in the development of British speedway. Only six of the riders had ridden before the Second World War, and only seven had been involved in the 1949 Final. In the *Speedway World*, John Wick wrote: "Many new faces will be appearing in this year's final ... and some of them with a fine chance of success ... Among these I expect Cyril Brine, Freddie Williams, Split Waterman, Danny Dunton and Wally Green all distinguishing themselves, and I shall be the first to applaud if one of the younger school of riders brings off a surprise." However, he said that he expected Tommy Price to retain his title, although he thought that Graham Warren, Vic Duggan and Aub Lawson would "be making a bold bid". He also said that "Veteran Jack Parker was very determined to win the title." The *News*'s Lionel Willis pointed out that there were eight Englishmen, seven Australians and Freddie Williams representing Wales in the final. They said it was the "most open" final ever. Their report commented that Tommy Price's supporters were confident that he would win, while Graham Warren, Jack Parker and Split Waterman were "names that instantly come to mind."

He did say that Freddie was the best 'outsider', adding "He turns out in the first race and should account for Ron Clarke, Wally Green and Jack Biggs. A win here should give him the necessary tonic and confidence. This, together with his knowledge of the Wembley circuit, may enable him to figure high in the night's honours." His forecast was Jack Parker to win.

Wembley manager Duncan King tipped Tommy Price, and of six other experts, none of them mentioned Freddie, although the office boy had a "sneaking regard" for him.

In the *Gazette*, Basil Storey commented that there had been a "poor standard" of racing in the qualifying rounds, but that there were new faces in the Final. He also said it was the "most open final of all time." He believed that Graham Warren was the "form horse and will start as favourite." He thought a shock could come from Ronnie Moore or Cyril Brine. He believed that anyone who beat Graham Warren would be champion.

The popular national newspapers also covered the final. In the *Daily Mail*, one of the sport's biggest backers at the time, Tom Stenner wrote: "The issue is very open. Youth puts in a big challenge, and 17-year –old Ronnie Moore has more than an outside chance, though this is his first final. Jack Young and Freddie Williams, both in their early twenties, and Danny Dunton and Split Waterman, a year or so older, will challenge the supremacy of Tommy Price, the holder, Jack Parker and Aub Lawson. But of all the young men, Graham Warren catches the eye. He has all the qualities needed to win the world title and this young Australian is the favourite.

Like Parker, Warren has to ride in successive races, which must be a handicap. In my search for the winner I give Lawson slight preference over Warren. Lawson has rare dash allied to superlative skill and will certainly not be troubled by the occasion. Price, Parker and Waterman may fight out third and fourth places."

The *Evening Standard* concentrated on the draw: "Number 13, drawn by Jack Parker, may prove to be lucky for the third time in the history of World Speedway Championship tonight. Bluey Wilkinson and Tommy Price won with it. Despite being the oldest rider in the final, Parker is still one of the best in the world. He has the right temperament for the big occasion and his track craft is second to none.

But it is stamina that may tell and Parker's big test will come early in the meeting when he meets Waterman, Warren and Moore in heat four. In the very next race he has to meet Clarke, Oliver and present champion Tommy Price. If Parker can win these two races, I feel sure that he will go on to win the title for the first time in his career.

Tommy Price is another man not likely to overawed by the occasion ... Form, of course, points to Graham Warren ... Rain shortly before the meeting would give Cyril Brine a great chance – he loves a wet track ... Vic Duggan cannot be left out but needs to make better starts."

In the programme for the Final, Tom Stenner emphasised the drama of the occasion. In an article headed 'The Great Night is Here!', he wrote: "This is the hour! The hour that millions of speedway followers, the world over, have been eagerly anticipating for many months. The *Sunday Dispatch* World Speedway Riders Championship – the greatest and most absorbing competition the sport has given us – has so captured the public imagination, that countless hearts will be beating with the rapid urge of a surging excitement as the hands of the clock quiver and touch 7.45pm."

Before the big night, Freddie discussed the meeting with his father. They agreed that Freddie should aim to break the track record in the first heat, which would lay down a marker to the other riders. Freddie was already joint holder of the Wembley track record, but he reduced it from 71.4 seconds to 71, beating Wally Green, Ron Clarke and Jack Biggs. Tommy Price had started with a win, but then fell in heat five. In heat six, John Wick said that "Williams gained a really brilliant victory." Vic Duggan was leading until the fourth bend of the third lap, but Freddie passed him on the inside to take the lead. Split Waterman also passed Duggan, but could not catch Freddie. After two races for each rider, Freddie and Graham Warren were on six points, Wally Green on five with Aub Lawson and Cyril Brine on four. Tommy Price and Jack Parker were both on three. To be certain of winning the title, Freddie needed three wins from his last three rides.

Heat 10 brought together the two unbeaten riders, Freddie and Graham Warren. Freddie was ahead from the gate, chased by Warren. On the first bend of the final lap, Warren tried to come through on the inside, but hit a slick patch and fell. He remounted, but finished last. Freddie's time of 71.2 beat the old track record.

Wally Green was now the main challenger to Freddie, and he won heat 12, beating Jack Parker. Parker was out again in heat 14, facing Aub Lawson, who was on seven points, and Freddie. John Wick described the race: "Lawson and Williams fought out the lead on the first lap. Lawson shot into the third bend a little too fast and drifted. In doing so he took Williams wide as well. Seeing his opportunity, Parker came through on the inside to take the lead with Lawson closing the big gap in second place. Lawson challenged Parker, but on the first bend, final lap, he again misjudged his speed and went wide, letting Williams through into second place." This left Freddie on 11 points with one ride left.

Wally Green's next ride was heat 16. He was facing Graham Warren, who led for two laps, Green then overtook him on the inside, before Warren got ahead on the last lap and held on to win. If Freddie could win heat 18, the title was his. He took the lead from the start, and although energetically pursued by Ronnie Moore, the young Wimbledon rider could not stop the title staying at the Empire Stadium for a second year. Wally Green finished runner-up with 13 points, and Graham Warren was third with 12. Had he not fallen in heat 10, he could have challenged Freddie for top spot, but it was not to be. So Freddie was World Champion at the tender age of 24, the youngest winner at that time.

Freddie was presented with the Trophy by Lord Louis Mountbatten, who was a distinguished officer in the Royal Navy, and uncle of the Duke of Edinburgh. Sixty two years later, Freddie himself presented the Trophy to the winner of the Cardiff Grand Prix, and joked that the status of the 'guest of honour' had gone down!

The *Speedway World's* sub-heading on its report was "Great Triumph for Youth" and it said that "After a meeting full of suspense and surprises, Wembley's Freddie Williams delighted a 93,000 crowd by carrying off the World Championship."

The *News* reported that "Naturally, Williams was tremendously excited when it was all over, and all he could say was 'I had the breaks.' At the halfway stage, when he had chalked up three wins in a row, he was so keyed up that he preferred to remain aloof from his rivals. Freddie wanted to get back on the track and finish the job, although he had to wait until heat 18 before he knew the title was his." The reporter also said that he thought that Graham Warren "was a beaten man" when he fell in heat 10. He also commented on how Freddie gave credit to his mechanic, Cyril Spinks, and insisted on having their picture taken together.

Tom Stenner's report in the *Daily Mail* emphasised Freddie's relative lack of experience compared to some of the older riders: "Five years ago Freddie Williams ... answered an advertisement for motorcyclists to try their skill on the speed tracks, Last night he won the *Sunday Dispatch* riders World Championship ... Williams, the only undefeated rider at the interval, was so excited that during the wait he pleaded for 'no talking' – even from his mechanic. His was a well-earned victory.

In Heat one Williams smashed the track record in 71 seconds. He won heat five comfortably. In heat 10 he led Graham Warren, also undefeated at that stage, into the first corner and stayed in front … In heat 14 Williams and Aub Lawson went at it with such a will that they let Jack Parker through on the inside. Williams eventually shook off Lawson, but he could not recover the lost ground. On his last race Williams streaked from the gate in front and he held off young Ronnie Moore to win cleverly … Vic Duggan was blotted out in this young man's final. Admiral Louis Mountbatten presented the trophy and £500 cheque to Williams."

Stenner also noted that the gate receipts were £22,600 of which £10,200 went to the Chancellor of the Exchequer in Entertainment Tax.

In the 1951 *Stenners Annual*, the same writer said that Freddie was a "worthy champion." He continued: Maybe he has not the glamour of some of the 'shoot-a-line' boys who can ride as well as they talk but on the big night he had the measure of everyone – except veteran Jack Parker." He also noted that Freddie's form dipped and "at first the limelight was a bit too much for this shy young man." In fact, in official meetings he had a couple of poor nights, at New Cross and Birmingham, but otherwise scored quite well as Wembley won the League comfortably.

In the *Daily Express*, Basil Storey pointed out that Freddie earned £100 a minute in winning the title. He also stressed the triumph of youth over experience: "Freddie Williams, 24 year old Welshman from Port Talbot, won the World Speedway Championship at Wembley last night. It was the most surprising triumph in the 21-years' history of the sport. … It was only at the beginning of the 1948 season, as an unknown reserve, that he first gained his place in the Wembley side. Before that he was an apprentice engineer at Portsmouth Dockyard. It was a complete triumph of speedway racing youth. Veteran Jack Parker, 43-year-old captain of Belle Vue, won only one race and scored eight points in what might be his last final before retiring. Jack has never won the title in 20 years riding.

Harringay's Australian captain, Vic Duggan, who two years ago was hailed as the most phenomenal rider of all time, scored only four points in his five rides.

Ronnie Moore, 17 year old Tasmanian and the youngest rider ever to reach the final, gave a plucky display against more experienced rivals, won one of his heats and scored seven points after being excluded in his first heat for a technical infringement – an unnerving experience for one so young."

The *Daily Mirror's* coverage was by Sam Leitch, one of their leading sports reporters. He wrote: "Freddie Williams, 24, a wiry little Welshman who learned to ride a motorbike in the mountains of Wales, is the new Speedway Champion of the World – and after only two full seasons in the sport!

The unfancied, unsung, smiling Freddie from Port Talbot toppled the cream of the world's best speed-men in the World Championship at Wembley last night before a 93,000 crowd. The flying Freddie charged through all opposition at £100 a minute – his five rides for a total of 14 points earned him nearly £600.

And in winning Freddie makes sure that the world title does not leave Wembley. Last year's holder was Tommy Price. This win by Williams is the most sensational of a speedway season already studded with shocks. Form went haywire, stars crashed. To add to a most amazing evening, Wally Green, West Ham, a 28 year old Londoner who used his Service gratuity to buy a motorbike and take up speedway in 1946, was second, one point behind Williams. The dash of Green, who was considered not to have a chance, earned him £300. Third was one of the fancied few – Graham Warren (Birmingham) who, in a burst of impetuosity, lost his chance by crashing in heat 10.

Williams startled the crowd of Cup Final dimensions in the opening heat when he won in a new track record time of 71 seconds. While the greying maestros of the sport were having bad luck – Tommy Price fell too in a desperate bid to overtake, and Jack Parker had the science, but alas not the speed, to be of much use – Williams was conquering all.

In the series only one man beat him – Jack Parker. It looked bleak for Freddie in heat 14 when he was passed first by Aub Lawson, Cyril Brine and then by Parker. But, where more experienced riders would have tailed away, Freddie hung on, slung his machine into the bends in daredevil fashion and pipped Lawson. He clinched the remarkable victory in heat 18, when Williams, challenged all the way by young Ronnie Moore of Wimbledon, crossed the line first to a deafening roar from the crowd.

The night's riding was put into the background by the surprise of Williams's victory, but the failure of Parker and Price illustrated vividly that Speedway is now a young man's sport."

Another critic was Freddie senior. He had travelled to the Final in a coach with friends and family members, including Freddie's brother Eric. Ian was away in Egypt on national service. When he met his son after the meeting, he questioned why Freddie couldn't beat Jack Parker! Interviewed in *Classic Speedway* in 2012, Freddie recalled that "This shows you what a hard taskmaster my dad was. After the meeting, I met him up in the restaurant and was expecting him to smile and offer his congratulations. Instead, he said 'Fancy letting Jack Parker beat you' – and he meant it too."

But at home in Port Talbot, Freddie winning the World Championship was the front page headline in the *Port Talbot Guardian*. The headline concerned his mother, Hetty: "World Speedway Champ's Mother 'dared not look'." It said that she was probably the last to realise that Freddie was the champion. It quoted her as saying: "I turned my back while the event was on" she said, "I don't really approve of speedway and I dared not look, and anyway, I don't understand the scoring, so I wouldn't have known until someone explained to me. Suddenly everyone around me started jumping and shouting 'Freddie, Freddie' at the tops of their voices and it seemed minutes before I could get them to tell me what had happened."

She also said that Freddie was "very calm" about winning the title, while Eric said that he "couldn't be happier if I had won it myself." The paper also reported that Freddie had been invited to a Civic reception by the Mayor, and that the Chamber of Trade had sent him a message of congratulations.

The next week, in the 6 October edition, the front page lead was "Port Talbot accords honour to World Famous son – Freddie Williams gets a great welcome." The previous Monday, he had been invited to a reception organised by the Borough Council in the Council Chamber. There was also a town parade, when his car was given a motor cycle escort of 14 bikes. Later this was followed by a public reception at the Odeon cinema, with a welcome from the Afan Ladies Choir, which included his sister Kate. Freddie said that he had more 'stage fright' at these events than he did at the World Final at Wembley.

The Mayor, Alderman TI Rees said that the town was very proud of him, and that "You may be feted in many places, but no greater compliment could be paid you by this town than the council meeting specially called to give you an official welcome." The Mayor spoke about Freddie's deep roots in the town and said that "We wanted with undisputed pride to welcome you, congratulate you, and wish you further success, because a championship had to be maintained.

The Guardian said that Councillor Richard Evans "said that all Wales could be proud that England had lost the glory of the world championship." He also hoped that Eric and Ian would have further success, and referred to the musical ability of Freddie's grandfather, Mr Griffiths, which he said that the Williams boys had matched in speedway.

Alderman Graham Griffiths pointed to the role of Freddie Williams senior in supporting his sons, and the practice the boys did riding on Margam Mountain. Councillor Fred Snook said that the town must be envied by speedway followers throughout the country. Councillor Paisley suggested that a speedway track should be built in Port Talbot. Further speeches were made about the Williams family, with Mrs G Nicholas saying that his mother should not be forgotten. In replying, Freddie said that "I am very, very proud to have brought this trophy to Port Talbot. I thank you for everything you have said about Mum and Dad and my family. I hope my brothers will do the same."

In the evening, "cheering crowds welcomed him at the cinema doors" and "deafening applause greeted his entry on to the stage. Councillor Richard Evans welcomed him, and said that the town knew he was good enough to hold the championship "for a considerable time." Superintendent Ewart Evans thanked the people for the "first class welcome" they had given Freddie, and said he hoped that Freddie would join the Special Constabulary in the mobile section.

In its 'Weekly Commentary' section, the *Guardian* said that "World Champions in the realm of sport are such a rarity in this country today that when one does appear on the scene it is only right that he should be accorded the honour due to him. When Freddie Williams returned to his native Port Talbot on Monday, together with the massive trophy he won when he carried off the world's championship in speedway... it was only fitting that he should have been given a civic reception and a warm-hearted welcome from his fellow townspeople.

Port Talbot rose to the occasion in grand style in welcoming home one of its sons, who has reached the pinnacle of his career and who has added his own singular contribution to that illustrious chapter of those who have gone out from the Borough to bring glory on themselves and honour to their native town."

Further celebrations followed. The Neath Motor Club organised a 200 mile motorcycle race, with different engine capacity machines having to do a different number of laps. A large crowd gathered at Aberavon beach in Port Talbot to enjoy the event.

A dinner for friends and neighbours was organised at the Walnut Tree Hotel. Freddie was presented with a gentleman's dressing set by Mr Jack Jones, a neighbour of the Williams family for many years. In reply, Freddie said that "I have attended many receptions since I gained the title, but never have I felt my hosts' appreciation to be so sincere."

One more duty that Freddie carried out at this busy time in Port Talbot was to be best man for his brother Eric. Eric married Helen Hogg from Glasgow at Margam Abbey. *The Guardian* said that Eric was a "well known speedway rider". Katie Williams, Freddie and Eric's younger sister, was the bridesmaid, and wore "a sage-green dress with hat to match and a spray of pink carnations". The reception was at the family home in Margam Road. However, the couple's honeymoon was postponed because Eric had to ride in Denmark the following Saturday. His bride was serving in the Women's Royal Air Force."

Freddie used most of the proceeds from his World Championship win to buy a new car. In *Vintage Speedway Magazine* (Vol 2 No.1), he recalled: "At the time I was running around in a little old Ford Popular. Alec Jackson ... suggested that I should use the prize money to get myself a nice car. You couldn't buy new cars then, but Alec said that he knew people at the Jowett factory in Bradford. I thought it sounded like a good idea, so I bought a new Jowett Javelin – for £500." He later reflected that maybe buying a house would have been better, but then he probably wouldn't have met his wife Pat, as he wouldn't have been staying at the hotel in Wembley where they met.

He also realised that there were few financial benefits from being World Champion. In the above article, he says that "Sponsorship for speedway riders was unheard of in those days. I was approached by Astorias who wanted me to say that I smoked their cigarettes. I didn't get any money – just cigarettes, which I had posted to Dad. I got absolutely nothing for being World Champion. I did get something once for riding for Wembley. Bill Kitchen and I were given a Philips shaver each."

He said that he knew that Split Waterman had received a percentage of the fee when he moved to Harringay, and felt that he was worth the same sort of money, so asked for a transfer. Sir Arthur Elvin refused to give him a transfer, or any extra cash, saying that it would be against Speedway's rules, and he was chairman of the Speedway Control Board. Fed up with the situation, Freddie threatened to pull out of the next meeting halfway through, saying that he wanted more money. Freddie said that "He threatened to have me banned completely – so my one and only attempt at blackmail failed." He does say that at the end of another successful season, the Lions riders were given an engine each by Alec Jackson, but believes that this was not sanctioned by Sir Arthur Elvin.

Freddie said that he believes that one of the reasons the Wembley riders only got "£2 a point and our bikes done" was because of Bill Kitchen. Freddie says that Bill "would have raced for nothing. He loved his motorcycling and if anyone so much as mentioned that we ought to get money on the side, Bill would think it was terrible. Yet he was my absolute idol."

On another occasion, Freddie recollected that he and Split Waterman were asked to do some publicity photos with film stars Diana Dors and Diana Decker. The riders thought that they "should get a few bob" for this, refused to participate and the camera crews left. The next day, Sir Arthur told them off for "wrecking such important publicity for speedway."

Despite his disputes with the Wembley management, Freddie stayed loyal to the club that had given him his start in speedway. And, given that the average salary in the UK in 1950 was around £250 a year (around £5 a week), and that footballers were paid a maximum of £15 a week during the season, maybe £2 per point wasn't so bad.

RIDERS' INDIVIDUAL SCORE CHART

RIDES	1st	2nd	3rd	4th	5th	Tot.	RIDES	1st	2nd	3rd	4th	5th	Tot.
1 F. WILLIAMS ...	3	3	3	2	3	14	10 D. DUNTON ...	1	0	1	1	2	5
2 R. CLARKE ...	1	2	0	0	0	3	11 A. LAWSON ...	2	2	3	1	2	10
3 J. BIGGS	0	1	0	0	2	3	12 J. YOUNG ...	0	1	2	1	3	7
4 W. GREEN ...	2	3	3	2	3	13	13 J. PARKER ...	2	1	2	3	0	8
5 D. OLIVER ...	F	3	1	2	0	6	14 S. WATERMAN	1	2	3	1	1	8
6 V. DUGGAN ...	1	1	1	0	1	4	15 G. WARREN ...	3	3	0	3	3	12
7 A. PAYNE ...	0	0	0	0		0	16 R. MOORE ...	Ex	0	2	3	2	7
8 C. BRINE ...	2	2	2	0	1	7	17 C. ROGER (Res.)	3	2				5
9 T. PRICE	3	F	3	1	1	8	18 M. ERSKINE (Res.)	0					0

The scores from the programme for the meeting.

Runner-up Wally Green, new World Champion Freddie and third placed Graham Warren after the 1950 World Final. (Courtesy JSC)

Freddie with Bernard Tussaud, the great-great-grandson of Madame Tussaud, the chief artist at Madame Tussaud's wax works museum. They are choosing eyes for the model of Freddie to go in the Sportsman's Corner at the famous museum in London. (Courtesy Peter Lush)

Freddie with his mechanic, Cyril Spinks, to whom he gave much of the credit for his World Final win. (Courtesy JSC – Peter Morrish)

7. 1951: Top rider for Wembley

Freddie did not ride abroad in the winter of 1950 to 1951. He had taken part in a short tour of Norway and Sweden with Wembley at the end of the 1950 season. In *Stenners 1951 Annual*, Lasse Akeby wrote: "Comparing the new with the old World Champion, Price gets my vote. Williams is a fast driver but seems to depend on a good start while Price can catch and outpace the rest."

Stenners's 1950 to 1951 world rankings had Freddie in sixth place, behind Graham Warren, Jack Parker, Aub Lawson, Tommy Price, and Ken Le Breton, although the latter was killed in a track accident in Australia in January 1951. An editorial by RM Samuel in the *News* also reflected doubts about Freddie's standing. Samuel said: "What of the 1950 riders? Freddie Williams, through winning the World Championship, should be accepted as the best performer of the season, but was he? I like Fred, he is a fellow Welshman and I have always found him good to watch on the track. Nevertheless, I confess to coming away from the Championship with an unsettled feeling. Analysed, it probably boiled down to the undisputable fact that while Freddie is certainly amongst the first 10 riders of today there are a few who would be ranked above him by the rank and file of speedway enthusiasts. I would go a short step farther, for I believe Freddie has, in his own team, one or two who would beat him three times out of five on current form.

I've added those last words because I am a believer in Freddie. He's young, and I think that he has every chance of becoming a star in a season or two that none could dare to do what I have just done – query his right to be considered the best rider of the year."

This is not the place to debate the merits of the 'old' World Championship culminating in one meeting with the current Grand Prix system. Freddie had been the best rider on the night at Wembley. In his first World Final he had beaten more experienced riders. Others may have been more consistent over the season, but he had the title.

Although Freddie did not ride in the winter, Eric rode for an England team in Australia that rode a seven match test series, but was not recognised as official by the Speedway Control Board, but was organised by Jack Parker. In early February, there were reports that Freddie was involved in trying to start speedway in Chapelizod in Dublin. His father was also involved, along with Howdy Byford, Split Waterman and Eric French. The latter was one of the few Irish riders in British speedway. Part of Freddie's role was in coaching riders to take part in the new promotion. Towards the end of March it was reported that he was involved in testing the new track. He also presented the trophy at the Irish Cycle Speedway Riders Championship.

At the end of March, a Freddie Williams team beat a Split Waterman team 50–34 at Chapelizod. The *News* reported that the large crowd had enjoyed "some of the most exciting racing seen in Ireland since the advent of speedway." Eric scored 12 points and Freddie 11, and according to the *Gazette*, the Williams brothers "swept all before them." The meetings were held on Sundays, so did not interfere with his Wembley commitments.

At the Empire Stadium, Bill Gilbert had decided to retire to concentrate on his business, although he later came back to ride for Norwich. Apart from that, the Lions were largely unchanged from 1950. They did not enter the Festival of Britain early season trophy, due to the usual unavailability of the Stadium until mid-May. The Lions rode seven challenge matches and five league meetings away from home to open the season.

At West Ham on 23 March, in the Lions' first meeting, Freddie rode the fastest time, 77 seconds, and was top scorer for Wembley. The *News* commented that "A winter's rest seems to have done him good." In March he was involved in a training school at Ringwood in Hampshire, "handing out advice to up-and-coming talent" according to the News.

In Wembley's second meeting, a challenge match at Wimbledon on 2 April, the News reported that Wembley "have three potential match winners in Freddie Williams, George Wilks and Tommy Price, but it was the World Champion, Freddie, who stole the show."

Freddie continued to ride regularly at Chapelzoid. The Dublin Eagles beat Bristol 42–41 with Eric scoring 10 points and Freddie and Split Waterman seven each. The next week, Odsal were beaten 44–39, with the Williams brothers top scoring again. Then on 2 May, Wembley drew 42–42 with the Dublin team, Freddie scoring a paid maximum for the visitors.

Freddie and Eric continued to ride regularly in Dublin. Opponents for the home team in May included a Bill Kitchen team and Walthamstow. However, *Stenners 1952 Annual* said that the crowds were not good despite the presence of star riders from England. A further meeting was held in June when an Abernethy Select was beaten 42–30. A different approach was taken at Shelbourne Park, where some young American riders were the nucleus of the team for the season, and rode some away meetings in England. This seems to have been more successful.

In April, Freddie strained his leg riding at Chapelizod. This was unfortunate as he had been chosen to challenge Aub Lawson for the Match Race title. At West Ham, Lawson won 2–0 with Freddie falling in one race. Freddie chose to ride his 'home' leg at Bristol, because it was the nearest track to his home, and his parents could come and watch him. The *Gazette* reported that "Aub Lawson (West Ham), the holder, beat Freddie Williams (Wembley) 2–1 to keep the Match Race Championship. Lawson's winning time of 62.2 in his first ride was the fastest clocked at Bristol this season. He was faster out of the gate but there was a great opportunity for Williams in the first race when the holder overslid coming out of the turn after three laps. Drawn inside for the second race, Williams made no mistake when he drove round the Australian at the pits turn and scored a great victory. But it was a fast getaway by Lawson in the final ride that proved the decider and Lawson deserved to keep his title."

Had Freddie won, he would have been the first rider to hold both the World Championship and the Match Race Championship at once. RM Samuel commented in the *News:* "Freddie Williams does not seem to have reached his best as yet. The season is young; maybe he'll settle down and be given another chance to have a cut at the champion later on. Riding his own track and before his own crowd could make a difference, though it is well to remember that some of Aub's best performances have been at Wembley."

As World Champion, Freddie was given more bookings for open meetings than before. In April he rode for a 'London' team against a 'Provinces' side at Wimbledon. At West Ham, he finished joint third in the Festival of Britain Trophy, with 11 points. And in June, he again came third in the London Riders Championship, with 13 points. But expectations were high. The report on Wembley's comfortable win at New Cross in April said that "Freddie Williams found himself unplaced in heat three, and did not really display the form expected of a champion."

There was an unusual incident in the league match at Wimbledon on the Monday before Wembley's opening night. Freddie and Bill Kitchen refused to ride in heat nine, saying that their gate slots had not been swept. The referee inspected them and said they were ok, so both riders were excluded for breaking the two minutes time allowance. Wembley went down by 10 points, but both riders rode later in the meeting.

Freddie celebrated the Lions' return to the Empire Stadium with a paid maximum against Wimbledon, and followed that with a maximum against Bradford the following week. These two meetings were the start of a run of 13 straight wins, which eventually saw the Lions retain the league title comfortably. In this run, after being unbeaten by an opponent in the first two meetings, Freddie scored a maximum at Bristol – becoming the first visiting rider to score a maximum at the Knowle Stadium that season – and a paid maximum at home to Birmingham, and was paid for four other double figure scores.

At the end of May, Freddie was invited to the Empire Pool to present cycling champion Reg Harris with victorious laurel wreaths after he had won a special match race. A rare visit to another two-wheeled sport, maybe reflecting the prestige that the Speedway World Champion had.

On 4 July, Freddie returned to New Cross, where he had been criticised earlier in the season. This time, reporting on Wembley's 24 point win, the *News* pointed out that the Williams brothers, along with Tommy Price, had ridden "magnificently to score more points between them than the whole of the Old Kent Road side." Freddie returned to New Cross a couple of weeks later to finish third in the Tom Farndon Memorial Trophy. In July he rode in the prestigious Laurels meeting at Wimbledon and finished fourth.

One curious incident occurred in the double header at Wembley against Harringay and then Bradford on 23 August. Freddie scored 11 points in the narrow win over Harringay, but then withdrew from the second match "because of unforeseen circumstances." He was subsequently fined £50 for withdrawing from the meeting.

A trophy that often eluded the Lions was the National Trophy, and this was the case again in 1951. In the first round, the Lions lost at home to Belle Vue in the first leg, but recovered to win comfortably in Manchester, with Freddie being paid for 12 points from five rides, a rare good meeting for him at Belle Vue. In the semi-final, Wembley comfortably beat New Cross, with Freddie scoring a five ride paid maximum in the home match. In the Final, Wembley lost by eight points at Wimbledon in the first leg, but were comprehensively beaten at home in the second leg.

The Lions did retain the London Cup, beating Wimbledon and then New Cross to reach the Final. Freddie scored a six ride paid maximum in the meeting at New Cross. The Lions then beat Harringay home and away to win the Cup.

Freddie continued to win more international honours with the England team. In the first match, at Harringay, Freddie was top scorer for England with 11 in a 60–48 defeat. Peter Foster in his history of the 'Speedway Ashes' said that he put on "a good show". Things improved for England at Odsal. They won by 10 points, and according to the *News* Freddie "was immaculate with four straight wins". He was again top scorer with 13. At Wembley for the third test, a 54,000 crowd saw Australia win to go 2–1 ahead in the series. Freddie's 12 points included three heat wins. Foster reflects that England "were served well only by Williams and Waterman." The *Gazette's* reporter commented that "On the form displayed only Freddie Williams and Split Waterman can hope to be retained for the fourth test at Birmingham."

Freddie was then named as captain for the test at Birmingham. The team was made up of riders who had only ridden post-war. RM Samuel commented in the *News:* "Many an old test favourite must have had something of a shock when the England team for next Saturday was announced. Truly the selectors have not allowed rather tattered reputations to influence them on this occasion. On paper it looks an odd side, but because I believe in experiments (without which nothing is ever learned) it is at least interesting. Freddie Williams, now presumably 'set' in his old form, should make a good skipper if he can master his shyness and show some authority – as I feel sure he can. If Freddie can repeat his Wembley test riding he should be a great inspiration to a side in which youth certainly predominates."

The average age of the England squad was 26, and it included 23-year-old Scot Tommy Miller, who was partnering Freddie. A Welshman and a Scot riding together for England. Miller won his first ride, but was then dropped for a ride before coming back for his last two, one of which he won. But Freddie had his worst match for England, scoring just two points before he was dropped for his last ride. The *News* reported: "Freddie Williams's worst night since he became an acknowledged star. Freddie scored one point in his first three rides, but team manager Les Marshall, probably thinking this was too bad to be true, persisted with him after the interval. Williams could make no improvement, and by the time he was pulled out in his last race, the match was all over." Tom Morgan wrote in the *News* that Freddie was "dropped like a hot brick" after the test at Birmingham. Before the team for the fifth test was announced, Reg Hay said in the *Gazette* that "Freddie Williams's inept performance at Birmingham should not be taken to heart. The Welshman has never been comfortable on the Birmingham track, but will do decidedly better at West Ham."

Freddie was then dropped for the final test at West Ham. The review in *Stenners Annual* commented that he was dropped because of a poor scoring record at West Ham, but said that "Evidently the selectors forgot that Williams won the vital before-the-final World Championship meeting at Custom House in 1950." Eric was called up by England, and scored nine points on his first home test for England. However, the *News* noted that Ronnie Greene, the England manager, "longed for riders such as Freddie Williams and Bert Roger."

Freddie also rode twice for England against Scotland. England managed to lose a five match series 3–2; Freddie scored 10 points in each of the tests that he rode in, and captained England in the last match.

The World Championship started at the end of May, with five meetings involving 80 riders, and just 18 going through to the next round. Freddie's future team-mate Trevor Redmond was one of them. In July, 17 meetings were held involving 136 riders having two meetings each. Of these, 51 qualified for the next round. Jack Young and Tommy Miller were the only unbeaten riders on 30 points. Eric entered at this stage, and qualified with 21 points. Bruce Abernethy went through with 26, and Trevor Redmond on 23, while Bill Kitchen went through with 20.

The top First Division riders entered at the Championship round stage. All nine First Division tracks held a meeting, with each rider competing twice. The final meetings were at Harringay and Bristol on 31 August, although the first seven were in a week from 13 to 18 August. One bad night could finish a rider's title hopes for another year. And no rider had ever, at this time, retained the World Championship.

Freddie was drawn at Wembley and Birmingham. The *News* reported: "Freddie Williams won the Wembley round with 11 points." He had been excluded in his first heat and "... won a run-off with Ernie Roccio, Bob Oakley and Tommy Miller to secure the £50 cheque for the meeting winner. Freddie shot like a rocket from the gate, gaining a narrow lead. Roccio gated equally well, and kept within a few lengths of the Wembley man for the whole course, but Williams romped home safely to secure the prize money."

At Birmingham two nights later, Alan Hunt won the meeting with 15 points, Freddie and Aub Lawson were joint second on 13. RM Samuel commented in the *News:* "Congratulations then to reigning champion, Freddie Williams, who did not allow a setback on his own track to lessen his intention to figure in the final. Many thought that his early disqualification at Wembley had robbed the Welshman of any hope. Instead he figures a point ahead of brother Eric, who has also ridden well."

Eric had scored 13 points at West Ham and 10 at Odsal to qualify comfortably. However, they were the only Wembley riders to qualify. Bruce Abernethy had won the meeting at West Ham in a run-off with Eric, but could only muster six at Harringay for a total of 19; Bill Kitchen scored 20, and Tommy Price 12. Twenty two points was the qualifying mark this time.

RM Samuel previewed the meeting for the *News:* "We shall see a terrific tear up between Split Waterman, Freddie Williams, Jack Young, Ronnie Moore and Jack Biggs ... If everything could go 'according to the book' I should say that the Championship lay between Split and Freddie Williams, basing my view, of course, on their intimate knowledge of the track. ... Fred has all the determination that his Welsh blood gives him; notice how he qualified – and well up too – after that loss of points when he was disqualified in his first championship round. That's mettle for you."

The magazine's editor, Len Went, forecast Lawson to win, followed by Biggs and Young. He commented: "Freddie Williams will make a big effort to retain the title and he'll scrap and fight as only a Welshman cam. But poker-faced Freddie seems to have 'gone over the hill' in recent weeks. His brother Eric could cause a surprise."

The *Gazette* said: "Freddie Williams: the reigning champion, at least until September 20. Is in the unenviable position of having more to lose than he has to win. The target for every rival present. They will all be keyed up to beat him. But, on his own track, should still be in the first three." Their joint favourites were Split Waterman and Aub Lawson.

They said that Eric: "... has a better chance than most people imagine. The mere fact that he is on his own track gives him something like a four point start over most of his rivals. Big snag, he is erratic. An outside chance – but a good one."

In their meeting preview, they commented: "Freddie Williams's road to final was not an easy one, the Lion having to ride all out at Birmingham to qualify. Never in the history of the

World Championship has any rider won the coveted trophy twice. Being a track artist, Freddie has the ability to make speedway history by lifting the sport's richest prize again."

Freddie and Eric were drawn to meet in their first race, heat three. Freddie won, with Eric last. But that was followed by a third place in heat eight and last in heat 10. Freddie's last two rides yielded a further three points for a disappointing seven points and tenth place.

Eric improved from his first ride to score six points to finish twelfth. The winner was a Second Division star, Jack Young, who beat fellow Australian Jack Biggs and Split Waterman in a three man run-off. However, the meeting is remembered for Jack Biggs's four wins, and then last place in his final ride, when one point would have made him World Champion. Split Waterman won that race, but the rider who kept Biggs in last place was … Freddie Williams.

The *News* reported that: "The Williams brothers had a lean time. Freddie, last year's winner, raised his supporters' hopes by winning heat three, but it turned out to be a false alarm. He didn't show up at all well afterwards, and a pointless pre-interval ride meant that Freddie's length of office as World Champion was rapidly drawing to a close."

Curiously, Freddie rode superbly at Harringay for Wembley the next evening and was unbeaten by an opponent in the league match.

Despite his disappointment in the World Championship Final, it had been a good season for Freddie. For Wembley, he was both top points scorer, and led the averages, 1.5 points ahead of second placed Bob Oakley (9.52 to 7.94). Remarkably, Wembley had seven riders averaging over seven points a meeting, with Jimmy Gooch on 6.25. The *News's* review of the Lions said that "Freddie Williams, another unsuccessful Match Race Challenger, carried the mantle of World Champion well and, riding like a champion all this season, more often than not finished as his side's top scorer." Nationally, in the League, National Trophy and London Cup, Aub Lawson was the top points scorer with 448. Freddie was second with 410.

In the First Division ranking published in the *1952 Stenner's Annual*, Freddie was fifth, behind Split Waterman, Aub Lawson, Ronnie Moore and Olle Nygren. In the 1951–52 World rankings, he was sixth, with Jack Young top and then the four riders who were above him in the First Division list. Freddie had now completed his fourth season as a team member at Wembley. In his review of the First Division in the *1952 Stenner's Annual*, Basil Storey said that Freddie and Eric "are sound but unlikely to improve". Howevery, both riders went on to prove him wrong.

In January 1952, the *Gazette* published their review of Wembley's 1951 season. It said: "It was the younger generation, Freddie and Eric Williams, Jimmy Gooch, Bob Oakley and Bruce Abernethy who stole the major honours." It continued: "Equalling him (Bruce Abernethy) for performance value was Eric Williams, Freddie's younger brother. He earned an international cap and, the way he was riding at the time, no man deserved one more. Eric has had an unlucky career to date, injuries holding him back time and again. But now he is blossoming out to the match-winner stage. No longer does Freddie overshadow him. Without doubt these two must now rank as one of the finest 'brother' combinations in the game. An indifferent early spell was gradually shrugged off until, away to New Cross, he notched his first league maximum of the season. Try as he would he just couldn't get full figures before his home crowd. That's a treat they still have in store. World Champion Freddie, as he was throughout the season, was a model of consistency. Only once or twice did he drop below his normal top scoring form. Freddie Williams was indeed, the rock around which the new Wembley was based.

Wembley with the National League Trophy at Harringay in September 1951: Tommy Price, Jimmy Gooch, Bob Oakley, Bruce Abernethy, Bill Kitchen (with trophy), Freddie, Eric and George Wilks.
(Courtesy JSC)

In the World Championship Final, as is so often the case for the defending champion, he disappointed. So, for that matter, did Eric Williams, who was riding at the last stage of the competition for the first time.

Freddie disappointed also when he was awarded the captaincy of England for the first time. After scoring 36 points in his first three tests, he met up with a night where absolutely nothing would go right for him. Result was two points for Freddie, an England defeat and his subsequent dropping from the last match of the series in favour of brother Eric."

Having had a winter off from racing before the 1951 season, Freddie decided to head for New Zealand for the winter, where Eric had ridden in 1950–51. It was a long journey, and the ship visited Port Said, Bombay, Aden, Colombo and Australia on the way. His time there is covered in the next chapter.

A classic action shot of Freddie riding for Wembley.

8. 1952: Just one point

Freddie started the year with a trip to New Zealand. However, the England team were riding a series in Australia, once again managed by Jack Parker. Wembley's up-and-coming youngster Jimmy Gooch was one of the tourists, and it seems surprising that Freddie and Eric were not involved. The selection for the England touring teams seems arbitrary, and maybe Freddie could get a better deal riding in New Zealand. However, one of the England party, Cyril Roger, was reported as saying in the *News* on 2 January that Frank Arthur had plans to bring Freddie over from New Zealand for the test series, and that if this happened "we will have the edge over our rivals." As it was, England lost the series 4–1, and Freddie was not called on to cross the Tasman Sea to help out.

Freddie did not arrive in New Zealand until mid-January. Ron Johnston reported in the *Gazette* that "great things are expected from Freddie Williams at Hastings", although the *News* had earlier reported that he was going to captain the Auckland team.

On 19 January, Johnston reported that "Freddie Williams has finally arrived here from Australia and is already proving very popular with everyone he meets. The folks out here have taken to him like a duck taking to water. Just wait until they see him ride. They'll go for him all the more if that's possible." In the *News*, Ronnie Moore wrote that: "Freddie Williams, having finally made his way over from Australia, is already terrifically popular here. … he's already being freely tipped to pick up a few of our championships. In fact he's already won the North Island title."

Freddie was proving to be hard to beat for most of the local riders, and won the North Island Championship at Palmerston North with a 15 point maximum. Jack Hart was runner-up on 14. However, not all his excitement was on the track. The *News* outlined how he had 'the scare of his life' in Auckland, when there was an earthquake just before one of his meetings. He said in a letter to his Wembley mechanic Cyril Spinks: "I've had the odd spots of excitement here and there, but this was the most terrifying yet."

The New Zealand league had five teams, and was run with four rider teams competing the matches over eight heats. Freddie's Auckland side finished top of the first round of the league, with six wins and two defeats, but the other four teams had each had a match cancelled due to rain, for which they were awarded a point each. In his first four meetings he only dropped three points. Ronnie Moore's Otago were one of their main opponents. Auckland won their home match against Otago 25–23, with Moore scoring a 12 point maximum and Freddie notching 10. In the return, Otago won by four points, but Freddie took 1.8 seconds off the track record and scored 11 points. Ron Johnston reported in the *Gazette*: "I can't help but go into raptures in praise of Freddie Williams. The Wembley man was going like a bomb and in his first ride lowered my track record by 1.8 seconds." Auckland won 32–16 at Christchurch. Freddie scored 10 points, and was said to "ride very well with Jack Cunningham."

As well as Ronnie Moore, Freddie would have expected to ride against his Lions team-mate Bruce Abernethy. However, Abernethy had been riding continuously since December 1947, and when he returned home from London "took to the bush for a lengthy holiday" according to EW Sullivan writing in *Stenner's 1952 Annual*. Norman Parker was another familiar opponent who rode for Canterbury. Not surprisingly, Freddie, Ronnie Moore and Parker were a cut above the rest of the riders. Freddie's average was 11.12 out of 12 in league meetings, and Moore and Parker both averaged above nine. EW Sullivan felt that they were too good: "Freddie Williams, Norman Parker and Ronnie Moore were in a class of their own. Except when opposing one another they usually came out on top and interest in them, as a draw, was somewhat lost. It was the weaker team members who provided the good close racing." He felt that the fans wanted handicap racing in the second halves of meetings.

A test series between England and New Zealand was planned. However, Freddie aggravated an old knee ligament injury when he hit a big bump on the track in the last race of the first test. He was told to take six weeks rest. The New Zealanders won the match at Hastings 31–17, with Norman Parker scoring seven and Freddie six. Ronnie Moore scored a maximum for the Kiwis, and Bruce Abernethy – back in action after his break – scored 11. With Freddie injured and Jack Parker unable to replace Bill Osborne, the rest of the test series was cancelled. Freddie was ranked as the top rider in New Zealand for 1951–52 in *Stenner's Annual*. The report on the New Zealand season said "Top spot goes to Freddie Williams for his fine league average, equipment and general consistency."

Freddie flew home from New Zealand – "quite a trip" according to the *News*, with stops in Fiji, Honolulu, California and New York. He arrived in the middle of March and was expected to be fit for the first league match.

Wembley's season started with the Middlesex Cup match at Harringay on 11 April. Bruce Abernethy had not returned from New Zealand, and – despite regular rumours to the contrary – never rode for the Lions again. Another departure was Bob Wells, who was now reaching the veteran stage and moved to Swindon, with Ian Williams as a team-mate. One new arrival was Trevor Redmond, a New Zealander who was signed from Aldershot. He became one of Freddie closest friends in the sport.

On 23 April, the *News* reported that Freddie's injury "may keep him out of the saddle for longer than expected" and that he had a try out at Wembley this week. Wembley team manager Duncan King said: "Freddie Williams has torn ligaments at back of one of his legs. The original damage was three seasons ago. He will have a minor operation next winter. He can ride this season. He has an occasional twinge, but is expected to be among top scorers for Wembley this season." The next week, it was reported that Freddie's knee was "progressing favourably one day, only to give him trouble the next."

Freddie returned to action with six points from four rides in a Lions' win at Belle Vue. But although he scored eight points at Wimbledon in a comfortable Lions' win, the match report said that he was "troubled badly by that weak knee" and "had to sometimes trail out of the bends to relieve the pain."

The Lions' home programme started on 8 May, against a weak Norwich side. Freddie scored a paid maximum, but away from home his form was inconsistent, as was the Lions'. While the Lions won their home league matches consistently, they lost at West Ham, Bristol, Birmingham and Norwich. Freddie only scored four at West Ham on 20 May, but dropped points when he went onto the centre green to avoid a crash with his old friend Howdy Byford. "Full marks to Freddie for that gallant and unselfish act" said the report. Freddie was also commended by the referee for his "smart thinking" and got a 'warm embrace' from Byford.

The *News* reported in mid-May that Freddie would have to treat his knee gently for some time to come. However, he did arrange to ride in Copenhagen on Whit Monday with Bill Kitchen and Jeff Lloyd. Also in May, the Lions rode a challenge match at Stoke. A crowd of 19,500 saw a narrow Lions' win. However, Freddie had apparently said to home skipper Ken Adams that "If you get more than 10,000 people in here, I'll give away my car." Fortunately Adams, a future Wembley team-mate, did not hold him to this pledge.

The 1952 Wembley Lions: Trevor Redmond, Eric, Bob Oakley, Tommy Price, Duncan King (manager), George Wilks, Den Cosby, Jimmy Gooch, Freddie, Tommy Barnett (trainer), Bill Kitchen (on bike).
(Courtesy Hayley Redmond)

The Lions' hold on the London Cup ended in the first round. Wimbledon won the first leg at the Empire Stadium by 10 points, and although Wembley put in a better performance at Plough Lane, they could not turn the tie round. The *Gazette* reported on the home match: "The Williams brothers ... are having a bad season. Tonight they hit their all-time low, nine points between them in 10 rides." Freddie's contribution was five, paid eight. He scored better at Plough Lane, with 11 paid 12 from six rides. In the *News*, Lionel Willis commented on the selection of the England team that "Freddie Williams seems to be riding under a cloud at the present time, but he could be useful held in reserve."

Freddie was chosen for the first test. Less than 20,000 turned up at Plough Lane to see Australia win by four points. England's cause was not helped when Norman Parker was injured in the first heat. Freddie rode with Alan Hunt and scored seven paid nine from his six rides. Previewing the second test, Willis wrote that "Cyril Brine and Freddie Williams, our third pair, have a points look about them. Freddie has been in-and-out these past few weeks because of his injured leg. But he did manage to score a maximum last Thursday [against Bradford at Wembley]."

England again lost by four points in front of a 36,000 crowd at Wembley. Freddie scored 10 paid 11, and kept his place for the rest of the series, which England lost 4–1. He had a poor night at Belle Vue, scoring just one paid two from three rides, but then scored eight paid nine at New Cross, and 12 paid 14 at Harringay in England's only win of the series. Freddie's third place, behind reserve Dick Bradley, secured a 3–3 draw in the last race, which meant England won the match.

Later in the season, Freddie again appeared for England in their annual series against Scotland. He rode twice, scoring a six ride maximum at Liverpool, and then 13 points at Motherwell in front of a reported 35,000 crowd. England lost both matches by four points, and the series 3–2. Eric was also in the England team for the meeting at Motherwell.

47

Gradually, Freddie's form improved. In July, he was unbeaten in four consecutive Wembley matches, although three were at home. A mid-season review of Wembley in the *Gazette* on 12 July said "Only recently has Freddie Williams recaptured the sparkling form which earned him world title honours two seasons ago." On 16 July, the Lions won by two points at New Cross, with Freddie unbeaten by an opponent. The *Gazette* said that he was "riding in his world beating form, was top scorer for the Lions with 11 points. Nothing showy about Freddie, just an honest to goodness workman."

After the Lions' defeat at Norwich on 14 June, they only lost two more league matches and in the end won the league quite comfortably, 11 points clear of runners-up Birmingham. In the league, from the beginning of July, Freddie's paid scores were only twice in single figures. In the season overall, he scored seven maximums and a further three paid maximums. He topped the Lions scorers in league and National Trophy matches with an average of 9.49, fractionally below his 1951 figure. He was half appoint clear of Tommy Price, who was the next best on 8.95.

As so often, the National Trophy was a forlorn hunting ground for the Lions. A comfortable aggregate victory over Bradford was followed by a 30 point defeat at Birmingham. Freddie had a rare poor night, with just two points from five rides. The Lions won the return home leg, but went out of the competition. Once again, in the *1953 Stenner's Annual*, Basil Storey did not want to acknowledge the Lions' domination of the league, saying that Birmingham, Harringay and Wimbledon were "colourful" and provided "the racing fireworks" in 1952. He said that "Wembley plodded through to the championship ... Even in victory there was a drabness in performance. Freddie Williams, always reliable, livened the closing weeks with a return to something approaching the fiery form which won him the world title in 1950." In the Stenners' rankings for 1952, Freddie was placed fourth, behind Split Waterman, Jack Young and Ronnie Moore.

Freddie just ahead of Harringay's Split Waterman. (Courtesy JSC)

Apart from helping Wembley win another league title, the other priority for Freddie was the World Championship. The championship was developing a wider geographical spread of entries, partly reflecting the development of the sport. Mid-European and Scandinavian rounds were held, with meetings in Vienna, Munich, Sweden, Norway, Denmark and Finland. This culminated in the European Grand Final, at Falkoping in Sweden on 22 June. The field was made up of the top four from the Munich qualifier, the top eight from the final Scandinavian meeting in Oslo and four British riders. The top eight qualified for the international round. In Britain, the National round was held at six tracks at the end of May, with 14 riders qualifying for the International round. A young Brian Crutcher was among the qualifiers. The riders now had two meetings each, with the top 62 out of 96 qualifying for the championship round. Eric entered at this stage, and qualified with 18 points. Of the 'international' contingent, Olle Nygren was the top qualifier on 26. Future Wembley team-mate Rune Sormander also qualified – just– with 13 from his two meetings.

Freddie's Wembley team-mate Bob Oakley was the top qualifier for the final with 28 points from his two meetings. Freddie scored 13 in the Wembley qualifying round, which was won in front of 45,000 fans by Jeff Lloyd with 14 points. He beat Trevor Redmond in a run-off to take the winner's cheque. Freddie then scored 14 at Birmingham to qualify comfortably with 27 points. At Birmingham he tied for top place in the meeting with Arthur Payne, and lost a run-off for the winner's cheque.

Also on 27 points were Ronnie Moore, Split Waterman and the current champion, Jack Young. Dan Fosberg was the first European rider to qualify since 1937. Belle Vue's Henry Long was the first South African to reach a World Final. Among those eliminated were Tommy Price, with 21 points, and Eric on 15. Future Wembley star Brian Crutcher was among the eight riders making their world final debuts, although Dick Bradley had been a reserve in 1951. A surprise was Trevor Redmond qualifying for one of the reserve places, along with Norway's Basse Hveem.

The *Gazette* said that "Freddie can do it again. In London the scales of popular opinion are beginning to weigh slightly in favour of Wembley's Welshman ... with Wimbledon's Ronnie Moore as co-favourite. Williams's recent return to form, plus the fact that he won the title two years ago and will be contesting the final on the Wembley track which he knows so well, are factors no shrewd judge of the cinders game can ignore." The article also said that Freddie had been "almost unbeatable" at Wembley in recent weeks. It also pointed out that the average age of the riders was 25, with Jeff Lloyd being the oldest at 36 and Brian Crutcher the youngest at 18.

In the *News*, Len Went said that Jack Young, Freddie and Ronnie Moore were the leading contenders for the title. He said that Freddie "the 'local hope' has the ground advantage but I can't see him matching Moore for cleverness or Young for speed." It was expected that Split Waterman would miss the final with a cracked kneecap. In the event he did ride, but was clearly restricted by his injury. Tom Morgan hedged his bets, saying that he expected Freddie, Moore and Young to finish level on points.

Since winning the title in 1951, Young had moved to West Ham, and thus had ridden more often at Wembley than in his previous final appearance. Freddie won the first heat in the fastest time of the night, 69.6 seconds. He beat Ronnie Moore, who had a puncture, but still managed to finish second. Young won heat three, and the two title contenders met in heat six. It was a "tremendous" race according to Tom Stenner's report in the *1953 Stenner's Annual:* "Williams ... slashed into the lead and stalled off every come-through manoeuvre for three driving laps. Then Young let loose in a desperate bid to dive through a narrowing gap on the outside as the pair swept down the straight for the last time round. Instead he scraped handlebar and footrest along the fence, somehow stayed on and, in spite of the terrific speed, angled into the corner to overtake on the inside."

The *Gazette's* report, probably by Basil Storey, said: "For more than three laps a grimly determined Freddie Williams defied all efforts of a slow-starting Jack Young to pass him. With Diamond Jack right on his back wheel, Freddie pulled every trick out of the bag in a masterly display of track craft. But cool, calculating Jack wore him down with that remorseless tenacity that has always been an outstanding characteristic of all speedway's Australian masters.

Freddie only made one slip, and that was sufficient for … Jack. Coming out of the first bend on the last lap, Freddie left a tiny opening and Jack was through. With the Australian on the inside coming down the back straight and approaching the last bend it was all over, including the shouting. How much that mighty duel cost gallant Freddie in stamina was proved in his later races. For he never again shaped like a challenger to Young's supremacy."

The 1952 World Final: Freddie (runner-up), Jack Young (World Champion), and Bob Oakley (third).
(Courtesy JSC)

Interviewed in *Classic Speedway* in the autumn of 2012, Freddie said that he made the start because he had a higher gear than Young, but then fought off the Australian for the rest of the race. He thought he had put the Australian in the fence, and momentarily relaxed, and that was when Young came up the inside of him. He said "I have to admit, that was probably the only time in my racing days when I deliberately meant to fence an opponent. Well, it was the World Final."

In heat 10, Freddie beat Long, Cyril Roger and Jeff Lloyd, but then was surprisingly beaten by Dan Forsberg in heat 14. This left Young needing two points from heat 17 to win the title, and he duly finished second behind Bob Oakley. Freddie won heat 18 to finish on 13 points and take the runner-up spot, just one point behind Young. It is interesting to speculate what would have happened if he had beaten Forsberg, but reports of the meeting say that Young knew he only needed two points in his last race for the title, and did not challenge Oakley, who finished third on 12 points.

Tom Stenner wrote that "Runner-up Freddie Williams was better than when winning the title in 1950 but unexpectedly dropped a point to Dan Forsberg." In the *Gazette*, William B Whitely said that Freddie was "a gallant runner-up" He also said that "clever as he is, and I am inclined to the belief that he is probably a trifle more track crafty than Young, Freddie just lacks that grimness that hallmarks a champion. Anyway, he was streets ahead of anybody else bar Young on the night's showing." A strange comment – Freddie maybe did not have the ruthless streak of Tommy Price, but was always a determined competitor, and had nearly fenced Young – uncharacteristically – to try to hold onto his title. Jack Young said about Freddie in the *News:* "A gallant loser but, boy, didn't I know that I had been in a race." A 93,000 crowd had enjoyed the meeting, where the Lions had taken two of the rostrum places, the only time that had happened in the history of the Championship.

Freddie stayed at home in the winter of 1952 to 1953. In November, the *News* reported that he was making a lot of trips between Port Talbot and London, and was doing a lot of shopping. His sister Kate was getting married in Port Talbot, and he seemed to be very busy with the arrangements. He had considered riding in South Africa, but the report said that the British riders had been 'left out in the cold' by the promoters there. In December, it was reported that he had been offered a trip to South Africa, but had turned it down. It could have been a holiday and some rides. Instead, he was spending the winter in South Wales. He was coaching novice riders at a newly built stadium in Neath, which had a 380 yard track, and in Cardiff.

Overall, it had been a successful year for Freddie. He topped the Wembley averages again, with 9.49 in league and National Trophy matches, half a point clear of Tommy Price. After his disappointing World Final in 1951, he had established his World Championship credentials again as runner-up to jack Young. And Wembley had won the league again. However, 1953 would see important developments for him on-and-off the track.

51

Above: Freddie and Pat (Courtesy Sarah Williams).

Left: An 'informal' photo of Freddie (right) with Wembley team mate Trevor Redmond, one of his closest friends in speedway.
(Courtesy Hayley Redmond and Sarah Williams)

52

9. 1953: World Champion again

1953 was a seminal year for the country, for speedway and for Freddie Williams. It saw the Coronation of the new Queen, Elizabeth II, in June; which dominated the national consciousness in the first half of the speedway season.

Speedway, as a commercially run business, at times lacked the stability of other major sports. In football and cricket, it was relatively rare for a team in the national competitions to go out of business. This happened from time-to-time in professional rugby league, particularly in new areas for the sport, which was forever facing the challenge of how to break out of its heartland in the north of England. Rugby union at this time was played by amateur players, with – certainly in England – attracting a crowd being a secondary consideration. But speedway was different. The sport had grown enormously since 1946, but some teams had – maybe inevitably – collapsed. This is not the place to discuss the reasons for the various teams going out of business – certainly the punitive rate of Entertainment Tax applied to speedway compared with other live sports was one important factor.

Another was the growth of television. In 1950, by the end of the year, there were 578,000 sets in use. With the coverage of the Coronation, plus the 'Matthews' FA Cup Final on 2 May, more and more people were buying sets. By the end of the year, there were nearly three million sets in use, a huge increase and a major social change in entertainment. It affected both cinemas, the theatre and live sport. As well as the attractions on television, and the novelty of pictures coming into people's homes, many of the sets were bought on hire purchase, with the weekly payments meaning less money to be spent on other forms of entertainment.

In mid-June, New Cross pulled out of the League. Their promoter said they needed crowds of 10,000 to be sustainable; only half that were attending the meetings. For the sport to lose one of the big London teams was a major blow, and the start of a downward spiral that lasted for the rest of Freddie's career.

However, for Freddie, the New Year had opened on a very positive personal note, with the announcement of his engagement to Olympic ice skater Pat Devries. The *Gazette* had a photo of the happy couple and said that the "serious looking fellow, with the attractive young miss, is none other than happily engaged former world speedway champion (and last year's runner up) Wembley Lion Freddie Williams. His bride-to-be is Olympic ice skater Pat Devries. Pat and Freddie met at a party two years ago and their engagement is no surprise to their friends. They'll announce the happy day soon."

The next week, Brian Crutcher asked in his column in the *Gazette*: "How many riders marry fans?" He said that Freddie's 'love match' was with the equally famous skater Pat Devries and that "they were each other's greatest fans. Pat has long been a Freddie Williams fan, even before she'd met Freddie."

The *News* featured Freddie on the cover, and said that "Freddie has a new partner … Congratulations to former World Champion Freddie Williams who has just announced his engagement to Miss Pat Devries. Pat was a member of the British Olympic skating team last year and has given exhibitions all over the country. She is naturally a keen follower of Freddie's performances on the track."

However, how the couple met is a little different from the version in the speedway press at the time. Interviewed a few months before he died by Tony McDonald for *Classic Speedway*, Freddie recalled that he was staying in the Treganna hotel in Wembley, which he used regularly and "was eating breakfast in the dining room one morning when I suddenly noticed this pretty young girl working there who I hadn't seen before. She brought me my meal and I went 'Wow!' Then I asked Mabel, the woman who ran the hotel: 'Hey, Mabe, who's that young bit of stuff who brought my breakfast?' She said: 'Do you mind, that's my daughter!'" Pat was his first real girlfriend, and according to the article, knew nothing about speedway and hadn't heard of, let alone knew, Freddie. She had her own successful career as a skater.

This was part of the reason that they had not met at breakfast before. Their daughter Jayne says that her mother would normally be training at the Wembley Ice Rink early in the morning, and would therefore not be around at breakfast time.

An incident a couple of years before this also may have prevented their meeting. Eric outlined what happened in *The Eric Williams Story* (part19) "Freddie was living in a family hotel called Treganna where he shared a cabin in the back garden with the infamous Kiwi brothers Bruce and Don Abernethy. This group wasn't very learned when it came to the precautions required when using gas. On returning from a meeting at Bradford in the early hours of a Sunday morning, they decided to have a bath. The setup at the hotel was such that it wasn't a simple matter of turning on a tap and getting hot water, the shrewd old landlady had installed a coin operated gas meter which required the bath taker to pay for their own hot water.

The three lads had put the required coins in the slot, turned on the gas, and then realised they didn't have a match with them to light it. They returned to the cabin in search of a match and, as all three were non-smokers, it took a while to find one. The three then triumphantly returned to light the gas. What they forgot was that the gas had been left turned on for the entire period they had been away in search of a match. As soon as the match was struck, there was an explosion when the accumulated gas ignited. This might sound funny now, but the three lads certainly didn't think so at the time it happened. It took a while for their singed hair and eyebrows to grow out. They were lucky they weren't seriously hurt. Naturally, they weren't too popular with the landlady and the other hotel guests who were all awakened in the early hours ... by the sound of the explosion."

Eric spent the winter riding in New Zealand. Freddie had decided not to ride in the southern hemisphere, and instead went with Pat to Switzerland, to enjoy some skiing and skating to strengthen his muscles on his injured left leg. In March, the *News* reported that Freddie had enjoyed his stay in Switzerland. It said that Freddie had found skiing "very tricky" although he had made one attempt on the Cresta Run (usually associated with tobogganing) and said it "takes too long to learn this game" and "speedway is a lot safer than that Cresta effort". Many years later, after retiring from speedway, he became an accomplished skier and returned to the Cresta Run. His daughter Jayne says that he did a record time for it.

In the *Gazette*, Harold Hastings's Wembley preview commented that: "Freddie Williams, quiet, reserved, and one of the few riders who does not insist on 'talking shop' whenever he runs into your scribe, has spent the winter here. He recently announced his engagement to Olympic skater Miss Pat Devries, and wedding bells may peal out this year. Freddie and Pat spent a few weeks skiing and skating in Switzerland and what better tutor could he have than his own fiancée? The pair have also been ice skating at the Empire Pool, for Freddie says that this strengthens the muscles and gives added poise. Now we wait to see him skid round the bends ... and it's no secret that he is keyed up to rip that world title from Jack Young."

Wembley 1953: Tommy Barnett (trainer), Eric French, Tommy Price, Duncan King (manager), Bill Kitchen, Freddie, Eric; front: Brian Crutcher, Trevor Redmond, Jimmy Gooch, George Wilks.

England 57 Australia 51 at Wembley, 13 August 1953. Back: Dick Bradley, Tommy Price, Charles Ochiltree (manager), Split Waterman, Freddie; front: Tommy Miller, Pat Clarke, Brian Crutcher and Eric. Eric started the night at reserve, but finished as England's top scorer with 15. (Courtesy JSC)

The Lions team that started the season was very similar to that which finished 1952. However, after three of the early season Coronation Cup meetings, Bob Oakley announced his retirement, to concentrate on his business in Southampton. So the Lions swooped to sign 18-year-old Brian Crutcher from Poole. The transfer fee of £2,500 reflected the rider's potential – he had reached the World Final as a Second Division rider the previous season. Buster Brown joined the Pirates in part-exchange. The signing of Brian Crutcher gave the side a younger image, although only three of the team were 'veterans' – Tommy Price, Bill Kitchen and George Wilks. The latter only rode five league meetings during the season. Rune Sormander became the first Swede to ride for Wembley in June as cover for the injured Wilks, but was then replaced by Eric French, who joined Wembley from New Cross when the south London circuit closed.

In a series about his career so far in the *Speedway Star* in 1955, Brian Crutcher recalled the influence that Freddie had in his decision to join Wembley. Interviewed by Eric Linden, Crutcher said how he was invited to a second half at Wembley before the 1952 World Championship Final. He was looking at the stadium, and said that Freddie came over and asked if he was feeling OK. He said he was feeling terrific.

He scored six points in the 1952 Final, his debut, and said they were the "hardest I've ever earned. Once again it was Freddie Williams who had an answer, a word of comfort. Freddie, who must have been feeling some slight disappointment himself, having just been pipped for the title by Jack Young. Yet the Welshman still had time for a raw young kid, raw as far as these big occasions were concerned. 'Six Points. But you'll do better next year.'" Crutcher replied: "Next Year, if I'm lucky enough to make a final again. I was outclassed tonight." "For you" said Freddie, Crutcher recalled, "There will always be another day."

In 1953, when Crutcher was looking for a move to a First Division club, he remembered the friendly attitude of Freddie Williams and signed for Wembley. He crashed three times in his first meeting, and then "saw grim faced Freddie Williams and Tommy Price walking purposefully towards him."

Wembley's campaign began with a couple of challenge matches. Freddie scored a maximum in a comfortable win at Birmingham, and the *Gazette* reported that "On this form Freddie Williams will take a great deal of holding this season. He gave one of the best performances by a visiting rider at Perry Barr for a long time, and only against Hunt in the opening heat was he any way pushed." To be able to enter the Coronation Cup, Wembley staged three home meetings at Wimbledon, losing twice. Against Belle Vue, Freddie had a rare last place in his first ride, then won the next three. In the *News*, Trevor Redmond wrote that Freddie was using American handlebars, and said that they were "very comfortable."

In April, the *Gazette* reported that "I hear that Freddie Williams is an accomplished 500cc motor car enthusiast. He would do more of it, but it is understood that the powers that be frown on the idea. When you consider that with fees and manufacturers' perks it'd be possible to get starting money at the rate of a couple of hundred pounds – well it makes you think." However, Freddie doesn't seem to have pursued car racing again, certainly not while he was a speedway rider.

The Lions also lost their first meeting back at the Empire Stadium, but two weeks later Freddie scored his first maximum of the season in an official meeting, again against Birmingham. The *News* reported that he led from start to finish in all his rides.

Freddie was nominated as the challenger to Jack Young in the Match Race Championship in May, but lost 2–0 in both legs. RM Samuel commented in the *News* that "Freddie Williams didn't put up much of a show as the May challenger. I don't think he was greatly interested; it seems hard to believe that he was the 'easy meat' that Jack made him look."

The Lions' hopes of winning back the London Cup finished in their first match. Wimbledon beat them in both legs, with the *News* reporting of the home meeting: "With the exception of Freddie Williams and young Crutcher, the Lions had little or no fight in them."

Brian Crutcher was an important signing for the Lions. He served the team well until the end of the 1956 campaign. Interviewed for this book, he recalled that Freddie was "a good trapper and technician." He remembered the race in the 1952 World Final when Freddie had been narrowly beaten by Jack Young to decide the title. Freddie had almost put Young "in the grandstand" but says that was not typical riding by Freddie. He always found Freddie to be a hard opponent, but a fair one. He was "a job to catch when he got in front". He never used bad language, and often was quiet in the pits.

On tour with Freddie in South Africa in 1953–54, Crutcher said that he got on well with Freddie and Pat, and says that Freddie was "good company" and had "a kind way with him". Crutcher recalls the life of a speedway rider in the early 1950s was riding "three to five meetings a week" and riding in Ireland on occasions. He says that he "made a good living from speedway" and went on to have a successful business career when he retired from speedway at the age of 25, having ridden for 10 years.

Crutcher found Wembley very different from Poole – he had a mechanic to prepare his bikes, and recalls the huge crowds that watched the Lions, although they declined gradually during his time at Wembley.

In the Coronation Cup, the two home defeats in meetings staged at Wimbledon made it difficult for the Lions to challenge for the trophy. Freddie still rode well, and against Belle Vue in June was "not troubled in picking up a maximum" according to the *News*. At Bristol in June, the *Gazette* said that "The Williams brothers were at their best with 19 points between them and the only rider to stop Freddie Williams getting an away maximum was local skipper Billy Hole in heat 11. That was one of the few times Wembley [riders] did not take a first bend lead."

The annual test series against Australia was due to start in June. The *News's* reporter said that he rated Eric slightly ahead of Freddie in the competition for team places, but two weeks later said that Freddie had "slipped into top gear at the right time." Eric Linden commented in the *Star* that "even if he isn't shining so brightly this season as of yore, [Freddie] must be found a place. So we make him first reserve. A more than useful man to have round to plug up any gaps that develop in the scoring." The first match of the three was at Norwich, but Freddie had a poor evening in front of a sell-out 27,000 crowd. He only scored three points (+1) as England lost to the Australians.

Despite this poor show, he kept his place for the second test at the Empire Stadium, where 34,000 enjoyed the action. Brian Crutcher was also in the team, along with Eric and Tommy Price at reserve. In the event, the two reserves were England's top scorers with 15 and 12 respectively. Freddie scored eight, but this was not enough for him to keep his place in the third test, which England won for a rare series victory. The *News* had commented on his omission: "...our selectors will pay the penalty for omitting Freddie. They say he's temperamental, but that excuse doesn't satisfy me." The English win at the Empire Stadium was the first time that the Australians had lost there since the War.

In September, England faced New Zealand in a three match series. Freddie rode in all the meetings. Barry Briggs fell in the first one and was injured, reducing the visitors' strength.

Brian Crutcher and Freddie with a Wembley fan. The award is one given for one of the second half events at Wembley. (Courtesy Brian Crutcher)

Freddie receiving an award from Alec Jackson, who originally signed him for the Lions in 1946. (Courtesy JSC)

Freddie practising at Wembley, with Pat keeping time. (Courtesy David Williams)

Left: Training together at Wembley. (Courtesy JSC – Peter Morrish)
Right: Freddie and Pat fixing a wheel. (Courtesy David Williams)

England won the series 3–0. Freddie rode in all three meetings, and scored an 18 point maximum in the second test at Bristol, a very comfortable 77–31 win. He also made one appearance for England against Scotland in a series held on Second Division tracks. He scored six points in England's only win, at Leicester in July.

The Coronation Cup had been the main competition for Wembley for the first half of the season, the National League was run mainly in the second half of the season. For once, the Lions were severely tested in the fight for the title. In the end they scraped home by one point, with 23 points from 16 matches, compared with 22 for their North London rivals. Harringay had won the Coronation Cup, and in *Stenner's 1954 Annual*, Basil Storey aggregated the results, which gave Harringay a clear lead. However, Wembley had ridden three 'home' matches at Wimbledon in the Coronation Cup, and lost two of them, so it was not really a fair analysis. A home-and-away double for the Lions over the Racers in two days in September was decisive, although Harringay were missing Split Waterman through injury for those two meetings. The *News* commented on the Lions' home win that the "bulk of the Lions scoring was done as usual by the Williams brothers and Tommy Price."

In 16 league matches, Freddie scored four maximums and a paid maximum. In eight other meetings he was paid for at least 10 points from his four rides. Against Norwich in July, the *Gazette* reported that he scored an "immaculate maximum". This was remarkably consistent scoring to win his – and Wembley's – last league title. Once again, Basil Storey, writing in *Stenner's 1954 Annual*, was critical of Wembley, saying that the team was 'workmanlike'. He said that Tommy Price and Bill Kitchen were the backbone of the team and that "there was a dour, 'old firm' look about the Williams brothers, Freddie and Eric; and at times Eric, in my opinion always a more spectacular character than the older Freddie, really threatened to sparkle." Tommy Price had a very good season, improving his average from the previous year. However, although Bill Kitchen may have played an important role as captain, his average fell to 5.74, and, at the age of 44, he was clearly approaching the end of his career. Freddie was again the Wembley top scorer, with his best ever average of 9.62, closely followed by Price on 9.27 and Eric on 9.20. On 31 October, in their review of Wembley's season, the *Star* commented: "Wembley ... owe a terrific debt to the two 'Taffies' in the team, Freddie and Eric Williams. In fact, they owe them their league title and their successes in other competitions."

Another competition where Freddie found more success was in the National Trophy. The 18 heat formula gave each rider six rides, and he scored a rare 18 point maximum against Birmingham in a runaway Wembley win in the semi-final. Harringay had been beaten by 40 points on aggregate in the previous round, again showing who were the top dogs in North London. In the Final, Wembley faced Wimbledon. Freddie had a poor night at Plough Lane, with just two points from four rides. The Lions lost by 28 points, but recovered three days later to win 66–42 at the Empire Stadium. Freddie was unbeaten by an opponent with 17+1, but the Lions lost on aggregate by four points.

Freddie's standing as Wembley's top rider and a former World Champion meant that he was given more 'open' bookings than before. He always said he didn't like riding with Eric as his partner, but they finished joint top in a pairs meeting at Bristol, despite both falling in one heat, and Freddie remounting for a point. In July they won a best pairs at Wimbledon in controversial circumstances. In the final, Freddie won, with Geoff Mardon and Ronnie Moore second and third. It was announced that the trophy was being awarded to the Williams brothers. There was uproar, so Freddie and Eric agreed to a rerun. Freddie won again, with Moore second, but this time Eric took third place.

And sometimes the brothers were rivals. In the London Riders Championship, Jack Young won with a maximum; Eric was third with 11 points, one ahead of Freddie on 10.

Once again, the World Championship was the main event in the last three months of the season. The tournament continued to develop more of an international base. Riders from seven European countries competed in six meetings leading to the Grand European Final at Kumla in Sweden, along with two British riders. The top eight qualified for the International round. Swedish riders dominated the meeting, taking four of the top five places. The meeting was won by Norway's Basse Hveem with a maximum.

For most British riders and tracks, the tournament started at the end of May, with 80 riders in five meetings, with the top 16 qualifying for the International Round. Ten meetings were held in July, with 54 of the 80 riders qualifying. Wembley's Brian Crutcher was one of the qualifiers, as were Bill Kitchen and Trevor Redmond.

Freddie and Eric entered in the Championship Round, which was held in August at nine tracks. Each rider had two meetings. Freddie's first meeting, at Norwich, was abandoned when he had seven points from three rides. His next meeting was at Wembley. Jack Biggs won the meeting with 14 points, Freddie was runner-up on 13 and Eric was third with 12. The *News* reported that Freddie was "loudly booed in heat 14 when he appeared to ride Ron How into the safety fence during a great fight for second place. An unusual occurrence this, Freddie on the receiving end from his own supporters." In the restaged meeting at Norwich, Freddie finished joint third with Rune Sormander on 12, and therefore qualified for the Final comfortably with 25 points. Eric also made it with 24, as did Brian Crutcher on 23. Former Wembley colleagues Split Waterman and Rune Sormander also made it through to the big night. Olly Nygren was the only survivor from the European entries.

In the *News*, Len Went said that "local knowledge counts for a lot. Freddie and Eric are magnificent battlers and they're bound to have a big say in the destiny of the championship. Former champion Freddie may outshine his brother on this occasion. He forecast Jack Young to retain his title, followed by Freddie, Jack Biggs and Split Waterman. In the same publication, RM Samuel said that Young "ought to win it". He felt that Eric was riding a little better than Freddie, and could "steal the limelight" along with Biggs or Nygren. Also in the *News*, Tom Morgan said that "Wembley's Williams boys will have track advantage which counts for a lot but at the moment they lack the dash of my chosen three: Nygren, Young and Ronnie Moore." The magazine also asked what the experts thought. West Ham's team manager Ken Brett not surprisingly tipped Jack Young, as did Major WW Fearnley of the Speedway Control Board. Wimbledon's Ronnie Greene, Wembley manager Duncan King, Harringay Manager Wal Phillips, Bradford's Ron Clarke, the SRA's Tom Garvey and Ian Hoskins from Scotland were all asked for their opinion. Garvey mentioned Eric, but none of them mentioned Freddie, despite him being the 1952 runner-up, 1950 champion and top scorer for the Wembley Lions.

In the *Gazette*, Bruce Valdar forecast Young, Waterman and Biggs, but said "I hate to leave out the Williams brothers." In the Speedway Star, Alan Hunt tipped Waterman to win from Young and Moore. Editor Eric Linden went for Young to complete a hat-trick of titles, followed by Jackie Biggs and Ronnie Moore, with Eric as the best outsider. He did include Freddie's name in his 'probables' list. Danny Carter also tipped young, and said he was the 'red hot favourite'. He mentioned Olle Nygren as another 'possible' along with Freddie.

In the *Daily Express*, Basil Storey tipped Split Waterman to win, with Young second and 'maybe' Ronnie Moore third.

It was a wet Thursday for the Final. Freddie, assisted by Pat, practiced starts in the Wembley car park in the afternoon of the meeting, to make sure that he was ready for the conditions he would face in the evening. In *Vintage Speedway Magazine*, interviewed by John Chaplin in 1993, he recalled: "It had been dry during the day, what if it got wet later in the evening when racing started? Pat and I went down to the stadium with a bucket of water. The concrete of the carpark was exactly the same as the Wembley starting area … we soaked the concrete and I practised starts on the wet surface all afternoon. And it did rain that night." Freddie also 'confessed' in that interview that the night before the final, he had gone with Pat, a team-mate and the team-mate's girlfriend for a night out in the west end.

They had a meal, saw a show and ended up in a club. They got home about 4am. His approach was that rather than worry about the meeting all day, he would get up late and arrive at the stadium an hour or so before the start. He knew that his bike would be ready and well-prepared by his mechanic Cyril Spinks. This way he avoided any big night nerves.

Tom Stenner, in the *1954 Stenner's Annual*, reported Freddie as saying "I practised starting nearly 1,000 times in 1953 in the Wembley Stadium car park and on odd pieces of gravel and the rider who snaps off first has a 90 percent chance. The others have to pass him, which is difficult in slippery conditions. Freddie also said that his grass track experience "stood him in good stead" particularly in the first half of the meeting. He outlined: "It was just like my grass days in those heats. I knew the answers before the skids occurred and but for that riding on the green years ago I would have finished well down the line. I had the break too at the start of most races, not because I am a Wembley rider –believe me there's no such thing as secret practice on our track – but because I have always concentrated on getting away."

Freddie won heat one, but only after Dick Bradley had led for the first two laps. In heat five, Freddie beat Jack Young and Ronnie Moore, "riding his home circuit brilliantly" according to Robert Bamford and Glynn Shailes. Tom Morgan said in the *News* that Freddie's win over Young was revenge for his defeat in the 1952 Final. In heat nine, he beat Graham Warren and Eric "without being troubled in the slightest" according to the *News*. After 12 heats, when each rider had taken three rides, Freddie and Split Waterman led with a maximum nine points, followed by Young and Geoff Mardon on eight, with Olly Nygren on seven.

In heat 13, Freddie was beaten by Jeff Lloyd, who had fallen in heat 10 and thus missed out on the chance of pressing for a rostrum place. The starting gate had malfunctioned, and several races, including this one, were started on the green light. An interview with Freddie in *Classic Speedway* says it was a 'ragged' start. Freddie did not make a good start, and had to overtake Geoff Mardon on the third lap to take second place.

Split Waterman won heat 15 and only needed to finish second in heat 17 to Freddie to secure a run-off for the title. If the former Wembley man won the race, Freddie would have to finish second to secure the runners-up spot again. So Freddie was not the favourite for the title at this stage. But there was further drama. The clutch plate on Waterman's number one bike had fallen apart. He was offered the loan of a bike, but came out for the race on his own machine, his mechanics had managed to replace the clutch. According to Jim Stenner, "Coolly, almost placidly, Williams sailed from the tapes on a £500 victory ride." Olly Nygren was second, hugging the white line, and Waterman could not get past him to force a run-off for the title.

The 1953 World Final: Geoff Mardon (third), Split Waterman (runner-up) and Freddie.
(Courtesy JSC – John Chaplin)

In the *News*, Len Went said that Freddie "unruffled and unchallenged, crossed the winning line amid a deafening roar, but he was not certain that the title was his until he returned to the pits."

In the *Star*, Eric Linden reported on heat 17: "Tension terrific. Long delay as starting gate decides to work again. From the gate its Freddie Williams. Nygren follows and in the jostling for position Waterman –on a different machine from earlier races – finds himself pushed right out. He just couldn't get back. A tremendous dive inside Nygren at the last turn only succeeded ion almost causing a Waterman fall. So its Freddie Williams's title."

For years after this, whenever Olly met Freddie, the Swede would remind him that "I fixed Split" to give Freddie the title without a run-off. Freddie said in *Classic Speedway* that "Nygren put tremendous effort into that race. Split must have been bitterly disappointed because he would have revelled in the fame of winning the World Championship. It would have been a very tough run-off between us."

Tom Stenner outlined that "Would Waterman have beaten Williams in a run-off? I doubt it. Williams had the faster winning times of 70.4 seconds (best of the meeting), 70.8, 72.8 and 73, compared to 73.2, 72.8, 72 and 72.6." In the *News*, Len Went said that Freddie's "night of glory" saw him earn £587/10s. Split Waterman was runner-up on 13 points, and Geoff Mardon beat Olly Nygren in a run-off to claim third place. Jack Young fell in his last ride and finished on 10 points. Eric secured four third places before a fall in his last ride saw him finish with four points.

Tom Morgan reported that "The entire Williams family was there to watch the triumph of Fred. Rarely have I seen Freddie looking so grim as he did all through the night in the pits. He always is quiet and reserved, but on this occasion he kept very much to himself and even shied at photographers. Apart from his actual racing, the only time Fred was galvanised into action was when he dashed out to see if brother Eric was all right after a spill.

That vital 17th race told the story. Fred did not know what the position was. He just threw all his concentration into his riding. I was the first to congratulate him as he came back from that vital win over Nygren and Waterman. 'Have I won?' said Fred. And for the first time during the evening he smiled and went limp with concentration."

RM 'Sammy' Samuel used his column in the *News* to address the issue of home track advantage for the Wembley riders. He said that there was nowhere else that could realistically stage the Final, and said "Freddie won fairly and squarely. He rode cleverly in each of his five races and I don't think anyone should grudge him his success on his form that night."

Ronnie Moore wrote in his column in the *Star* that "fast riding, fast gating and never-give-up tactics won Freddie the title for the second time in his career."

So Freddie became the first British rider to win the World Championship twice. He was presented with the Trophy by Sir Edmund Hillary and Sir John Hunt, the famous mountaineers who had just conquered Everest.

Even if he did have home-track advantage, he faced an international class field to win the title. In the days of one-off World Finals deciding the title, the only other British rider to win twice was Peter Craven, with wins in 1955 and 1962. Of course, Tai Woffinden has since matched and overtaken the feat in the Speedway Grand Prix, and has now won the most titles by a British rider.

Oddly, the report in the *Gazette* did not welcome Freddie's success. Editor Bruce Valdar commented: "Williams' fifth race found him performing in his usual unspectacular yet immaculate home racing style. Never flurried … always unhurried … almost infuriatingly unshowy and entirely without that so-vitally speedway necessary asset of a dash of exhibitionism – that is Freddie Williams, 1953 Speedway World Champion. Socially a nice, shy guy, Freddie Williams is not, I'm afraid, speedway's idea of a World Champion – but you've got to hand it to the Welsh-born, one-time Portsmouth Navy Dockyard fitter, he has the ability and temperament ideally suited to big occasions …" The article then said that Split Waterman was "obviously speedway's idea of a champion". But Freddie was the top rider in the country's top team. Split Waterman may have been a more flamboyant personality, but Freddie was arguably the more consistent rider, and had had his best season in the sport for the country's top team. One does wonder if Valdar was continuing Basil Storey's approach of often being critical of anything associated with the Wembley Lions. To be fair, Basil Storey always acknowledged the key role that Sir Arthur Elvin played in supporting speedway.

However, the *Gazette* did subsequently name Freddie as their 'rider of the year.' Frederick Philpot wrote: "A heated argument developed [among those making the choice] between World Champion Freddie Williams and Jack Young. The latter has been in the forefront all the season whilst Freddie had bursts of brilliance such as the World Final evening. Eventually we settled for Freddie, because of his world triumph. For sheer individual brilliance the World Champion must be the rider of the year."

In the national press, Basil Storey in the *Express* recognised that "On the night's racing Freddie just deserved the title, for he came out best in a triangular battle of nerves involving himself, England captain Split Waterman and Australian ace Jack Young. As early as heat six, the championship had resolved itself into a struggle between these three." However, he did say that there was so little between Freddie and Split Waterman that "it was a pity they could not have held the title jointly."

In the *Daily Mail*, Freddie said that the £500 winner's cheque was "a nice wedding present" and that it would help pay for his honeymoon in South Africa." The *Express* had noted that Freddie had earned £587/10/0 for winning the title.

Once again, Freddie's success was front page news in the *Port Talbot Guardian*. Under the headline 'Speedway Champion does it again', the paper reported that on arrival in Port Talbot, Freddie had visited his mother's wool shop and put the World Championship trophy on display in the window, surrounded by wool, cards and pattern books. The report said that "his mother naturally wanted to show her new neighbours in Morrison Road what her eldest son can do", so as soon as he arrived home, the cup went on display. The report also stressed the support he had received from his parents in his speedway career. He also said that his grass track experience was an advantage on a wet night at Wembley: "When I knew that the track at Wembley was wet and slippery, I knew that I had an advantage. Unlike many of my opponents, I have had a lot of experience of riding on slippery grass tracks, thanks to my father. That gave me the necessary boost to enable me to win. Many times have my brothers and I raced on top of the Margam mountains after heavy rain, and so now we know how to deal with it." The week before his wedding, he was given a civic reception by the Mayor, Alderman Percy Wiseman, and other town dignitaries."

A month later, Freddie had another important fixture. Just before his big night at Wembley, he and Pat had arranged their wedding for 17 October, at St John's Church on Wembley High Road. Tom Morgan previewed the wedding in the *News*, saying that both speedway and ice stars would be present. Skaters John and Jennifer Nicks were invited, with Jennifer being one of the bridesmaids. From speedway, Sir Arthur and Lady Elvin were invited, along with Howdy Byford, a particular friend of Freddie's, his Wembley team-mates and former Wembley star Split Waterman. Around 150 people were invited, and the reception was to be at Pat's aunt's house in Sloane Gardens.

The *Wembley News* reported that Miss Devries was given away by her uncle, Captain F. Barrett. She wore "a dress of white net in Victorian style" and "had a head-dress of gardenias and orange blossom, and carried a bouquet of gardenias, stephanotis and lilies of the valley." There were five bridesmaids, and the wedding was conducted by the Rev. ED Buxton. The report, with two photos, was front page news in the paper, which actually gave very little coverage to the speedway team.

Both the *News* and the *Gazette* featured a photo of the happy couple on their front covers. Hundreds of Wembley fans had come to the wedding, and police had to control the crowds. Freddie and Pat had to leave the church by a side door.

Ian was Freddie's best man and was in a photo in the *News* with his dad and two brothers, all suitably regaled in top hats. Ian had to read all the telegrams, but there were so many that he did not have time to read them all.

Another photo showed Freddie and Pat cutting the three-tier wedding cake, which had been made by Pat's grandmother. Freddie and Pat had to leave the reception early to appear on the radio programme *In Town Tonight*. The following day, they flew to South Africa for a honeymoon combined with racing action for Freddie. Jayne recalls how her mother told her that she had had injections for the South Africa trip just before the wedding and was still feeling the effects of them on her big day.

The happy couple on their Wedding Day.
(Courtesy Sarah Williams)

Left: Going onto the flight to South Africa for their
honeymoon. (Courtesy JSC)

Above: Both the main speedway magazines made
the wedding front page news.

10. A trip to South Africa

South Africa had a small, but well-established speedway set up for Freddie to ride in during the British autumn, winter and early spring of 1953–54. He captained an unofficial touring squad, the third one to visit South Africa since the War.

The sport had started in South Africa in 1928 and had first been visited by a British team in 1930–31. A small number of South African riders had come to compete in Britain. The most successful was Henry Long, who reached the World Final in 1952 when he was riding for Belle Vue. One recruit for Wembley was Fred Lang, who joined the Lions for the 1954 season.

Speedway was not a major sport in South Africa, but did have a following among the white community. The country had undergone political change in 1948, with the election of an Afrikaner-led National Party government, who introduced 'Apartheid' (separate development) laws which formalised and developed the racial divisions that already existed. There was opposition to this among the African and 'Coloured' (mixed race) communities at this time, but the issue had not yet developed into an international political one, and there was no sports boycott in place. British cricket and rugby union teams toured South Africa regularly, and a number of South African footballers played for British football teams.

The previous unofficial English touring teams had consisted of mainly Second and Third Division riders. Freddie's Wembley colleague Trevor Redmond had ridden in South Africa the previous winter, and three of his Wembley team mates were in the England squad. Apart from Freddie, Brian Crutcher and Bill Kitchen were chosen, along with Freddie's brother Ian, Don Perry, Howdy Byford, Bill Griffiths, Reg Duval and Gerry Hussey. For Freddie and Ian, the tour gave them the only time in their careers that they were team-mates, and certainly Ian's scores improved throughout his stay in South Africa.

As well as riding in the test matches, the British riders joined local teams. Trevor Redmond had developed a new track at Springs, in the East Rand, and Bill Kitchen and Reg Duval joined him there. Gerry Hussey rode for Durban, Freddie and Ian joined Pretoria, Brian Crutcher and Bill Griffiths were with Randfontein and the Wembley Lions (who had no connection with the London team) recruited Don Perry and Howdy Byford.

For the first few seasons after the War, the sport had been based in Johannesburg. A team opened in Durban in 1952, so the League became the National League. However, the Pretoria team did not seem to have had a home stadium of its own, and rode home meetings mainly at the Wembley track. Certainly, speedway had a good base in the Transvaal, with supporters clubs starting and better crowds attending meetings than watched club rugby union or cricket. Speedway was also establishing a base in Northern Rhodesia, and Freddie took a team there to face a Dominions side.

Trevor Redmond reported on speedway in South Africa for the *News*. He said that Freddie and Pat "were amazed at the reception handed out to them. Freddie looked completely overwhelmed and was quite flabbergasted by all the publicity. Believe me, he was sort of expecting lions, tigers and natives. Instead, he was greeted by newsreel cameras, newspaper reporters, and then whipped smartly away to a crackerjack cocktail party. Freddie has been doing some broadcasting over the radio network and, for the first week, was installed in one of the leading luxury hotels in Johannesburg and was lord over everything he surveyed!" Redmond also reported that Wembley had its biggest crowd of the season for his first meeting. Freddie scored a 12 point maximum, won the scratch race final and broke the track record. His Pretoria Eagles beat the Springs Stars 40–38.

Redmond's next report said that Freddie and Pat had "managed to find a very modern flat in the best part of Johannesburg" but that the peace was likely to be disturbed when the rest of the British riders visited them. In mid-December, he reported that Freddie and Pat had spent a week in Durban, and "spent a good deal of time sight-seeing and also managed a trip to the Zulu reserve. The weather wasn't too good but they enjoyed themselves just the same." He also said that Pat was not allowing Freddie to have all the limelight. She had given a skating exhibition at the Olympic Rink in Johannesburg on the same night that South Africa's ice hockey team played an Overseas team. Tom Durling, the Canadian coach to the South African team, said that "...she's a great skater – one of the best ever to be seen on a rink in this country." Howdy Byford reported in the *Star* that Freddie had won the Welcome Trophy with a 15 point maximum, and had a brand new Zephyr car.

On the track, Redmond said that Freddie had been beaten twice when Redmond's Springs side beat the Pretoria Eagles 45–39. Freddie was still top scorer for his team with 10. The first test had been twice rained off, but was eventually staged on 2 December. A 9,000 crowd saw a 54–54 draw. Brian Crutcher top scored for England with 17, with Freddie and Bill Kitchen scoring 13 apiece. The South Africans came close to winning. It took Bill Kitchen to grab second place in the last race to retrieve a draw for England.

Freddie was also an attraction in the club meetings. A record crowd of over 5,000 saw Springs beat Pretoria 44–40. Trevor Redmond beat Freddie in the first race, and set a new track record. Freddie ended up with 11 points, and Ian scored 10, his best for Pretoria so far. At Wembley, Freddie won the South African Match Race Championship, beating Henry Long twice.

Freddie and Brian Crutcher were a dominant force in the second test, staged before a 2,000 crowd a week before Christmas. Crutcher got an 18 point maximum, and Freddie scored 17 to help England to a comfortable 62.5 to 45.5 victory. Freddie was only beaten by Henry Long. Freddie also broke the track record.

As well as showing top form in the test matches, Freddie was close to unbeatable in other meetings. For Pretoria, Trevor Redmond reported that he had given "another first rate performance" with a 12 point maximum in a 47–36 win. Ian contributed 11 points as well. In a Commonwealth Best Pairs in Bulawayo in North Rhodesia, a 550 mile drive from Johannesburg, which Freddie did in one day, he rode for Britain against the Dominions. The British won 58–50. Freddie top scored with 15 points and was "cheered every time he went to the starting line" according to Christian Weber in his *75 Years of Speedway in South Africa*.

Alongside a picture of Freddie, the 9 January 1954 edition of the *Star* said that "The Wembley star is at present delighting the speedway public in South Africa with his skill ... For Freddie, its more than just a speedway tour, although that is a big enough matter for him. Married at the end of last season, he has his wife, ice skater Pat Devries, along with him to delight the Springboks with her own brand of magic on ice. Certainly, the country seems to suit them both. Reports are that Freddie has never ridden better, nor Pat skated with more grace and charm."

Also in Bulawayo, Freddie scored 14 out of 15 points for Wales, although not partnering Ian, in a pairs meeting; the meeting was won by Redmond and Dick Campbell for New Zealand. Riding again for Pretoria at Wembley, Freddie scored 11 of his team's 40 points in a four point defeat.

The 1953–54 British tourists to South Africa: Howdy Byford. Ian, Bill Griffiths, Dom Perry, Reg Duval, Freddie; back: Bill Kitchen, Brian Crutcher. (Courtesy Hayley Redmond)

Left: The first issue of this magazine featured Freddie on the cover. Right: The programme cover from one of the Pretoria Eagles meetings – Freddie and Ian's team. (Courtesy Hayley Redmond)

Freddie and Ian waiting to ride. Roy Bester is next to Ian on the right.
(Courtesy Hayley Redmond)

Speedway in Durban – the stand is packed. (Courtesy Hayley Redmond)

This could be the Golden Helmet that Freddie won by beating his great friend
Trevor Redmond (right) in a match race in a meeting in Bulawayo in early 1954.
(Courtesy Hayley Redmond)

Freddie speaks to the fans in South Africa as Trevor Redmond looks on.
(Courtesy Hayley Redmond)

Freddie and Pat also continued to enjoy life away from the track. They visited the Kruger National Park. Pat was scared – she had been told stories by the riders of the possible dangers. They had told her that the Lions could jump the fence – she hardly slept according to Freddie. Freddie was fined 10 shillings for coming back after the 7pm curfew. He said that the staff were worse than the speedway stewards. However, he was back at 6.30pm the next night.

A 10,000 crowd saw a Dominions team beat England 59–48 at Wembley. Freddie scored 17 points for England and broke the track record. The test series resumed on 22 January, with a virtually identical result to the second test. This time the tourists won 62–45, with both Freddie and Brian Crutcher scoring 18 point maximums. Ian also showed his development with an 8+1 score.

Another outing for the riders was to visit a gold mine. At Wembley, Freddie was runner-up to Brian Crutcher in the Overseas Championship.

A month after the last test match, on 19 February 1954, Henry Long had his best meeting of the test series to steer South Africa home 56–51. Again Brian Crutcher and Freddie were England's top scorers, with 16 and 15 respectively. Another international fixture saw the Dominions beat England 55–53, with Freddie scoring 13 points.

Freddie then broke his collarbone in a South African Match Race against Brian Crutcher. Despite missing Freddie and Bill Kitchen for the final test, England won 57–51 to take the series. After his second victory against Henry Long, Freddie had beaten Fred Lang 2–1 and 2–0, then Trevor Redmond 2–0 and 2–0 before the clash with Brian Crutcher.

In the race against Crutcher, Freddie lost control on the bend and was somersaulted onto the track. The accident finished his season in South Africa. He had slight concussion as well as a broken collarbone. Trevor Redmond reported that Freddie "has ridden brilliantly out here during the past few months and has made a great impression with everybody. He was detained in hospital for observation – he had slight concussion – but now he's out and about and quite cheerful." His collarbone was expected to have healed by the time he got home. Also, the riders had visited the Kruger National Park. Freddie and Pat flew home in March, a day before the other British riders.

John Bunton's report on the South African season in *Stenner's 1954 Annual* put Freddie at the top of the rider ratings, ahead of his Wembley team-mates Trevor Redmond and Brian Crutcher. Bunton commented that "From the off there was never real doubt about the all-round superiority of World Champion Freddie Williams."

11. 1954: National Trophy winners

Freddie and Pat returned from South Africa at the end of March. Freddie was recovering from his collarbone injury, and was undergoing special strengthening exercise under the direction of Wembley trainer Tommy Barnett. The *News* reported that the fracture was proving to be "troublesome" and that he had startled Pat by bringing home a medicine ball each evening. He commented "When anybody else breaks a bone it heals up without any bother, but with me there's always complications."

Freddie missed Wembley's first two meetings, a four team 'inter-track challenge' at Wimbledon, and the Middlesex Cup match at Harringay. The Wembley team was largely the same as 1953, although two veterans were in the final stages of their careers. Bill Kitchen only rode one National League meeting for the Lions, although he was still involved at Wembley, while George Wilks took part in just seven meetings.

The only new recruit was Fred Lang, who had travelled from South Africa with Freddie and Pat. However, he did not fulfil his potential at Wembley, and may have done better to have started his British career in the Second Division.

The post-war 'boom' in speedway was clearly coming to an end. The First Division still had eight teams, but the second tier started with 15, but four withdrew during the season. The reasons for this have been covered elsewhere; it was clearly not a good time for the sport.

The Lions' season opened with the RAC Cup. Wembley rode all their six matches away from home. Freddie's first meeting was at West Ham, with a meagre return of 4+1 points from four rides. He managed 13 (+1) in a challenge match at Wimbledon the following Monday, but the News reported that he was not happy with his form. He outlined that "In one race I went into a bend like a novice and when I was back home and in bed I kept thinking to myself, what a lousy effort for a World Champion." Weightlifting was helping him restore strength to his shoulder. Despite his concerns, he had been Wembley's top scorer at Plough Lane. He was also top scorer in a 44–40 defeat at Birmingham, and beat local favourite Alan Hunt, ending his unbeaten record in the RAC Cup. The *Star* said that "Freddie Williams has already shown plenty of fine form this season despite the fact that he had not reached peak fitness following his unfortunate crash when racing Brian Crutcher for the Match Race title in South Africa. The Springboks did not rerun the Match Race, so Freddie is the holder." Given the problems with the injury the race had caused, one suspects that Freddie wasn't that bothered about being the holder.

Wembley narrowly beat Harringay 45–39 on their first meeting back at the Empire Stadium. Freddie scored 10 (+1) from his four rides and was the Lions' top scorer. But two league defeats by Wimbledon the following week were an indication of a shift in the balance of power in speedway. The Dons were potentially stronger than the Lions this season. In the first meeting, Wembley lost by three points, and Freddie was excluded for 'unfair riding' in heat nine, which was very unusual for him. Three days later, the Dons won 51–33 at the Empire Stadium. The *News* reported that "The Williams brothers, with eight apiece, did their best for the Lions."

Freddie scored his first paid maximum of the season for the Lions in a 65–19 home massacre of a weak Birmingham team. The London Cup was now reduced to four teams with the demise of New Cross. The Lions faced Harringay in the semi-final over two days at the beginning of June. Before then, Freddie had four teeth extracted and had to miss a meeting at Wimbledon. He was unconscious for a couple of hours and felt 'groggy' for a couple of days. The Lions won 63–44 at Green Lanes in the first leg and the *News* reported: "Just recovered from a dental operation, Freddie Williams gave the sort of display expected from a World Champion. Unbeaten by an opponent in his first five rides, he was finally caught on the hop by Waterman in the nominated event. Brother Eric was the next best in a very well-balanced Lions outfit." The Lions won the second leg 60–48, and the *News* said that they qualified for the final "chiefly due to the brilliant exploits of the Williams brothers." Eric scored 15 points and Freddie got 14 (+1).

Freddie and Eric were in demand for open meetings. In June they rode in Vienna, where local star Fritz Dirtl won the meeting, with Freddie and Eric second and third respectively. There was a feeling among the local fans that they had team ridden in the meeting heats, and they were booed. Another Austrian rider, Josef Kamper, told the Williams brothers not to do this, and things calmed down.

They also rode together in a Pairs meeting for the Television Trophy at Harringay. They represented Wales, with Ian as reserve, a rare joint appearance for the three brothers. Freddie stood down from heat eight to give Ian a ride. He took the first bend too fast and sent Eric flying. Later in the season they all rode together in a more important meeting – the World Championship qualifying round at Wembley. Freddie and Eric, along with Brian Crutcher and Tommy Price from Wembley, were seeded to the final qualifying round of the World Championship.

As World Champion, Freddie was seen as one of the riders to beat. In the *News* in June, Gerry Hussey commented: "I managed to win against Freddie Williams. The Welshman isn't World Champion for nothing you know. He's a wizard, a great artist and a fine opponent. To defeat Freddie is a feather in anyone's cap – and I had to travel pretty fast to get the better of him." This was in West Ham's 46–38 win over the Lions.

On 24 June, Freddie got his second paid maximum for the Lions, 9 (+3) from four rides in a 67–17 slaughter of a struggling Belle Vue team. The Lions were only beaten twice at home in the League, both times by Wimbledon. The eight team league format was that each team faced the others twice at home and twice away. Although Freddie rode well with 11 from four rides, the Dons' 48–36 win at the Empire Stadium on 29 July made it difficult for the Lions to catch them. The final table had Wimbledon top with 44 match points from their 28 meetings, and Wembley second with 40 points. The Lions losing all four league matches to the Dons had been decisive.

The Lions fared better in the knock-out competitions. The London Cup was – in reality – decided on 19 August, when the Lions beat Wimbledon 69–38 in the first leg of the Final. The *News* reported that Freddie was "outstanding" and the "man-of-the-match" with Eric, Tommy Price and Brian Crutcher not far behind. Freddie scored 17 from his six rides, Eric got 12. Eleven days later, the Lions won 61–47 at Plough Lane, with Freddie scoring 8 (+2) from his six rides.

In the National Trophy, the Lions won both legs against West Ham to reach the semi-final. Freddie had a poor night in Custom House in the first leg, with just seven points, but scored 14 (+2) from his six rides two days later in the second leg. In the semi-final, the Lions scraped through by one point on aggregate against Bradford. The Final was much more straightforward. The Lions built up at 15 point lead against Norwich at home, with Freddie scoring 8 (+1) from five rides. Two days later, Wembley won by 16 at The Firs, with Freddie scoring 10 (+2) from five rides. So at least there were two cup successes for Freddie and the Lions to celebrate.

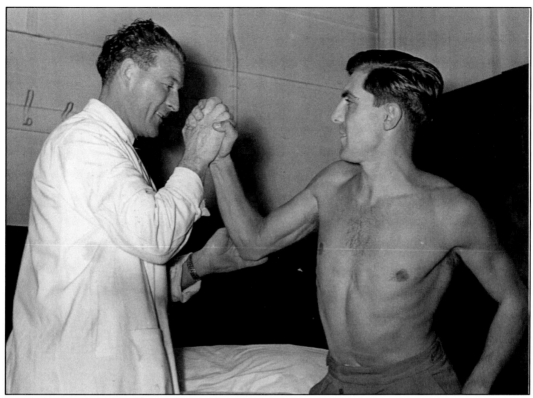
Freddie working with Tommy Barnett, the Wembley trainer.

On the international scene, there was a three match series between England and Australasia, which included Wembley's Trevor Redmond. Freddie only rode in the first test at West Ham. He scored 5 (+1) in a 60–48 win for England. Eric scored one point from reserve, but was chosen for the final two meetings, scoring 11 and 9 points. England won the series 3–0.

As always, the final part of the season saw the culmination of the World Championship. Freddie was drawn at Belle Vue, not a track where he had a good record. He crashed in his first race, and only got four points from his next three rides. He won his final heat to secure seven points. With each rider only taking part in two qualifying rounds, he needed a maximum from the Wembley round to have a chance to being able to defend his title on the big night at Wembley.

Ian was also drawn to ride in the Wembley qualifying round, and it is the only official meeting where the three brothers rode together. Wembley invited Ian to take part in a second half a couple of weeks before the qualifying round. He won the scratch race final, beating Brian Crutcher and Jack Young. The *Star* said that "Not since Ken Le Breton have Wembley fans been more impressed with a Second Division rider."

Freddie nearly made it. He tied for top place with Eddie Rigg on 14 points. Eric finished with 10 points, and missed out on the Final, and Ian scored a respectable seven. And who was the rider who scuppered Freddie's hopes? It was Eric. There have been stories over the years in speedway of collusion between riders in qualifying meetings for the World Championship. This was clearly not the case here, nor would Freddie have expected any 'help' from his siblings.

Freddie, Ian and Eric at the 1954 World Championship qualifying meeting. This is the only time all three brothers rode together in an official meeting. (Courtesy JSC)

Freddie won a run-off with Gerry Hussey to take the second reserve place at Wembley. But on the big night he did not get a ride. The *Star's* World Final preview said that "second reserve, local Freddie Williams could be a nuisance. Although the edge has gone right off his riding in recent weeks, he is capable of beating any rider in the game even now." Ronnie Moore won the title with a 15 point maximum. Wembley's Brian Crutcher beat Olle Nygren in a run-off for second place. Tommy Price and Trevor Redmond both finished on five points, for both it was their last World Final appearance. Two Final debutants were noteworthy. Barry Briggs finished sixth with nine points and Ove Fundin in last place with two. Within three years both had won the title.

Clearly, Freddie's form had declined slightly since 1953. Brian Crutcher was now the top rider at Wembley, with a 10.10 average in the National League and National Trophy meetings. Eric was the second highest in the Lions' averages with 9.41, while Freddie was third, with 8.89, a drop of 0.73 from his 1953 figure. The *News's* review of the Lions season, published in January 1955, commented that "The individual honours in the Lions were shared by Crutcher and Eric Williams. These boys rode hard and true all season. Many were surprised to see Eric displace his brother Freddie in the scoring honours. Yet the ex-World Champion had a fairly good season...".

Wembley Lions with the National Trophy at Norwich. This was the last trophy the Lions won.
Back: Unknown, Tommy Price, Bill Kitchen, Eric French, Eric, Brian Crutcher, Duncan King (manager);
front: Jimmy Gooch, Fred Lang, Trevor Redmond, Freddie.

In the *Star*, Dave Nelson also noted that Eric had outscored Freddie: "Among the heat leaders the Lions were very, very strong indeed. Perhaps most surprising of all is the fact that Eric Williams took over the top-scoring mantle from brother Freddie. Undoubtedly Eric is a classier rider than many think. But just as undoubtedly, he has never shown that fiery spark which blazed Freddie to two world titles. He has shown brilliant form, its true, but it needs brilliance plus to win a World title, or to top the scoring for a power packed side like Wembley."

In October, the Lions went on a short tour to Sweden. Both Freddie and Eric were part of the team. The Lions won their four matches, and Freddie won an individual meeting at Eskilstuna with 13 points, beating Geoff Mardon in a run-off.

After Freddie's trip to Sweden, he and Pat headed off to South Africa. Freddie was originally planning to ride as a freelance, but then secured a place with the Durban Hornets. He captained the side, and scored a maximum against the Springs Stars in a 42–38 win. He also set a new 4-lap track record. Pat was offered a coaching job at the Johannesburg ice rink.

In December, Freddie was the guest of honour at a Sportswriters dinner in Durban, which reflects the impact speedway was making. Normally their guest would have come from rugby union or cricket, which were the most popular sports for the South African white community.

There was no England team in South Africa this time. Freddie captained an Overseas team against South Africa in January at Port Elizabeth. He scored 12.5 in a 56.5–51.5 victory. He was also the team manager of a Commonwealth team that raced five tests against South Africa from early December to the end of February.

Freddie and Trevor Redmond with Buddy Fuller, one of the mainstays of South African speedway.
(Courtesy Hayley Redmond)

Why he did not ride in the series is not known, maybe it was to give an opportunity to some of the younger riders to gain international experience. Trevor Redmond managed the South African team.

Freddie and Pat stayed in South Africa until the end of March 1955, enjoying what the country had to offer. Freddie was third in the 100 Guineas Trophy, and lost 2–1 to local hero Henry Long in the Match Race Championship. Freddie lost the first leg at Wembley 2–0, won the second in Durban 2–1, and then lost the decider at Springs. The *Star* also printed a photo of a visit Freddie and Pat made to a wildlife park.

In the South African League, Freddie's Durban Hornets and Springs Stars had finished on the same match points. Trevor Redmond claimed the title for his Springs team because of a slightly higher points average. However, Durban threatened to withdraw from the League unless there was a run-off to decide the title. This duly happened, and Durban won on aggregate 56–51 to claim the title. Freddie and Dick Campbell won the last heat 5–0, with Ronnie Genz falling and Trevor Redmond excluded. Springs had won the first match 54–53 on their own track, with Freddie scoring 14 for Durban. South African writer John Bunton said in the *News* that "freelance stars of the magnitude of Freddie Williams added glamour and lustre to the programmes [in South Africa]."

12. 1955: "Magnificent for England"

In the latter half of the 1954 season, Harringay had staged a series of double-headers to conclude their league programme early. Their crowds had shrunk and made continuing the team unsustainable, and it was no great surprise when they did not return to the track in 1955. This also meant that the London Cup was abandoned, as there were only three teams left in London.

This meant just seven teams competed for the National League. In the Second Division, 11 teams started the season, but two withdrew during the campaign, so just nine teams were left by the end of the season.

In the First Division, each team was scheduled to face the others twice at home and twice away. However, concerned about the crowds some league matches were attracting to the Empire Stadium, Sir Arthur Elvin decided that the Lions would only have one league match at home against the other teams, and would ride away from home three times. He planned to stage high profile individual meetings in the vacated home slots, although only four actually happened. He felt that these meetings would attract better crowds.

Eric Williams felt that he would lose out financially from this arrangement and asked for a transfer. He was put on the list, but at a price that no team was going to pay in a sport that was struggling financially. So, at the end of the season, Eric and his wife and daughter emigrated to New Zealand, with Eric saying that he would never ride for Wembley again.

For Wembley, Sir Arthur's decision effectively ended any chances of winning the league title. The Lions finished third, with 23 points from their 24 meetings. Wimbledon won the league, with 34 points, and Belle Vue were second with 32.

Fred Lang did not return from South Africa. He was replaced by Ken Adams, an established Second Division rider with Stoke. He performed adequately at reserve, but was hardly the sort of recruit who was going to attract fans to the Empire Stadium. During the season, Jimmy Gooch was loaned to Swindon, where he found some success.

The Lions' league averages reflected the preponderance of away fixtures. Brian Crutcher's average fell to 9.33; next best was Tommy Price with 7.12, then Eric on 6.96, and Freddie on 6.75. For Freddie, this was a drop of over two points a meeting, and his lowest average since his first season as a regular rider for the Lions.

In the four 'open' meetings at Wembley, Freddie had 16 rides and scored 30 points. In one he only rode twice due to injury, scoring one point. In a league match, a fair estimate for him would be five rides in the match for 10 points, and two in the second half for (say) a further four. So, for the whole meeting he would have seven rides for 14 points. It is not known what the pay rates were for the individual meetings, although there were cash prizes for the winners. But most of the Wembley team would have lost out, along with the extra travelling – and lower scores – for the six extra away meetings. Clearly the Lions camp was not a happy place.

The Lions' season, as usual, started with a series of away meetings. Another problem for the team was that the stadium was let out for two weeks in May for religious services, so the Lions first home meeting was two weeks later than usual, on 26 May. The season opened with three challenge matches, then five away league fixtures. Two of these were won, at West Ham and Bradford. Freddie only scored double figures, from five rides in the league matches, once – in the win at West Ham. RM Samuel wrote in the *News* that he "seems to be far below his usual brilliance and I should class brother Eric as the better rider today".

The next week, the *News* commented that "The former World Champion is not riding with his usual zip at the moment and is being overshadowed by younger brother Eric. However, both are immaculate riders and there's hardly a point between the brothers." A week later, on 1 June, the magazine said that "The Williams brothers ... are now approaching peak form and places must be found for them [in the test team]." Freddie's form had picked up, with 10 points in the first night win against Wimbledon, when he was the Lions' top scorer, and then 11 (+1) against Norwich the following week. In fact, neither Williams brother was chosen in the test team. Tommy Price and Brian Crutcher were the Lions' representatives. However, Freddie was called up as a last minute substitute, replacing Crutcher who failed a fitness test. He was one of only two home riders to win a heat as Australasia won 67–39. Riding from reserve, he was joint top scorer with Arthur Wright on 10 points.

On 15 June, Samuel wrote in the *News*: "Will you agree with me if I suggest that Freddie Williams, though still a comparatively young man, has lost much of the zest of a couple of seasons back? I would like to think that this was merely a bad patch, but it is lasting too long for the suggestion to be really convincing. I hope I am mistaken." Freddie's scores had been better for the last two weeks, but were not good when he was riding out of London. After the test match, Samuel wrote that "A satisfying thought is that Freddie Williams is really getting going again."

Both the Williams brothers were in the England team for the second test, at Wembley. Captained by Brian Crutcher, the Lions avenged the defeat at Wimbledon with a 67–41 win. Freddie top scored with 17, followed by Brian Crutcher on 16. Eric scored 11 and Tommy Price seven. Peter Foster, in his *History of the Speedway Ashes*, said that "Both Freddie Williams and Brian Crutcher were magnificent for England."

The *News* reported that Freddie had pointed out that Ronnie Moore's frame was cracked, and said: "That typically sporting action by rival-rider Williams may easily have saved the World Champion [Moore] from serious injury or something even more tragic." Their reporter also said that the England victory was made possible by the "clever, but always fiery", riding of Freddie and Brian Crutcher. The *Star* said after the test: "Battling back to peak form, just in time for the test matches, came Wembley's Freddie Williams, and never was a return to his sparkling best more welcome. His zest put the sting into the English side in the second test, that had been so sadly missing in the first match of the series – even though Freddie did well in that one too. But at Wembley, it helped transform a side with a small chance, to say the least, into a team of world –beaters. And to think he was so nearly overlooked in the opening match of the series."

Freddie's form for the Lions had also improved. He scored a 15 point maximum – his only one of the season – in a 48–48 draw at West Ham. This followed a paid maximum at Wembley against Belle Vue. However, Freddie injured his foot in a fall in his first heat in the Laurels at Wimbledon on 27 June, and it was badly swollen for the third test at West Ham. He only scored one point from his first two rides, was then replaced by Eric, who was one of England's reserves for two rides, and then took his last two for a score of 4 (+2). He had his ankle ligaments strapped during the meeting after his first two rides. The *News* said that he probably should not have ridden in the meeting. With Ronnie Moore and Jack Young both scoring 18 point maximums, the Australasia side won comfortably, 66–42. Freddie was dropped for the next test, at Bradford, as the selectors followed a policy of including some home riders more familiar with the track. England won the last two matches to take the series. The meeting at West Ham was Freddie's last test match. It was a poor way to finish his international career.

England team versus Australasia at West Ham on 5 July 1955. England lost 66–42. Back: Gerry Hussey, Freddie, Brian Crutcher, Eric; front: Ken McKinlay, Alan Hunt, Ron Mountford, Arthur Wright. This was Freddie's last appearance for England. (Courtesy JSC)

Left: Freddie speaking to the crowd after riding for England. The rider behind him is Phil Clarke. (Courtesy Williams family)

A significant event in Freddie and Pat's life was that he opened a motorcycle shop in Wembley at the end of June. An advert in the *1956 Five Star Speedway Annual* said that "Freddie Williams invites all motor-cyclists to call in and inspect his large display of NEW and USED MOTORCYCLES." It was based at 422, High Road, Wembley. The sign for the shop reminded prospective customers of Freddie's two World Championship successes.

On the track, Freddie continued to show generally good form at home, but could be inconsistent away from the Empire Stadium. With the handicap of the fixtures they faced, the Lions were never in with a realistic chance of winning the league. Even the teams that dominated the sport a few

Above: Freddie's motorcycle shop in Wembley, which he opened in 1955.

Left: To be able to ride motorbikes on the road, Freddie had to have a licence. Apparently, he never did pass the test.

(Both photos courtesy JSC)

years before would have struggled with riding threequarters of their meetings away from home, as happened in 1948 when they were exiled to Wimbledon for home meetings until the end of August while Wembley staged the Olympics.

They fared better in the National Trophy. In July, Freddie scored 17 at home against Belle Vue, but only five from five rides in Manchester in the second leg. The Lions went through comfortably by 12 points on aggregate. In the semi-final, the Lions faced Wimbledon. Again, Freddie rode well at Wembley, scoring 13 (+2) from six rides. The Lions had an 18 point lead to take to Plough Lane 11 days later. They made it to the final, but Freddie had a very poor evening. Three rides without scoring, and he withdrew from the meeting. It is not clear if he had an injury or bike problems, but it was unheard of for him not to score. The report in the *News* said that he was "hopeless" and that Tommy Price wasn't much better. Fortunately, Eric rode well for 12 points, and with Eric French also scoring 12 (+2) from the reserve berth, the Lions reached the Final by four points on aggregate. Eric Williams's win over Barry Briggs in heat 15 clinched their place in the Final.

There they faced Norwich, who finished the season in sixth place in the League. However, they had recruited up-and-coming Swedish star Ove Fundin in June. Wembley had beaten Norwich in the Final in 1954, and would have expected to build up a good lead from the first leg at Wembley. But instead it was Norwich who took a 21 point lead with a 64–43 win. Freddie scored six points from five rides, but that made him the Lions' third highest scorer. Brian Crutcher scored 15 and brother Eric got nine. Freddie won heat 17, one of eight heats won by a Wembley rider, but the *News* said that "Freddie Williams, Redmond and French were a big disappointment to everybody."

The Lions improved at the Firs, and won 63–45, but lost on aggregate by three points. Freddie scored 5 (+1) from four rides. At the end of August, RM Samuel had written in the *News* how Freddie, Tommy Price and Split Waterman were 'off form' this season. Interestingly, both Freddie and Split Waterman had business responsibilities away from speedway, and Tommy Price was now in his mid-40s. Samuel commented on Freddie: "What can I say about Freddie except that this has been his most inconsistent season since he joined Wembley. Possibly the reason lies in staleness. Remember that he had a pretty hard time last year, and followed it by riding right through the winter. You will tell me that many boys do this, and probably point to Ronnie Moore and Barry Briggs as examples. Granted, but Freddie is considerably older [aged 29]. Further, he has responsibilities which must restrict his dash. At the moment I should not class him as being quite so good as his younger brother Eric."

In the *News's* report of Wembley's 61–35 win over Bradford, the writer said: "Freddie Williams continues to disappoint. There's precious little fire about the ex-champion's riding these days." In the last month of the season, the Lions arranged a two-legged challenge encounter with Wimbledon. The Lions won 67–40 at the Empire Stadium, but collapsed to lose 77–31 at Plough Lane. Freddie scored a point from four rides, and the *News* said that, along with Trevor Redmond, he had "another shocking match".

In the World Championship, Freddie was drawn at Wembley and Belle Vue in the final qualifying round. He scored 12 at Wembley, and nine at Belle Vue. However, his total of 21 was not quite enough to reach the Final. Brian Crutcher, Eric and Billy Bales tied for the last place on 23. However, Doug Davies withdrew from the Final due to illness, so two places were available. Brian Crutcher and Eric duly qualified. Bales did make it to the big night when Aub Lawson withdrew. It was Eric's best World Final. Peter Craven won the title for the first time with 13 points. Eric, Barry Briggs and Ronnie Moore all finished on 12.

Left: Back: Freddie senior and Freddie; front: Ian and Eric. (Courtesy JSC)

In the run-off, Briggs and Eric fell, and Briggs remounted and rode home to claim third place. The week before the Final, Eric had cracked a bone in his hand, and had to ride with it strapped up.

Despite his World Final success, Eric had decided to emigrate with his family to New Zealand and kept to that decision. They left on the RMS Rangitani in November, with Eric declaring that he would not ride for Wembley again. It was a great pity that he was unable to build on his showing in the World Final. He did not ride again in England until 1960, and lived for most of the rest of his life in New Zealand.

In November, Basil Storey commented in the *News* that "Freddie Williams is never likely to experience another spell as indifferent as his 1955 performances. After all, Williams was World Champion as recently as 1953, and I'm sure this dour Welshman from Port Talbot wouldn't thank you for suggesting that maybe, at the ripe old age of 30, he can no longer expect to hold his own in current racing company." On 28 December, the *News* said that Freddie "never seemed to recover from a bad knock to his leg at the Laurels meeting."

In the *Star* in December, Danny Carter said that "Eric Williams popped off to New Zealand and does not intend riding for Wembley again, Freddie Williams has his motorcycle business – and it certainly didn't help him having all the worries of the business and riding on his shoulders last season. Brian Crutcher is going into business, I hope it doesn't affect his form as seems to some people to have affected Freddie Williams."

When interviewed by Tony McDonald, Freddie did say that away meetings on a Saturday, the busiest day for his business, did cause problems for him. He had to arrange cover for his absence, which must have been a cost to him as well.

Another point that should be considered is that Freddie had ridden for two consecutive winters in South Africa. While he and Pat clearly enjoyed their time there, it meant that he had been riding without a long break since the start of the 1953 season. Trevor Redmond also had the same schedule, and his form also seemed to drop off towards the end of the season. However, Freddie was in fact only 29, and most speedway riders, if they had good fortune with injuries, could continue into their mid-30s, or even further. It remained to be seen if he would benefit from a winter's break.

13. 1956: A sudden retirement

One piece of good news for the Wembley riders was that the Lions management had abandoned their programme of open meetings instead of league matches that had run in 1955. The Lions would face their opponents in the First Division on an equal footing.

West Ham announced in March that they were withdrawing from league speedway. Decreasing support and the decision by Jack Young not to return to ride in Great Britain were given as the reasons. With Harringay and New Cross also out of speedway, London was left with just two teams – Wimbledon and Wembley. The First Division had seven teams, including Poole who had won the Second Division in 1955. The Second Division also had seven teams, Exeter having pulled out of speedway. There were also four teams in the Southern Area League, and plans to run some open meetings at Glasgow's White City Stadium. Even the speedway press was in decline. The *News* closed in February and was taken over by the *Speedway Star* with the first 'joint' edition on 14 April.

The Southern Area League was a potential source of new riders for the bigger teams, and the Lions signed Mike Broadbank from Rye House for a £150 transfer fee. Another early season recruit was Australian Ray Cresp, who after a couple of meetings for Eastbourne showed he had the potential to ride at a higher level. Another recruit from the SAL was Merv Hannam, who also came from Eastbourne. He was Brian Crutcher's uncle, although he was only just under three years older than his nephew, but did not ride regularly in the first part of the season.

And an 'old boy' returned to Wembley. Split Waterman had ridden for West Ham in 1955, but was now allocated to Wembley. He was not the force he had been in the early 1950s, but was still a useful heat leader. He had sold his motorcycle business and was now running a garage in New Malden. Brian Crutcher had also gone into business and was running a garage in Hampshire.

The Lions had lost Eric Williams who had emigrated to New Zealand. Ken Adams moved on to Ipswich in the Second Division in early June. During the season, Jimmy Gooch moved to Bradford. Tommy Price also announced that 1956 would be his last season as a rider. At the age of 44, this was maybe not surprising.

At the end of March, the Lions announced a retained list of 12 riders, although five were 'inactive'. In practice, Brian Crutcher was clearly the Lions' top rider, followed by Split Waterman, Freddie, Eric French and Trevor Redmond. Both Broadbank and Cresp ended season with averages of over six points, commendable for their debut seasons in the top flight. The Lions also had a new manager, John Evans.

As always, the Lions started with a series of away fixtures before opening night at Wembley on 17 May. Two challenge match defeats, at Belle Vue and Wimbledon, saw Freddie score 7 (+1) and 6 (+1). In a 42–42 draw at Norwich, in front of a 'disappointing' crowd of 6,948, he scored just 3 (+1) from four rides. Two weeks later, in a 20 point win at Odsal, he won his first two races before finishing last twice. His run of poor scores continued; the Lions lost by eight points to Wimbledon in their first home meeting, Freddie scored four points from his four rides. He was not alone, at Poole in a 55–29 defeat, Freddie, Tommy Price, Split Waterman and Trevor Redmond only scored four points between them.

Once again, the Lions riders were in conflict with the team's management. On 19 May, the *Star* reported that the riders were upset at missing meetings because the Lions had refused to join the inter-divisional tournament. They were the only team to do so, and it meant that the riders had lost early season rides. Eric Linden said that the Lions had not broken any regulations, but that some people considered they were being snobbish. In the same issue, Danny Carter speculated that Freddie and Jimmy Gooch were in danger of losing their team and reserve places respectively. He said that Mike Broadbank justified a team place.

The report in the *Star* on the Wimbledon meeting said that some of the Lions riders needed a 'dose of the Dons' team spirit'. Ken Adams was replaced by Ray Cresp. Freddie's form picked up against Birmingham at Wembley, with 8 (+1) from four rides, and then 5 (+1) from three rides against Belle Vue. When a not particularly strong Odsal side came to Wembley, he scored 8 (+2) from four rides. In the *Star*, Basil Storey, often a critic of the Lions, said that Tommy Price, Freddie and Split Waterman had "an old time look" about them.

On 9 June, the Lions were away to Belle Vue. Freddie had an engine failure in his first ride, and finished last in his second. He then told the Wembley management that he was packing it in. They assumed he meant for that meeting; but no – he was retiring from the sport. Belle Vue had often been a track where Freddie found it hard going in his last two or three years in the sport. In 1954, his score there in the World Championship Qualifying round saw him miss out on a Final spot.

On his way home, he stopped at a café in St Albans which was a common meeting place for speedway riders, and sold his equipment to a young rider. It was the end of an 11 year career in speedway, from his early trials at Rye House to two World Championships.

The *Star* reported that "Close associates of Welshman are not surprised" at his decision, and that there was "not much likelihood of a comeback." Basil Storey wrote that: "Freddie Williams's retirement is a blow to Wembley, in spite of his indifferent form this season. Freddie runs a motorcycle business, but his current loss of form is the reason for his retirement. Freddie is only 30. The Wembley management are worried, … Alec Jackson tried to talk Freddie into a change of heart." He continued: "Attendances at the Empire Stadium this season have been shockingly low … and although Williams has never been a particularly big crowd puller at other circuits, he has retained a good following at Wembley." He said that the Wembley management regard Freddie's retirement decision as a calamity. Tommy Price is to retire at end of season, and Wembley's experienced riders are slipping out the back door as fast as promising new talent enters at the front.

Writing in 1994 in *Vintage Speedway Magazine*, Freddie recalled that "In the end I began to lose interest in speedway … Tracks had changed, there was no dirt on them at all and I was feeling pretty depressed. In one race someone started to come round me and I found myself easing back. I rode into the pits and said to Duncan King … 'That's it, I'm finished…'" Freddie did say that he regretted selling all his speedway equipment on the way home, and wished that he had kept something.

In his interview with *Classic Speedway* in 2012, he outlined that the Belle Vue meeting "was another of those occasions where I was in a miserable mood driving up there and I was no longer riding as hard as I should have been." He concluded: "I didn't miss it at the time but I did a bit later on when sponsorship came into the sport and there was more money to be earned again." Clearly, growing business commitments with his motorcycle business, and family responsibilities – Pat was five months pregnant with Jayne – were influences in his decision to leave the sport that had been the major part of his life since 1946.

Freddie's average for the 10 league meeting he rode for the Lions was 5.14. It was a sad end to what had been a very successful speedway career. As a speedway rider, Freddie is rightly remembered for his two World Championship titles and his part in the remarkable

Wembley Lions team which dominated speedway for the first 10 years after the War. The Lions finished runners-up in the league to Wimbledon in a seven team league. And the following year, the sudden death of Sir Arthur Elvin saw the Lions withdraw from league speedway just before the start of the 1957 season.

Once, there was the possibility of a comeback. A couple of years after he retired, his brother Ian recalls that Charlie Knott, the Southampton promoter, approached Freddie about joining the Saints. Ian says that Knott offered Freddie £500 to sign, and gave him the money in cash. Freddie had come with Ian to the meeting, and did a few laps on Ian's bike. He decided not to come out of retirement, and gave the money back to Charlie Knott, saying to Ian "No, I don't want to start again." Ian points out that £500 was a lot of money in those days.

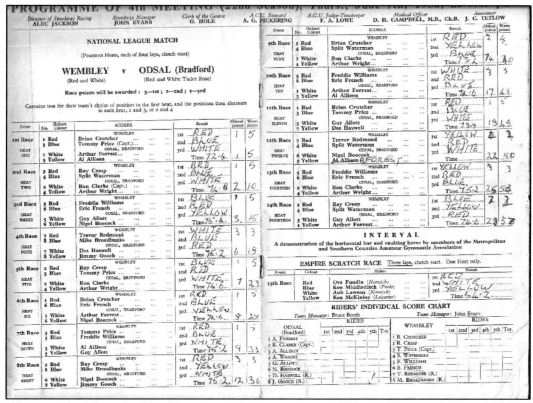

The scoresheet from the Wembley versus Odsal programme on 7 June 1956. Freddie scored 8 (+2) from his four rides. The Lions won 57–27. Two days later, Freddie retired.

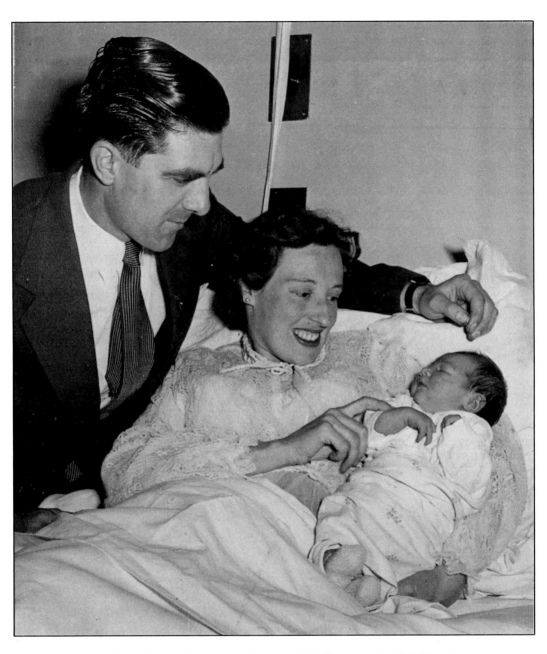

Freddie and Pat with Jayne in October 1956. (Courtesy Sarah Williams)

14. Life after speedway

Freddie kept an interest in speedway, the sport that had been the main part of his life from 1946 to 1956, and one of his daughter Jayne's childhood memories is of regularly going to meetings at Wimbledon, where her dad would sit with the family for a few races before heading off to the pits to mix with the riders.

Freddie's next formal link with the sport came in 1970. Trevor Redmond and local businessman Bernard Cottrell revived the Wembley Lions, buying a First Division licence from the Coatbridge Monarchs, who had struggled financially since losing their Edinburgh Stadium in 1967 to new building development for the Commonwealth Games. Bill Kitchen had been Redmond's first choice as team manager, but he was then appointed as the national track inspector for the sport, so was not available for a club position.

Freddie was a good connection with the past glories of the Wembley team, and while his new team did not match their predecessors in terms of winning trophies, they got excellent attendances in a sport which had grown again in popularity since the dark days of the mid-1950s.

Leaflet courtesy Hayley Redmond.

Bert Harkins, who captained the 'new' Wembley Lions for most of their two years at the stadium, says that he had never met Freddie before joining the Lions. He had heard of him, of course, but was at school when Freddie won his world titles. As team manager, Bert says that "He was very good, as a former rider he understood the rider's point of view. He understood what happened on the track, and was always on the rider's side. He could give us advice about riding, what to do and how to ride the Wembley track. Off the track, he was very friendly."

Freddie also returned – very briefly – to the track when other 'veterans' from the 1950s were invited back for a second half race in one of the early Wembley meetings. In fact, at the age of 44 when he became Wembley team manager, he was a year younger than Tommy Price in his last season with the Lions. Sadly for the legions of new – and old – speedway fans, the Wembley team only lasted for two seasons. The demands of football for more matches at the stadium saw the team withdraw from the league – temporarily at first – in 1972, but then it became clear that they would never return. The last meeting at the stadium was in the memorable World Final in 1981. Freddie was involved in 2000 when, just before the 'old' Wembley Stadium was pulled down, he and other former riders, including Bert Harkins, had the chance to visit the Stadium they had raced in for the last time.

Freddie continued to attend speedway events and often riders would stay at the family home in Hertfordshire. Jayne recalls Tommy Jansson staying, and Bert Harkins says that he would stay after Wembley meetings once he got to know Freddie. He met his wife Edith through Freddie and Pat – she was their au pair when they first met in 1971. Bert was living in Glasgow while riding for Wembley, and would stay with Freddie and Pat rather than make the long trip home to Glasgow after riding at Wembley.

Wembley Lions 1970: Dave Jessup, Bert Harkins, Tim Bungay, Freddie Williams (manager),
Wayne Briggs, Reidar Eide, Brian Collins, Ove Fundin on bike.

Wembley Lions 1971: Dave Jessup, Tony Clarke, Brian Leonard, Gote Nordin, Sverre Harrfeldt,
Brian Collins, Peter Prinsloo; on bike: Bert Harkins (captain), Freddie Williams (manager)

Freddie with David at the celebration of the 40th Anniversary of Speedway at High Beech in 1968.
(Courtesy John Somerville)

David, Ivan Mauger and Freddie. (Courtesy David Williams)

91

Bert Harkins, Halifax's Eric Boocock and Freddie at Wembley. (Courtesy JSC)

Brian Crutcher, Jack Geran and Freddie at one of the veteran riders dinners.
(Courtesy Brian Crutcher)

In 1981, Freddie became President of the Veteran Speedway Riders Association. Bert Harkins, who had just retired as a speedway rider, remembers being signed up by Freddie to become a member of the VSRA. Later it became the World Speedway Riders Association. In both organisations, Freddie and Pat often attended dinners, meeting former teammates and opponents. They also often attended the veteran riders lunches held in Bournemouth, meeting friends such as Brian Crutcher and Ken Middleditch.

In 1998, Freddie was nominated to be in the Welsh Sports Hall of Fame, which had started in 1990. He was the first person – and at the time of writing the only one – to be chosen from any form of motorcycle sport, and of course was the first speedway rider. Other people who were chosen in 1998 included Gareth Edwards, one of Wales's greatest rugby union players, Cliff Jones who played football for Tottenham Hotspur and Wales, and was a member of the famous 1961 'double team' that won the league and the FA Cup, and Lewis Jones who won international honours in both rugby union and rugby league. In the same year, he was involved in the 70th anniversary of speedway celebration at High Beech. A month later, Freddie attended a memorial event at the Meadowbank Stadium in Edinburgh to put up a plaque in memory of Peter Craven, who was killed there in a track accident in 1963.

In 2000, Barry Briggs had organised a final speedway dinner at Wembley to celebrate speedway's role at the 'old' stadium which Freddie and Pat attended, and Freddie was in a group photo of 14 former World Champions taken at the Stadium. 600 people attended the dinner, and took part in tours of the stadium in the afternoon.

In 2003, Freddie attended a service at Liverpool Cathedral to mark the 40th anniversary of the death of Peter Craven and to commemorate the 175 riders who had been killed in track accidents in speedway. Freddie gave the Second Reading from Corinthians and Timothy. The next week, a letter in the Speedway Star from Craven's family passed on their thanks to people who made the Service of Commemoration and Thanksgiving a day they would never forget. They expressed their gratitude to Canon Bayling, Rev Michael Whawell and to Freddie "for his heartfelt reading of the lesson."

When Freddie and Pat moved to Newbury, they went to watch speedway at Swindon with Ian and Jen, enjoying hospitality in the legends lounge.

In 2012, Freddie was invited to present the trophies at the Speedway Grand Prix in Cardiff. John Chaplin was involved in persuading the Grand Prix officials that Freddie should present the trophies with members of his family also invited.

Many family members attended to watch the ceremony. It was a far cry from an incident at the 1990 World Final at Odsal, where Freddie and Eric were refused complimentary admission because nobody recognised them. Strange, because although Eric had lived in New Zealand for many years, Freddie was renowned throughout the sport in Great Britain.

Overall, Freddie was one of the great British riders of the post-war era, when thousands of fans attended speedway each week, and the sport had large coverage in the newspapers. The second World Championship in Freddie's career in 1953 coincided with the season that can be seen as the turning point in the sport's fortunes. The reasons for this have been discussed elsewhere, but the sport was struggling when Freddie retired, and the question can never be answered whether Sir Arthur Elvin's head would have over-ruled his heart – and the other Wembley directors – and allowed the team to continue in front of ever declining crowds in 1957. As it was, his premature and sudden death in February 1957 saw the Lions leave league speedway a month later.

World Champions Group at the dinner held in 2000 to mark the end of the 'old' Wembley Stadium. Freddie is in the front row on the left. It is very unlikely that the sport will ever return there.
(Courtesy JSC)

Freddie with Mark Loram at Cardiff in 2000, the year he won the World title.
(Courtesy JSC – Mike Patrick)

Left: Freddie signing some World Final programmes for fellow former World Champion Peter Collins, who won the title in 1976.
(Courtesy JSC – Peter Morrish)

Below: Celebrating the 75th Anniversary of speedway at Rye House in 2003. Freddie is on the left, with Ronnie Moore next to him, Mark Loram, Ove Fundin in the Norwich Stars body colour and Michael Lee.
(Courtesy JSC – Mike Patrick)

Freddie's achievement in winning the World Final in 1950 is remarkable. It was his first final, albeit at Wembley, where he was familiar with both the track and the large crowds. But how many debutants have won a World Final? Only two others: Jerzy Szczakiel in 1973, and Gary Havelock in 1992. It was only Freddie's third season as a team member at Wembley, and only the second time he had entered the World Championship.

His win was also significant as it represented the triumph of the new generation of speedway riders, taking over from those who had ridden before the war. He was only 24 years old, maybe not young in today's terms, but certainly young for a top speedway rider at that time.

He was the first British rider to win the World Championship twice, and is still one of only three riders to do so. His record of two World titles, jointly held with Peter Craven, was only overtaken in 2018 when Tai Woffinden won his third title.

After retiring from speedway, Freddie ran his motorcycle business. After a few years, he switched to selling cars, after a couple of his customers were killed in bike accidents. He was a Subaru dealer for many years, and insisted that his coffin be taken to his funeral in a Subaru.

In 1967, the family moved to Delgarth, a seven-bedroom house in Hertfordshire. This remained their base for many years, and Freddie developed the property over the years to include a swimming pool and sauna, a tennis court, and a stables block. After family members had moved away, they moved to a smaller house in Newbury to be near Ian, Jayne and Sarah.

Pat and his family were clearly very important to Freddie. His and Pat's support for their children and grandchildren in their endeavours was very strong, as is shown in the chapter about their achievements. The values he had learnt from his own experience, and also from his father, about the importance of fulfilling potential and achievement in sport are clear in the successes of his children. He also very much enjoyed the company of his grandson, Sarah's son, also called Freddie.

His and Pat's legacy is not just their own sporting achievements, but those of their family. Of that, they could justifiably be very proud.

Pat's 80th birthday party. (Courtesy Sarah Williams).

Freddie with Brenda Leat (Peter Craven's widow) and Brian Craven in 2008. (Courtesy JSC)

Right: Freddie with the World Championship trophy at the speedway exhibition at Donnington Park. The rider next to Freddie in the photo is Split Waterman. Sadly, the exhibition is no longer there.
(Courtesy Sarah Williams)

Sarah and Freddie ready for a practice horse ride before his famous ride on Aldaniti. Freddie looks ready to ride a speedway bike, and had borrowed the helmet and Wembley body colour from Bert Harkins. (Both courtesy Sarah Williams)

Freddie feeding a lion at Paradise Wildlife Park.

Freddie and Freddie together at Cardiff 2012 (Steve Hone Photography)

Family group at the 2012 Cardiff Grand Prix: Standing: Nick Anthony, Joanna, Sarah, Charlie Morlock, Jayne, Pat; front: Freddie and Freddie. (Courtesy Jayne Ross)

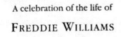

A celebration of the life of

FREDDIE WILLIAMS

12th March 1926 – 20th January 2013

St Gregory's Church, Welford
Wednesday 30th January 2013

*"Hide not your talents, they for use were made.
What's a sundial in the shade?"*

Freddie Williams

Wembley & Wales
World Champion 1950 & 1953
1926 - 2013
Husband, Father, Grandfather & Great Grandfather
RIP

Top: The Subaru which took Freddie's coffin to the funeral.
(Courtesy Jayne Ross)
Left: The brochure for the funeral.
Right: The plaque at the Speedway Memorial Garden at Paradise
Wildlife Park. (Photo: Peter Lush)

100

15. Eric Williams

Eric Williams was an important part of the Wembley Lions team from 1950 to 1955. He rode in three World Championship Finals and missed another after qualifying, won 23 caps for England, including tours of Australia and New Zealand, and won the National League – four times – the National Trophy and the London Cup while with Wembley.

Eric was born in Port Talbot on 17 November 1927. He was christened William Eric Williams, but was always known as Eric, and was just 18 months younger than his brother Freddie. His lifelong love of motorcycles came from his father, and his first competitive motorcycling was initially in trials riding, and then in grass track events. He was discharged from the Army in 1945, having had TB while an apprentice at the Army Technical College, and always felt that he was badly treated by the military authorities.

He became an apprentice fitter and turner at the steelworks in Port Talbot where his father worked, and joined the local motorcycle club. He got the first motorbike of his own in 1946, but almost destroyed it by going into deep water on a trials event, ignoring his father's warning not to cross a stream there.

There was a story behind his first bike, which he told to Ross Garrigan in one of his *Eric Williams Stories*, which they published on the internet. He had gone with his father to buy the bike which was in a miner's cottage in the valleys. It belonged to the son of a woman who had looked after it while he was away fighting in the War, but she had received a telegram saying he was 'missing presumed dead' and now the War was over she accepted that he would never return. Freddie Williams senior told the woman that she had kept the bike in immaculate condition, which it was, and paid her £35 for it. Eric said that every Armistice Day he thought about that visit to the depths of the mining valleys to buy his first motorbike.

Eric moved onto grass track racing, which could be a lucrative business. The £5 he got for winning a meeting was the equivalent of a week's wages. But with Freddie on Wembley's books and riding second half races for the Lions, a move into speedway and the Wembley Lions was almost inevitable.

He was invited to Rye House for a trial, and then after joining the Lions, was sent on loan to Birmingham to get more experience. But after three meetings, he broke his thigh in a track accident, which finished his season. The story is told that he broke his thigh again falling out of bed in hospital, but he says this is not correct.

His first full season was with Cradley Heath in the Second Division in 1949. Despite his lack of speedway racing experience, he achieved an average of over eight points a meeting. Alan Hunt was Cradley's star and *Stenner's 1950 Annual* says that "Eric Williams and [Gil] Craven backed Hunt stoutly". Eric recalled that "I had acquired confidence in my own riding ability following the most enjoyable 1949 season I had spent with … Cradley. Girlfriend Helly and I had experienced a wonderful time at Cradley Heath and in the surrounding rural districts." Matt Jackson, in a profile of Eric says that "His form at Dudley Wood was nothing short of outstanding as he rattled up a succession of high scores … Eleven maximums and an end of season run that put him among the best in the Second Division meant an inevitable call up to the Lions…"

Peter Foster, in his *Heathens – Cradley Heath Speedway 1947 – 1976* book says that Eric "had a splendid season" and noted that his partnership with Alan Hunt gained "a fearsome reputation".

Prior to the 1950 season, Wembley had sold Split Waterman to Harringay, and needed a replacement. Eric went straight into the team, and while he had been reluctant to leave Cradley, he was contracted to Wembley and had to move to London. There, he recalls not been made particularly welcome by the established Wembley riders. He had not had to work his way up from reserve, and said to Ross Garrigan "I now realise what an honour this really was...".

He clashed with Tommy Price, who expected a second string to allow him room to win races, and not 'fill him in' with cinders. The message was passed on by brother Freddie, which annoyed Eric even more, as Price had not spoken to him directly. However, Eric was clearly ready for the top level. The *Speedway Echo* said he was "a polished rider, almost a finished product" after an early season meeting at New Cross.

Freddie always worried about riding with Eric as his partner, not because of his brother's riding, but because of the additional responsibility of watching out for a partner who was also his brother. In a meeting at Harringay, it was reported that Freddie brought down Eric in the last race. Eric remembers it very differently – that he and Freddie had made a good start, when Split Waterman cut across from the outside gate to try to come up the inside. The result was Eric's footrest hitting Freddie's back wheel, and ripping all the spokes out. Eric was the only rider left on his bike, but inevitably the race was stopped. Eric's foot was injured by the wheel sprocket of Freddie's bike. Eric ended up in hospital, and Freddie was annoyed – apart from his concern for Eric – at being excluded.

Eric missed a couple of weeks racing, including a return to his old club in a challenge match at Cradley. Overall, he rode 44 meetings for the Lions in 1950, with a commendable average of 7.43 in league matches, less than a point below what he had achieved with Cradley in the Second Division the year before. *Stenner's 1951 Annual* said that "There's a new backbone forming to the Wembley line-up – the Williams brothers, Freddie and Eric, and Bob Oakley." Eric finished fifth in the Lions averages, and had medals for winning the League and the London Cup from his first season in the top flight. In the World Championship, he entered the competition in the third round, but could only manage four points in the meeting at Cradley. Only the top two qualified from each meeting, so he did not reach the Championship round.

At the end of October, Eric had a fixture more important than any speedway one. He married Helen Hogg at Margam Abbey. Freddie was his best man, and the *Port Talbot Guardian* said that he was a "well-known speedway rider." Kate Williams was a bridesmaid, and the bride was given away by Mr G. Edwards, a family friend.

The report said that their honeymoon was postponed because Eric had a riding engagement in Denmark the following Saturday. Helen was serving in the Women's Royal Air Force at the time.

For the 1950–51 winter, Eric was selected for the England team, led by Jack Parker, that toured Australia. Helen accompanied him for a 'working honeymoon'

It was an 'unofficial' tour, not backed by the Speedway Control Board, but organised by Parker. Although the Lions lost the test series 7–0, it was good experience for Eric, at this stage of his career, to be able to ride in Australia. He ended up as the Lions' third highest scorer in the test matches, with 58+2 from six meetings. He missed the third test through a bout of tonsillitis. He scored double figures in five of his six test matches, and had a fall and engine failure in the fourth test where he only scored five points.

It was not a great performance by a 'makeshift' England team. Eric was seen as a second string at Wembley at this time, but was the third heat leader for this England team. Peter

Foster says in his *History of the Speedway Ashes* that "Tommy Miller and Eric Williams had done themselves proud" in the series.

Sadly, the test series was overshadowed by the death, following a track accident, of Australian star Ken Le Breton. Also, fellow Australian Graham Warren was badly injured while riding in New Zealand. It was believed that his career could be over, but he did return to action later in 1951.

Eric returned to England to continue his career with Wembley. Once again, the Lions won the League and the London Cup. For Eric, the season marked a number of 'firsts' – his first full maximum in a league match for the Lions; his first appearance in an 'official' test against Australia, and his first appearance in the World Championship Final.

Basil Storey, in his Division 1 Review in *Stenner's 1952 Annual*, was, as so often, critical of the Wembley team, saying that despite winning the title, they had problems. He said that "... the Williams brothers, Freddie and Eric, are sound but unlikely to improve..." However, the review of Wembley's season in the same publication said that "Much of Wembley's success revolved around the consistency of the Williams brothers." In terms of National League and National Trophy points scored, Eric was second highest for the Lions, his average improved to 7.70, which would have made him a heat leader in most teams, but he was only fourth best for Wembley.

In the World Championship, Eric entered the competition in the Championship Round. His first meeting was at West Ham. In heat 18, Eric, with 10 points, lined up against Wembley colleague Bruce Abernethy (12 points) and local favourite Aub Lawson (10 points). The race was rerun after a first corner accident. Eric made the gate in the rerun; Lawson worked his way past Abernethy but could not catch Eric. So, the two Wembley riders finished on 13 points; Abernethy won the run-off for the £50 cheque for winning the meeting. For his second meeting, Eric had to travel to Bradford, and a joint fourth place with Wembley colleague Bob Oakley was enough to give him 23 points from his two qualifying meetings and a place in the Final.

There, Eric was up against Freddie in his first race, heat three, and finished last. Two third places and two seconds gave him a total of six points. He finished in 12th place, just a point behind Freddie who had faded after that first race win. Still, it was good experience for a rider in only his third full season of speedway and second in the top flight.

England had already lost the test series to Australia when Eric was called up for the fifth test at West Ham. Freddie had had a poor night at Birmingham in the fourth test, and was dropped along with several other changes to the team. Split Waterman dominated England's scoring with 17; while Eddie Rigg scored 14. Eric was third highest scorer with nine as England went down 58–49 to complete a 4–1 series defeat. He finished last in his first ride, missed his second, but then secured three second places and a heat win.

Eric's progress was reflected in the Division 1 Rankings in *Stenner's 1952 Annual*. He was in 12th place; the only other Wembley rider listed was Freddie who was fifth.

Eric did not ride abroad in the winter of 1951–52. In 1952, he continued to improve for Wembley, increasing his average again to 8.20, and finally achieving the third heat leader spot, behind Freddie and Tommy Price. He was also the Lions' third highest points scorer, with 328 including bonus points in the National League and National Trophy.

The Lions "plodded through to the Championship" according to *Stenner's 1953 Annual*. Bruce Abernethy had failed to return from New Zealand, and was replaced by Trevor Redmond. The Lions won the National League comfortably, but lost in the first round of the London Cup to Wimbledon, and in the National Trophy to Birmingham.

In the World Championship, the international growth of the sport saw an International Round introduced, and Eric qualified from that with 18 points from two meetings. But in the Championship Round, he could only muster 15 from his two meetings. Once again, he was drawn away from home for both meetings, having to travel to Norwich and then Harringay. A poor night at Norwich saw him score just five points. With no chance of qualifying for the Final, he scored a more respectable 10 at Harringay. Despite his improved form for Wembley, Eric was not selected for any of the England versus Australia test matches. The visitors won the series 4–1, with England winning the last test.

In the winter of 1952–53, Eric rode with an England team touring New Zealand. Another England team, led by Jack Parker, was in Australia, and got heavily beaten in three test matches. Eric's group in New Zealand was led by Bill Kitchen. The riders also rode for local New Zealand teams and Eric joined Hawkes Bay. The report in *Stenner's 1953 Annual* said that they were "the team to beat", with Eric supported by Maury Dunn and Peter Clark. The league racing was over 12 heats with five-man teams. However, the test matches were run with the more usual six rider teams, but over 12 heats. The New Zealanders won the series 3–2. Eric scored 39 points in his six matches; only Bill Kitchen fared better. In the New Zealand Rankings for 1952–53 in *Stenner's 1953 Annual*, Eric was in fifth place, behind fellow tourist Ken Sharples, Ron Johnston, Maury Dunn and Geoff Mardon.

Helen did not go on this trip, and at the end of his visit Eric was clearly looking forward to seeing his family again. However, New Zealand had made a very favourable impression on him, which was going to be important for his future.

Back home, he had diversified from speedway and bought a partnership in an electrical goods business. They sold and repaired televisions and radios, and reconditioned electrical stoves. With television about to experience a huge growth in 1953, this was clearly a good investment. The company's advertising used Eric for publicity. An advert said "For everything Electrical, consult Eric Williams – new partner in Fieldson's Service Ltd." The company was based in Willesden, near where Eric and Helen lived. The company was big enough to advertise in the *Daily Mirror*, and sent out goods all over the country.

While television benefitted Eric's business, the growth in use of this new leisure item was an important factor in speedway's decline in popularity in 1953, which would eventually lead to Eric leaving the Wembley Lions.

The 1953 season saw the National League programme reduced, with just 16 meetings. The first half of the season saw the National League teams competing for the Coronation Cup. The Lions won the League title by a point from Harringay. They fared less well in the Coronation Cup. With the Empire Stadium unavailable for speedway as usual until mid-May, they raced three home meetings at Wimbledon, and lost two of them. There were changes in the team as well. Bob Oakley retired early in the season, and the Lions signed Brian Crutcher from Poole, who had reached the 1952 World Final as a Second Division rider. George Wilks only rode five league matches for the Lions, and Bill Kitchen was at times at reserve.

Eric maintained his improvement in his scores. His average in League and National Trophy matches went up to 9.20, marginally behind Freddie on 9.62, and Tommy Price on 9.27. The Lions reached the National Trophy Final, but lost by four points on aggregate to Wimbledon. Eric was the only Lions rider to reach double figures in a poor display in the first leg at Plough Lane.

On the international scene, Eric's consistent form saw him recalled by England for the second test at Wembley, after the Lions had lost the first of the three-match series at

Norwich. Eric and Tommy Price (at the age of 41!) were chosen at reserve for the meeting that could settle the series. The England team manager gave Eric six rides and Price five, ruthlessly axing Tommy Miller and Dick Bradley after two and one rides respectively. It paid off – Eric top scored for England with 15 points – three wins and three second places, with Price scoring 12 (+1). For the third test, they both were given full team places, with Freddie, Brian Crutcher and three other riders being dropped. England won 61–47, with Eric scoring 8 (+1) after a fall in his first ride.

In the World Championship, Eric entered the competition in the Championship Round, and qualified for the Final with 24 points from his two meetings. The lowest qualifiers were on 23, and four riders with that score raced-off for three places in the big Wembley meeting. Eric had the benefit of being drawn at Wembley for one of his qualifying rounds, and scored 12 points. A couple of days before, he had achieved the same score at West Ham, and by 28 August, when the round finished, knew that he had reached his second World Final.

However, he did not challenge for the top positions. Freddie won the title, and Eric finished with four points from four third places, before falling in his last ride. But he had more experience of the big night, which would benefit him in 1955.

Eric stayed at home for the 1953–54 winter, looking after his family – his young daughter Linda was now attending meetings with Helen to watch her dad race – and to look after his business. Freddie and Ian spent the winter riding in South Africa.

For the Lions in 1954, Brian Crutcher was now clearly the team's leading rider, with an average of 10.10. However, Eric improved on his 1953 figure to average 9.41. Both riders scored 341 points, including bonus points, in National League and National Trophy meetings. Fred Lang, one of the leading South African riders, had signed for the Lions, with Bill Kitchen having retired from league racing, and George Wilks only riding in a handful of meetings.

For only the second time since the end of the War, Wembley did not win the National League. Wimbledon had recruited well, and finished top of the table. However, there was some compensation for the Lions with both the National Trophy and London Cup being won, so Eric added to his collection of winner's medals.

In the National Trophy Semi-Final, Wembley beat Bradford by just one point on aggregate. Eric came second in heat 17 at Odsal, meaning that all Wembley had to do was secure one point from the final heat to win. The other riders carried him back to the pits shoulder-high after his crucial ride. The Final was won much more comfortably, with the Lions beating Norwich home and away.

One honour for Eric was participating in the Golden Helmet Match Race Championship. Ronnie Moore was the holder, but had to relinquish the title after a crash while riding in Denmark. The Speedway Control Board looked at riders' recent form to decide on the contestants, and Eric was chosen to face Bradford's Arthur Forrest. The two riders were friends, and Eric recalls in *The Eric Williams Story* part 21 how he and Helen would go out for fish and chips after meetings at Bradford with Arthur and his wife, and then stay with them before travelling back to London the next morning.

Eric won the first leg 2–1 at Wembley. Two days later at Bradford, Eric lost 2–1. He had stopped for a break on the trip up north, while running in a new van. He had dozed off and was nearly late for the meeting at Bradford. Alan Hunt warmed up his bike for him. The decider was at a neutral track, Birmingham. This time Arthur Forrest won 2–0 on a rain-soaked track.

In the World Championship, Eric was one of four Wembley riders nominated to the Championship round. A first race engine failure saw him end up with nine points from his five rides in his first meeting at Birmingham. To have any chance of reaching the Final, he would need at least 14 points from the meeting at Wembley. This meeting was also notable as it was the only time the three Williams brothers rode together in an official meeting. Eric's chances of reaching another World Final in reality ended with a last place in his first ride. Freddie was also in the position, after a poor first qualifying round meeting at Belle Vue, of needing a maximum to have any chance of reaching the Final. He nearly made it, but was beaten by Eric in his second ride. Freddie made a poor start, and had to pass Ian and Bob Oakley, which he did, but could not catch Eric, who won the race. Eric finished up with 10 points from another win and two second places. Freddie was reserve for the big night at Wembley.

The Williams brothers had ridden together under the banner of Wales, in an international best pairs meeting at Harringay earlier in the season. Freddie and Eric were the main pairing, with Ian at reserve. Freddie stood down from his last ride to give Ian a race, and his younger brother promptly knocked Eric off!

England faced an Australasia team in a three match test series, and won 3–0. Eric was chosen at reserve in the first test at West Ham, and scored a point in his only ride. England won by 12 points, with the visitors clearly missing the injured Ronnie Moore. Freddie and Wally Green were dropped for the second test at Belle Vue, with Eric and Peter Craven coming into the team. Eric rode with Brian Crutcher, and scored 11 (+2) in his contribution to a 20 point England win, despite Ronnie Moore having returned for the visitors. His and England's good form continued into the third match of the series at Bradford. England won 56–52 with Eric scoring 9 (+1).

Eric did not ride abroad in 1954–55, and the forthcoming season proved to be his last one with Wembley. With the speedway team losing money, Sir Arthur Elvin announced that the Lions would forego six of its home fixtures. The league schedule was to ride against each other team twice at home and twice away. Sir Arthur felt that some of the provincial teams were not a big draw, and more fans would be attracted to watch 'big money' open meetings.

One immediate effect of this was to undermine the league championship. Wembley had finished runners-up to Wimbledon the previous year, but would have little chance of taking the title back with only six home meetings. And so it proved, with the Lions finishing in third place, their lowest position since the War, except for 1948 when they raced most of their home fixtures at Wimbledon. In the team, Fred Lang had not returned from South Africa, and was replaced by Ken Adams. Jimmy Gooch moved to Swindon, although he remained a Wembley rider and continued to ride for the Lions in National Trophy meetings.

In the end, only four open individual meetings were held at Wembley. Eric had protested about the decision to have only six home league meetings and had been put on the transfer list at over £2,000. But with little money in the sport, there were no takers for him. He said that the Wembley riders would be financially penalised because they would earn less than in a normal league meeting. In a league meeting, Eric would expect to have five rides and score – on average – between 10 and 11 points, and have one or two rides in the second half. In the open meetings, he only had five rides, and scored two, seven, five and eight points. The last meeting was a handicap one.

The burden of racing so much away from home also hit the riders' averages and scores. Brian Crutcher was the top Wembley scorer, with an average of 9.33 and 380 points. Tommy Price was second with a 7.12 average and 258 points. Eric was third, with a 6.96 average and 268 points, marginally ahead of Freddie. It was his lowest league average up to that time.

Left: Eric wearing a Wembley body colour.
(Courtesy JSC)

The Lions did find some success in the National Trophy. They reached the Final, where they again faced Norwich. But the outcome was very different. The Lions went down 64–43 at home in the first leg, their biggest ever home defeat. Nine days later, they went to The Firs hoping to at least salvage some pride. Norwich were missing two key riders, Ove Fundin and Aub Lawson. The Lions came very close, winning 63–45, but lost on aggregate by three points.

Eric was involved in a nasty accident during the meeting. In heat seven, he was up against Billy Bales, a big favourite with the Norwich fans. Eric's throttle cable got entangled with Bales's left handlebar, resulting in Bales ending up in the fence and being taken to hospital. Eric was excluded, but completely denied intentionally injuring another rider. Some Norwich fans bore a grudge against Eric for many years as a result of this incident, continuing it even when he rode for them in 1962.

England again faced Australasia, this time in a six-match series. Eric was not selected for the first match, which England lost heavily, but was one of four Wembley riders chosen for the second test at the Empire Stadium. England won comfortably, 67–41, with Eric scoring 11 (+3) from his six rides. However, he fared less well at West Ham in the third test. Despite being England's third highest scorer at Wembley, he was dropped to reserve. He scored two points from his two rides as England lost. He was not selected for the last three meetings of the series, which England won to take the series 4–2.

The highlight of Eric's season was the World Championship. Once again seeded to the final qualifying round, he was drawn to ride at Wembley and Norwich. Eric took 12 points from his first meeting, at Wembley, and 11 from the meeting at Norwich. After the qualifying rounds were completed, 15 of the places were decided, with Eric, Brian Crutcher and Billy Bales all tied on 23. A run-off would have to take place to decide who got the final place. However, then Doug Davies, a young South African rider with Birmingham, became seriously ill and could not take up his place in the Final. The run-off took place at West Ham, with two places in the Final now available. Brian Crutcher lost control on the first bend, and Bales ran into him. However, the impact knocked Crutcher upright and he then pursued Eric, who had taken the lead, leaving Bales at the back. Brian Crutcher caught Eric on the line, but it did not matter, both Wembley riders were in the Final. Bales later joined them when Aub Lawson had to withdraw from the Final with a collarbone injury.

However, between the run-off and the big night, Eric experienced bike problems. But his Wembley team-mate, Eric French, lent him an engine for the Final. Eric won his first race, but then came third to Peter Craven and Arthur Forrest. His defeat to Forrest, by inches, proved to be crucial at the end of the meeting. In his third race, heat 10, he was second to Ronnie Moore. After all the riders had undertaken three rides, Peter Craven and Barry Briggs were on eight points, Ronnie Moore and Brian Crutcher had seven and Eric was fifth with six. In heat 13, Eric was up against Barry Briggs and Brian Crutcher. The three riders clashed with Crutcher caught between the other two. The race was stopped and Crutcher was excluded, which Eric later said was "ridiculous". Eric won the rerun, pursued throughout the race by Barry Briggs. So, after four races for each rider, Peter Craven was on 11 points, Briggs was on 10, and Ronnie Moore and Eric on 9. Brian Crutcher beat Craven in heat 17, to leave the Belle Vue man on 13 points. Ronnie Moore won the next race to reach 12 points, and Eric won heat 19, overtaking Olle Nygren on the second lap. Briggs needed to win heat 20 to force a run-off with Craven, but was beaten by Ove Fundin.

So, Peter Craven was the new World Champion, with Briggs, Moore and Eric in a run-off to decide second and third. Moore raced away from the start, with Eric second, being fiercely chased by Briggs. However, on the first bend of the final lap, Briggs overtook Eric, only to fall on the final bend. Eric had to lay his bike down to avoid hitting Briggs. The referee did not put the red lights on, so Briggs remounted, as did Eric, but Briggs's bike started first and he got to the line ahead of Eric.

This was Eric's last World Final appearance. He saw out the rest of the season with Wembley, but then announced that he was emigrating to New Zealand with Helen and their family. His relationship with the Wembley management had not recovered, and he saw a better future for him and his family in New Zealand.

Eric did not ride again in Great Britain until 1960. Speedway continued to decline after Eric left, and a handful of teams kept the sport alive in the late 1950s. A new decade saw a revival, with the launch of the Provincial League in 1960, revitalising venues that had last staged the sport in the early to mid-1950s. Johnnie Hoskins had staged a short season of eight meetings at New Cross in 1959, and then entered a team, the New Cross Rangers, in the National League in 1960, bringing the senior league up to 10 clubs.

It was announced in February that Eric had agreed to return to British speedway and join New Cross. While the New Cross team looked strong on paper, with Barry Briggs – recruited on loan from Wimbledon – and former Wembley star Split Waterman as heat leaders with Eric, a review in the *1961 Speedway Star Digest* said that they were a 'run of the mill' team. They finished in eighth place in the league table, with seven wins and a draw from 18 meetings.

Eric made his debut for the Rangers in a challenge match at home to Norwich on 11 April. He won three races and fell in the other. Given he had not ridden in league racing for four years, he was remarkably successful. He finished the season as New Cross's top scorer, with 237 (+10) points from 22 matches. However, in National League meetings, Briggs had the better average, at 9.81 compared to Eric's 9.40. Eric's scores included two full maximums.

Eric qualified for the World Final. He scored 22 points in the Great Britain second round meetings, with 10 at Belle Vue and 12 at Oxford. Nine riders qualified for the big night at Wembley from the semi-finals, and Eric finished in seventh place with 23 points. However, his season in England finished early, with his last meeting being the Tom Farndon Memorial Trophy at New Cross on 24 August. Norman Jacobs notes in *Out of the Frying Pan*, his history of New Cross Speedway, that Eric "left early to return home to New Zealand because of domestic problems". He thus had to withdraw from the World Final. Eric later commented that although he had qualified for the Final, there were very few other meetings for him to ride in towards the end of the season, and therefore he returned to New Zealand. However, it does seem remarkable that he would forego a final big speedway night at Wembley without good reason.

Eric had also resumed his international career. Peter Foster, in his *History of the Speedway Ashes*, says that Eric was "riding as well as ever" when he was recalled to the England team to ride against Australasia at Ipswich. England lost by six points, but Eric scored 9 (+2), with three second and three third places. He kept his place for the next test at Leicester, a track where he had not ridden before the 1960 season, but only scored one point and was dropped for the last two tests. After this season, England became Great Britain, including Australian and New Zealand riders, which made the competition for selection for places far tougher.

In 1960, another innovation was the World Team Cup. England raced in a qualifying series against Australia, New Zealand and a Challengers team, presumably there to make up the numbers. It is a pity there weren't two more Welsh riders available, as Ian and Eric could have competed for Wales for a change. Eric was chosen for the first two meetings, at Wimbledon and Oxford, scoring six and five points respectively. Former Wembley team-mate Trevor Redmond was at reserve for New Zealand. Eric was not selected for the final two qualifying rounds, or the final.

Norman Jacobs said in *Out of the Frying Pan* that Johnnie Hoskins had taken a gamble in bringing Eric and Split Waterman back out of retirement, but that "the gamble paid off handsomely with Williams, who rode as well as at any time in his career."

Johnnie Hoskins could not persuade Barry Briggs to stay with the Rangers, and it was a weak New Cross team that started the 1961 season. South African Doug Davies was signed by Hoskins as a replacement for Briggs.

Hoskins had agreed with Eric to pay for the cost of bringing him and his family to London. Eric settled his business affairs in New Zealand, where he had been selling cars, and left Wellington on a cruise liner for London. However, the ship had problems en route, and they were stranded in Lima for a time. When they arrived at Southampton, they were met by Freddie, who told Eric that his speedway bike and equipment had been stolen from the store at Freddie's business.

Eric made his return to action at New Cross on 10 May, when he scored three points for a London team against the Rest. He was lent a bike by the New Cross management, but was not impressed with it. However, he then scored nine points from three wins in the next home meeting. Eric finished the season with a 6.58 average in National League and National Trophy meetings. He was third in the team's scorers, behind a resurgent Split Waterman, who had an average of 8.17 in league meetings, and Doug Davies on 7.02.

New Cross finished the season in eighth place in the National League, with seven wins from 18 meetings. The team finished their league fixtures in early August, and Eric's last meeting at New Cross was the Supporters Trophy on 20 September, when he scored 11 points from five rides.

In the World Championship, Eric reached the British semi-finals, but scores of three points at Belle Vue and four at Norwich were not enough for him to progress further.

Sadly, the Greyhound Racing Authority, who owned the New Cross Stadium, told Johnnie Hoskins that he could not run speedway there in 1962 because they wanted to run stock car racing instead. Eric recalls having to take legal action to get his fares back to New Zealand paid by Hoskins, which he eventually did. He found work outside speedway with a 'self-drive' car hire business. The job also came with a flat for Eric and Helen and the children. He also did some work connected to the business as a chauffeur.

Eric and Jimmy Gooch moved from New Cross to Norwich for the 1962 season. Eric's average from 16 National League and National Trophy meetings was 5.54. Norman Jacobs, in his *Speedway in East Anglia*, says that "Williams couldn't settle down and retired before the end of the season." The National League was now down to just seven teams, and Norwich finished in fifth place. Eric made his debut for the Stars on 5 May, riding off a 10-yard handicap – the National League had a complex handicap system at this time to try to make the racing more entertaining. He rode fairly regularly after that. One highlight was a five ride maximum at Oxford on 14 June in a National Trophy meeting.

Eric's last meeting for Norwich was a best pairs meeting on 18 August, which he won with John Debbage. The records of Norwich for that season note that Olle Nygren was signed after that meeting to replace Billy Bales who was injured, and Eric, who had gone home. However, Eric's memoirs say that they left London in February 1963, after he had settled his legal case with New Cross, and wound up their affairs in England. He bought three motorbikes from Freddie which he planned to sell in New Zealand to give them a start there.

His time with Norwich was the end of his speedway career, at the age of 35. He subsequently worked in the car and newspaper industries. He took up golf, and played off a single figure handicap for many years. He maintained his love of motorbikes, and rode in amateur trials meetings in the 1970s and 1980s.

Helen died in 1993. A year later, Eric linked up with Margaret, whose husband Harold had died a few years before and had been a friend of Eric's. They subsequently moved to the Gold Coast in Australia to be near Margaret's daughter.

One enjoyment in later life was working on his *Eric Williams Stories* with Ross Garrigan, which were enjoyed by former riders and fans.

Eric died on 24 July 2009. He had been ill with multiple myeloma, but Dr Robert Green recalled in a eulogy at Eric's funeral that a few days before he died, Eric had gone to watch a pro-am golf tournament at Mackay Golf Club and enjoyed it. His funeral was held in Mackay. A memorial service was also held by Linda and Mandy in Hastings in New Zealand, and a service was held at Margam Abbey, attended by Freddie, Kate and Ian. His friend Reg Fearman said in a tribute: "The bravery, dignity and courage that he showed despite knowing, as he put it, his sentence, was an example to all." He also said that he and Eric had been the last two surviving members of the 1950–51 British Lions tour to Australia. Bob Andrews said that Eric had established the New Zealand Veteran Speedway Riders group and that he was carrying it on. He said that Eric "was a hard rider in his time, but also a very sensitive man."

Eric was cremated in a white coffin with red and white flowers – the Wembley Lions colours. A few months before he died, he was photographed in his Wembley racing jacket, putting his left foot out speedway style while on his walking frame. A Lion to the last.

16. Ian Williams

Ian Williams never planned to become a speedway rider. But he did, following in the footsteps of his two older brothers, and was "one of the finest riders ever to wear the Swindon colours" according to Robert Bamford in his history of Swindon Speedway.

Ian was born in 1931, which made him five years younger than Freddie and four years younger than Eric. He recalls that "Our dad was very keen on motorbikes and he got us all bikes. Freddie and Eric rode in trials, scrambles and grass track meetings. I loved being with them, so I went to the meetings, and would have a ride round. I rode mainly to please my dad, but I did grass track for a couple of years, and remember that if I won a meeting, I got £5." When the war started, Port Talbot was a target for German bombers because of the steel works. Fred Williams senior was in the Home Guard, which gave him access to bikes that needed repairs. He recalls a hill climb event organised by Swansea Motorcycle Club, where Ian managed to get about 100 yards up a local mountain.

When he was 17 years old, Ian became the Welsh grass track champion. He also enjoyed trials and scrambling, although he did not take his riding as seriously as his two older brothers. While his dad was a hard taskmaster with Freddie and Eric, he wasn't with Ian, who maybe had a more relaxed approach than his older siblings. Ian's mother hoped that he would become a musician, and he had violin lessons for a couple of years. But he came home from violin lessons one day, and heard the bikes being revved up. He went round to see what they were doing, still carrying his violin. Eric said 'bugger off and take that silly box with you'. Ian went indoors, put the violin on the settee, and never touched it again. His mum begged, Eric apologised and he still never touched it again.

When he left school, he got an apprenticeship in the steelworks. He had some time off after some minor injuries in a grass track meeting, and was called in by the man in charge. When asked which was his priority, bikes or the rest of his life, Ian answered 'Bikes' and was sacked!

He did go and watch Freddie and Eric practising at Rye House, and with Freddie's encouragement, did have a ride, but recalls that he "didn't really like it." In 1949, Ian was called up for National Service, and was stationed in Egypt. There were political tensions in Egypt, and it was not an easy place to serve. He says that he "loved being in the Army, and made friends for life there. He was in 42 Company in El Ballah, part of the Middle East Land Forces (MELF). He says that "People knew about Freddie in the Army, so I was asked to look after all their motorcycles, even though I didn't know anything about them. It was a small Company based in the 'middle of nowhere', near the Suez Canal. Most of the men were regulars, and they sorted out us conscripts – they made men out of boys." There were some opportunities for motorcycle sport – unofficially – as well. There was a Matchless bike that was used for races, watched by the officers.

Ian missed Freddie's 1950 World Championship win because he was in Egypt at the time. However, he did manage to meet Eric and his wife Helen when his ship stopped at a nearby port. Eric was on his honeymoon on the way to Australia. Ian managed to pass his Army apprenticeship while in Egypt.

He came home after two years national service, and still had no strong plans to become a speedway rider. However, he was called to the phone (a half mile walk) to speak to a Mr Woodcock about riding for his team. Ian can't recall which team it was, and believes that he was only offered the opportunity because of his two older brothers. Nothing came of this, but then Freddie arranged for him to have a trial at Wolverhampton after their meeting against Swindon. They drove up there, but then the trial was cancelled. Ian says that "Freddie did his nut" after their wasted journey, but Swindon joint promoter Reg Witcomb said to them that if Ian came to Swindon on the following Saturday, he would get a place in the team. Reg Whitcomb had not seen Ian ride, and in fact Ian didn't even own a bike.

The brothers returned to London, and on the Saturday Ian borrowed Freddie's Jowet Javelin car and one of his brother's bikes and drove to Swindon. He was not given a warm welcome by the other riders, who no doubt thought this was a flashy, privileged youngster who had come to take one of their team places. Bob Jones did make Ian welcome, and always supported him after that.

Ian had two rides for Swindon that evening at reserve, scoring paid four points. However, the meeting was subsequently deleted from the official records after Long Eaton withdrew from the league. He says that "Swindon were a weak team at the time. The riders were men who had come out of the Army and were trying to earn a few bob. We were paid £1 a point and £1 a start. My Dad was earning £8 a week in the steelworks and I could earn £10 in one meeting. It didn't seem right."

Ian's lack of speedway experience did not show in his first season. Riding in the Southern League, Swindon finished sixth out of 10 teams, with 18 wins and 18 defeats. Ian scored 169 points, for a very creditable average of 6.11. He scored a paid maximum against St Austell on 21 June (9+3) and then a full maximum against Aldershot in September. The averages were based on four rides.

The 1953 edition of *Coming Speedway Stars* included a profile of Ian, headed "Best novice of 1952". It said that he "enjoyed a really brilliant season. Scores of nine and 10 became almost commonplace... He improved as each week went by." The writer concluded that "If his improvement is maintained – and there is no reason why this should not be so – it is quite on the cards that within a year or two the Williams trio will be as well known at Wembley as the Roger threesome is at New Cross."

In *Stenners' Speedway Annual 1953*, the review of Swindon's season said that the recruitment of former Wembley veteran Bob Wells and Ian was "extremely successful. The review also said that the Robins were a team, rather than having one or two 'stars', which arguably was true for much of Ian's time at the club.

The next season, 1953, Ian "continued to progress at a rate of knots, posting several double-figure scores" according to Robert Bamford. On 1 August, he blasted round the 410 yard Blunsdon track to break the track record that had stood since July 1951. He broke it again twice in that meeting. Swindon finished fourth out of eight teams in the Southern League. Ian's progress was shown by his place at the top of the averages, with a figure of 8.39 from 28 meetings.

Stenners Annual 1954 put Ian at number 10 in their rider rankings for the Southern League in 1953, quite an achievement for someone only in his second season of league racing. The review of the Robins' season said that the team lost confidence after a narrow home defeat to Exeter. It said that every match saw one rider or more "out of touch" but that "Only Danny Malone and Ian Williams kept at peak all season." The *News* review of Swindon's season said that Ian was the team's outstanding rider. Inevitably, comparisons with his brothers were made: "He had a spell of indifference in mid-season, and it cannot be denied that he has yet to master certain away circuits, but one needs no psychic powers to discern that here is a young man who will wear the England test jersey many times in the not too distant future. Ian may yet prove the best of the three brothers. He has all Eric's tenacity and much of Fred's skill."

One of his team mates was Bob Wells, now reaching the veteran stage, who had ridden for Wembley from 1946 to 1951. There were always rumours linking Ian with a move to the Empire Stadium. He did ride some second-halves there, but says that he was never approached to join the Lions, and would not have wanted to anyway. He says that "Freddie didn't like Eric riding with him, and didn't want me to go there. Anyway, it was more fun in the Second Division. If they had a bad match, Sir Arthur Elvin would have them in the office; I was perfectly happy with Swindon. I had offers to go to other teams, but I wasn't interested."

Ian also rode second-halves at other First Division tracks, such as Harringay and West Ham. He once beat Tommy Price at Wembley in a two-lap match race with a rolling start. He followed Freddie's advice about how to manage the flying start, accelerated at the right time and Price could not catch him.

Ian broke his wrist in the last meeting of 1953, a matter of a few weeks before he sailed to South Africa. Howdy Byford cut the plaster off on the ship. For the winter season of 1953–54, Ian had arranged to travel with Freddie to ride in South Africa. They rode for the Pretoria Eagles. Ian was rated number 11 in the South African rider rankings in the *Stenner's 1954 Annual*. He spent six months in South Africa, and rode five times for England against South Africa in test matches at the Wembley Stadium in Johannesburg. England won the series and Ian scored 19 points; his best being 8+1 in the third test. He got to know Trevor Redmond, one of the main organisers of speedway in South Africa, well on the tour. Reg Duval, Bill Kitchen and Don Perry were also in the touring party. Another British rider there was Freddie's young Wembley team-mate Brian Crutcher.

In the South African Match Race Championship, Crutcher clipped Freddie's back wheel, causing Ian's big brother to break a collar-bone and be concussed. Ian was furious with Crutcher, blamed him for the crash, and had to be restrained from attacking him. Freddie did not blame Brian Crutcher, but the youngster did learn how the Williams brothers would stick up for each other. Years later, the two riders would joke about the incident when they met up at social events.

Apart from that, the tour was a great experience for Ian and included a visit to the Kruger National Park, and to a gold mine. Apartheid was in force in South Africa at the time, and Ian does recall finding it "awfully bad" how the African population were treated. However, overall he says it was a "wonderful experience" and that they were "looked after very well".

Back home, Ian continued to enjoy further success with Swindon. Now riding in the National League Second Division, Swindon finished third behind Bristol and Poole. New team manager Norman Parker recruited new riders to strengthen the side, and one of the new boys, Bob Roger, finished top scorer for the Robins, with a 9.71 average, ahead of Ian on 8.26. In April, Belle Vue visited Blunsdon for the first time, and went away defeated 46–37. Ron Swaine and Ian "performed brilliantly for the super Swindon side" according to Robert Bamford. At the end of the season, Ian finished runner-up to Ken Middleditch in the Second Division Riders Championship at Belle Vue with 13 points; Bob Roger was joint third on 11.

This was also the season when the three Williams brothers rode together for the only time in an official meeting. It was the World Championship qualifying round at Wembley on 26 August. Ian finished on a respectable seven points from his five rides. In his first race he beat Bob Roger, Les McGillivray and Phil Clarke. Then in heat five, he faced Freddie and Eric, and finished third, ahead of former Wembley Lion Bob Oakley. Eric's win in the race effectively finished Freddie's chances of a World Final spot.

The three brothers also rode together in the Television Trophy at Harringay in June. This was an international best pairs event. Ian was reserve for Wales, who were represented by Freddie and Eric. Freddie pulled out of one of his rides so that Ian could have a ride in the tournament, and he promptly knocked Eric off.

In 1955, Swindon finished eighth in a nine team Second Division. Ian was made team captain. He finished third in the averages, behind Bob Roger and George White, on 8.09. However, he did win the World Championship qualifying round at Blunsdon, with a "brilliant" 15 point maximum. The team used a lot of guest riders to cover for injuries, including Eric on one occasion. Ian missed the chance to race against Freddie and Eric when he missed an end of season challenge match against Wembley. The Lions recalled Jimmy Gooch from his loan at Swindon for the meeting, and won 67–29.

Arguably the best two seasons of Ian's career were 1956 and 1957. Speedway's decline saw only seven teams in the Second Division in 1956, but with a strong heat leader trio of Bob Roger, George White and Ian, they won the league by a point from Southampton. Ian remembers that the team were always confident they would win the league. It was very much a team effort, with the heat leaders backed by Ernie Lessiter, Ray Harris and Ron Swaine. Ian finished with an average of 9.52, 0.01 behind Bob Roger. Wembley returned for a challenge match in September, and were beaten 49–47. But by now Ian was the only Williams brother involved – Eric had left the Lions to emigrate to New Zealand at the end of the 1955 season, and Freddie had retired in June. He did score 10+1 against the Lions.

In those days, for long trips the team travelled in convoy. Ian had a former post office van for his speedway trips. On the way to St Austell from Exeter, it rolled off the road and he had to be rescued by his team mates. They managed to get the van going again, but later in the trip had to abandon it and he got a lift to the meeting from team manager Bob Jones. He recalls that the team had great team spirit and would always help each other out.

In 1957, further track closures saw Swindon in the National League. Eleven teams were all that were left, although some of the sport's top riders, including Ove Fundin, Brian Crutcher, Barry Briggs and Peter Craven were all still racing. Swindon recruited Ken Middleditch, Neil Street and Mike Broadbank and won the league by a point from Belle Vue. Ian finished third in the averages on 8.17, a very creditable return in what was still a competitive top flight. Looking back in 2017, Ian said that the signing of Neil Street had made a big difference, and that he was a "fabulous rider who arrived at Swindon at just the right time". Ian also gives credit to Bob Jones, who he says was "a wonderful team manager".

The Robins struggled early on in the season, but in the league won 15 of their opening 17 matches to secure the league title.

Ian also reached the World Final for the first time, along with Bob Roger and George White. But he admits that he just didn't ride well on that night, and feels that maybe he was out of his depth. After a second place in his first race, he finished with three points in 14th place. But his appearance does mean that the Williams brothers are the only trio of brothers to appear in a World Championship Final. Freddie acted as Ian's mechanic in the final.

In 1958, Swindon could not repeat their remarkable feat of the previous season and finished sixth. Bob Roger had been involved in a nasty accident early in the season, and his absence hit the team hard. Ian finished third again in the team averages, with 8.34. However, a new honour was being selected for England against Australasia at Swindon. Ian was one of three home riders in the team and scored four paid seven.

The following year saw a slight decline in Ian's scoring, although he was still third in the Swindon averages on 7.22. The team also dropped slightly, to eighth in a nine team league. Ian was again chosen to ride for England against Australasia in September. At Southampton, England lost by four points with Ian scoring six from three rides at reserve, but in the final match of a three match series, at Swindon England won by two points. Ian scored 8 (+1), including two heat wins.

In the late 1950s, as well as his commitments for Swindon, Ian often rode at St Austell, where Trevor Redmond was promoting open meetings. Ian recalls that "I got on well with Trevor. It was a long way to go; we went once and the weather was terrible. But Trevor said that he couldn't afford to have the meeting rained off, so we all rode for him."

In 1960, there was something of a revival in the sport's fortunes, with the launch of the Provincial League. The National League also expanded, with New Cross reopening. Eric joined the South London team, and Ian recalls riding against him – and beating him. But Swindon finished bottom of the league, with just five wins in 18 matches. Ian maintained his third place in the averages, but his average of 6.92 was below seven for the first time since 1952. He was chosen by England as reserve in a World Team Cup qualifying meeting at Blunsdon, and scored one point. Swindon improved in 1961, finishing fifth. Ian's average fell to 6.22, although he was ever present for the league meetings. Swindon reached the final of the RAC National Trophy, but lost to Southampton.

At the start of 1962, there were reports that Ian would be leaving Swindon to join the new Provincial League team at Neath, which had been set up by Trevor Redmond. However, the Speedway Control Board vetoed the move, as he was felt to be too good for the lower level, and he stayed at Swindon. Only seven teams competed in the National League, and Swindon finished sixth. Ian's average of 6.00 put him in fourth place of the regular team members. George White had retired, and only Neil Street and Mike Broadbank remained, along with Ian, from the 1957 Championship winning team.

Ian was ready to retire at the end of the season, but was persuaded to do one more campaign. Swindon moved up the table by one place to fifth. Ian handed over the captaincy to Mike Broadbank at the start of the season. He still rode in 22 league matches, but finished with an average of 5.01. He recalls that his first wife, Josie, became more nervous about him continuing to ride as he got older.

He was remarkably consistent in his 12 year career with the Robins. He missed just 13 meetings in 12 years for Swindon, rode 447 matches and scored 3,452.5 points. Matt Jackson comments that "Ian will certainly be listed amongst the all time greats of Swindon Speedway and along with Freddie and Eric is one of the finest Welsh riders ever to have competed in the sport." Ian had the chance to ride for other teams, but was happy at Swindon, and is glad that he never moved

Ian certainly deserved a testimonial meeting from Swindon, but these didn't happen in his day. However, in June 2006 he was the first rider to be inducted into the Legends Lounge at Swindon, and with his second wife, lifelong Swindon supporter Jennifer – known as Jen – attends the meetings regularly, after losing touch with the sport for a time. He says that the club look after him very well and there is a table with his name on it, which he thinks is better than a testimonial.

Away from the sport, outside the speedway season he worked as a lorry driver for British Road Services, and then worked full-time for them when he retired from racing. He still lives in Swindon, and looks back on all the enjoyment he had from speedway racing, something he never originally planned to take up.

Ian and Jen in April 2017. (Photo: Peter Lush)

17. A sporting family

Pat Devries

Pat Devries was born in Fylde, near Blackpool, on 6 July 1930. She started skating, and her mentor in Blackpool advised her that to develop her career she should move to London. She was aged around 16 at this time, just after the War. Her family had run a hotel in Blackpool, so they sold up and moved to London in 1946, buying a small hotel in Wembley, conveniently near the Wembley Ice Rink.

The *Wembley News* had an article on its front page on 11 January 1952 about her selection for the Winter Olympics. It said that she did "most of her skating at the Empire Pool where she has given figure skating exhibitions. At present she is training at the Queens Ice Club [in] Bayswater." In 1948, aged 18, Pat won the British Junior Ladies Figure Skating title.

She used to get up very early to be able to train on the ice before the rink was open to the public. She would then go back to bed, which is why she had not met Freddie before serving him at breakfast at the hotel early in 1952.

At Queen's Ice Club she met Peri Horne, another aspiring Olympic skater. The two became life-long friends and they both competed in the European Championships in Vienna, the Winter Olympic Games in Oslo and the World Championships in Paris in 1952. They had qualified for places in the team for all three events through the National Skating Association of Great Britain Olympic Trials at Richmond Ice Rink on 5 December 1951. Pat, who was listed as representing Wembley ID & FSC, finished second in her trial. Peri qualified with her partner, Raymond Lockwood.

They left for Vienna, for the European Championships, on 31 January 1952. Peri points out that there was "no funding" for them to train, and it was a very different environment from today. She worked as a librarian, and fitted in her training around her shifts. Full-time training was not an option for her.

The *Wembley News* report said that Pat had "already taken part in international competitions at St Moritz, Davos and Paris." It also said that she had been invited to be on the *Calling all Forces* radio programme, presented by Ted Ray.

Peri had never been abroad before. She says that it was "fantastic" to go to the Olympics. No equipment was provided for the team, and she remembers that they wore ARP (Air Raid Precautions) black trousers and ARP berets. Lilywhites had managed to get some red jackets and boots for them. The Olympic Association gave them some "lovely" scarves and "we bought some little woollen caps in Vienna", so could discard the berets.

They "just made do as much as they could," she recalls. First of all, they went to Vienna for the European Championships, which was still "very war-torn" and armed soldiers took them to the ice-rink. Pat was a solo skater while Peri was part of a pair with Ray Lockwood. Pat finished 15th in the European Championships. Peri and Ray Lockwood finished fifth.

The team then went onto Oslo. Peri says that "We felt so proud when we marched through the middle of Oslo and everyone clapped." British journalist Ralph Hewins reported that "Twelve winter sports girls from Britain held people from 29 nations spellbound today at the official opening of the Winter Olympic Games. They marched into the ice-bound stadium at Bislett in perfect step and swinging their arms in the red blazers like Guardsmen. Twenty-four thousand people were hushed. Then there was a terrific burst of cheering for the girls.

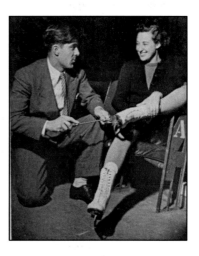

Top and bottom left: Pat in action on the ice. Bottom right: Freddie repairing Pat's skate.
(Courtesy Williams family)

The 1952 Winter Olympics

LADIES				
1. Miss E. Batchelor	...	...	...	N.S.A.
2. Miss M. Beatty	...	...	...	Richmond A.I.S.C.
3. Miss C. Cowley	...	...	...	Brighton I.F.S.C.
4. Miss P. Devries	...	...	...	Wembley I.D. & F.S.C.
5. Miss A. M. Kay	...	...	...	Liverpool S.C.
6. Miss V. Osborn	...	...	...	N.S.A.
7. Miss A. Robinson	...	...	...	Richmond A.I.S.C.
8. Miss E. Skevington	...	...	...	N.S.A.
9. Miss Y. Sugden	...	...	...	N.S.A.
10. Miss B. Wyatt	...	...	...	N.S.A.

The number against the competitors' names corresponds with that on the armlet, but does not indicate the order of starting.

The period of Free Skating for each skater will be four minutes.

Top left: The Bislet Stadium in Oslo.
Top right: The list of competitors from the programme for the Olympic trials in December 1951.
Left: Peri Horne, Raymond Lockwood (partly hidden) and Pat.
Bottom: Pat, Barbara Wyatt and Peri Horne after being given medals to remember 1952.
(All Courtesy Peri Horne)

A commentator said on the Norwegian radio: 'The other teams shuffle past. The British girls are like a well-trained ballet ... They might be parading down Bond Street ...' The commentator paused. Then he said: 'Words fail me. I cannot tell you how marvellous they look. What a proud moment for the British. We shall hear more of this team.'"

The event was at an outdoor rink, which was a new experience for some of the British skaters. Coverage in the British press was limited, despite British skater Jeanette Altwegg following up her win in the European Championships with gold in the Olympics. *The Times* reported that it was "bitterly cold" and "Miss Wyatt's figure was also very good and undermarked, as were those of Miss Osborn and Miss Devries." The report by Marylin Hoskins in *The Skater, Skier and Ice Hockey Player* magazine said that Pat was "making her first big international appearance" and she "skated with great confidence". She also reported that in the free skating, three days after the compulsory events, Pat "had an unlucky evening" and "had a nasty fall at the beginning of her programme, but made a remarkable recovery and carried on."

Pat was in 14th place after the first five compulsory events, and finished 17th after the second day's competition. In her event, Peri finished 11th.

Just before the Olympics started, King George 6th died, and Peri remembers that "we had to find black dresses or armbands for the memorial service." The team then went to Paris, for the World Championships, which were at an indoor rink. Peri also remembers training at the Kulm Hotel in St Moritz, where the team was given free hotel accommodation, because they were an attraction for the hotel guests. There was "chocolate and loads of food" she says, different from the austerity at home.

In the World Championship, Pat finished 12th. Her granddaughter Joanna says that as a skater: "She was known for being good at figures, drawing patterns in the ice with your blade, very precise and specific."

Pat then turned professional, and did ice pantomime and an ice show before she retired after she got married in October 1953. Freddie later said that he regretted asking her to retire. When they were in South Africa she performed on ice in Johannesburg, and was very well received. In 1955, during their visit, she coached ice skating in South Africa.

Pat's granddaughter Joanna Anthony (neé Webber) won the British Junior Ladies Figure Skating title in 2004, also at the age of 18, repeating her grandmother's feat. Pat supported her granddaughter, who went on to become a professional skater. Joanna recalls about winning the British Junior title: "It wasn't just me. Everyone had played a part in making it happen, Granny [Pat] for driving me to the rink and putting me on the ice, Grandpa [Freddie] for getting up in the morning to make tea and make sure the car was warmed up for us, and the rest of the family for the hours of travel and support they had given me. It was a team effort." Later, on a visit to Oslo, Joanna skated at the rink where Pat had competed in the Olympics, watched by her mother Jayne, aunt Sarah and family friend Jo Powell.

As well as supporting Joanna, and backing her children and grandchildren in their careers, Pat also became an international judge in figure skating. She died in November 2014.

Jayne Ross

If Jayne Ross was competing in a sport that was better known, and featured in the Olympics, it is no exaggeration to say that she would be a household name. Having first won a title at the Horse of the Year Show (HOYS) at the tender age of nine in 1966, she can reflect on over 50 years in equestrian sports, primarily in Showing.

And she still competes at the very top level. At the 2018 HOYS in Birmingham, she won the Supreme with Time 2 Reflect, having won the Hunter – Ladies Side Saddle Championship with Time 2 Reflect to qualify for the Supreme. For readers who do not follow Showing, the Supreme is the final event of either the HOYS or Royal International Horse Show (RIHS) and is made up of all the riders & horses who have won a competition at that particular show The RIHS is held at Hickstead in July each year. To even qualify to compete in the HOYS or RIHS, it is necessary to win or come second in selected other shows. Winning a Supreme is similar to winning a World Championship. Over the years, Jayne has won six, and an amazing 55 individual Championships at the HOYS.

Interviewed after her success in 2018, Jayne gives great credit to the horse, saying that "She's such a special horse – she's everybody's favourite. She gives 110 per cent every time – you just can't fault her." However, *Horse and Hound* pointed out that it was Jayne and owner Diane Stennett's second consecutive win in the Ladies Side Saddle Championship, and that Jayne has "dominated this particular Ladies championship for four years". The report by Alex Robinson also says that "Her [Jayne] pre-judging supreme performance was stand out. Jayne rode the mare to produce a lovely rein back and two gallops also showing of flawless transitions."

Part of the skill of this sport is to be able to ride with different types of horse and different sizes. In the 2018 HOYS, Jayne entered 11 Championships, won three; was runner-up in six, and had a fourth and a sixth. Ivan Mauger style consistency!

So how did this all start? She recalls "Dad had finished with selling motorbikes – he worried about young lads having accidents – and turned to selling cars. He sold someone a car, and the customer said 'you've got a daughter, little girls love ponies, come and meet the ponies. I fell in love with ponies, and [at the age of five] after five or 10 minutes could ride one. I was a natural. Then all I wanted to do was play ponies."

As part of a remarkable sporting family, Jayne says that "It's in the genes." The topic under discussion was being competitive, but as both her parents did sports that involve speed, balance and agility, all qualities needed to ride a horse, maybe her heritage has helped her as well.

When she first started riding, the family were living in Harrow, and she recalls "I learnt at Suzanne's Riding School. Mum and dad were great believers in doing things to the best of your ability. I was bred to be competitive, to do it properly. Mum wanted me to go to the best riding school. I must have been around six to eight years old when I met a couple of knowledgeable people experienced in show ponies, Richard and Marjorie Ramsay. Later on, they helped me get an important break in my career."

In 1966, she won the Pony of the Year award at the HOYS, riding the Gilbert Scott family's show pony Cusop Pirouette. She was nine years old! She recalls "There were classes for that age group. I hadn't been riding all that long compared to some of them. I had no 'horsey' connections at all, most of the others had been very focussed on riding from an early age."

She carried on riding ponies, and at the age of 17 was chosen to ride for Great Britain in Germany at the Junior European Team Pony Championships. She recalls: "I had a choice –

either stay and do my exams, or go to Germany. I went to Germany. Mum and dad supported me. I have made my living from sport ever since. I had a great time at the Euros, although I didn't win a medal."

Although Showing has been her main equestrian sport, she also took part in Eventing, which combines Dressage, Show Jumping and Cross Country Jumping, where she reached Advanced Level. She represented Great Britain in Combined Training, which combines Dressage and Show Jumping skills. She has also ridden in Point-to-Points as well as training 43 winners, and has held a National Hunt racing licence.

However, much of her work, as well as riding, is in 'producing' the horses – preparing and training them for the Shows. Part of Showing is that one of the judges ride each horse, so the horse has to be ready to be ridden by a stranger, as well as being immaculately prepared and look their best. Often, people do not do both riding and producing, but Jayne does. She says that when working with horses, she treats each one as an individual. She says "I inherited Freddie's calm and settled attitude; I learnt from him and his level temperament. But we are all perfectionists, and it was Mum and Dad who put the competitive drive there. I can be competitive at anything – I get annoyed if I lose at Chess."

Some of Jayne's best memories of the HOYS are from when it was staged at Wembley, a place that had special connections for her because of Freddie's history there. In the programme for the 2018 HOYS, she said that "Some of my fondest memories of HOYS come from the days it was held at Wembley, for no reason other than my family had such a strong association with the place ... I used to get a shiver down my spine whenever we drove the horsebox in, thinking of Dad competing there back in the 1950s in front of packed grandstands. So, to compete and win at Wembley myself was unbelievably special for me." Jayne won the Riding Horse Championship in the 2001 HOYS on Soldier Brave, the last year that it was staged there before it moved to Birmingham.

In the past, with her first husband, Anthony Webber, a former national hunt jockey, she ran a training yard and equine rehabilitation centre in Lambourn. Their work there included breaking in 150 yearlings a year. In 1998 to 1999, she worked with flat racing horses in South Africa.

When she returned from South Africa, she rode a horse for Richard Ramsey, who had broken a hip. This led to a partnership with Carol and Bill Bardo for 12 years, producing horses at Moor Farm in Maidenhead. Jayne's first HOYS title was won on Carol's horse Soldier Brave. Many other successes followed.

Pat and Freddie would always come and support her at the HOYS. A great memory of Freddie is when he took part in an event to raise money for the Bob Champion Cancer Trust. He had to ride a mile on Aldaniti, the famous Grand National winning horse ridden by Bob Champion in 1981, who was recovering from cancer at the time. He borrowed a Wembley Lions body colour and a tartan motorcycle crash helmet from Bert Harkins, and nervously completed the ride.

One important and unusual accolade for Jayne was being inducted into the British Horse Society's Hall of Fame. She is only the third person from Showing to receive this honour, which is open to all British equestrian participants, including the horses, except for those involved in racing. "Dad would have been proud" she says. This honour is marked with a plaque on the wall of the Household Cavalry in Hyde Park on the South Carriageway. She added that "Alan [her second husband, Alan Ross] used to ride past it when he practiced as a dentist in London and he would polish it!"

Jayne in 1966, when she first entered and won a class at the Horse of the Year Show.
(Courtesy Jayne Ross)

Alan also has a sporting background. In his younger days as a student, he won the Northern Ireland Junior and Senior Foil Championship in fencing, and competed in the World Student Games on two occasions. Through a dental colleague, he discovered riding and enjoyed hunting, particularly with the County Down Stag Hunt when he was still working in Belfast. Later, he bought a horse called The Busby Soldier. Alan said that he was a 'moderate' rider, but the horse went on to great success with Lucinda and David Green, including winning at Badminton six times. He met Jayne in 1999, and they got married in 2012. He says that Jayne is a "phenomenal rider, who lights up an arena."

Away from horses, Jayne enjoys skiing, and has taken part in bobsleighing. She remembers going to speedway as a child, watching Wimbledon as a regular family outing, but was never interested in participating in motor sports.

Her daughter Joanna has followed in her grandmother's footsteps, and became a professional skater. A particularly fond memory for Jayne is travelling to Oslo, to watch Joanna skate in the arena where Pat had competed in the 1952 Olympics. She says that "Pat was disappointed that I wasn't keen on skating. I didn't want to fall on the ice; I was ok on a pony. But Joanna never minded, and Pat was an important influence on her." Her other daughter Harriet trained as a singer, following in the footsteps of Freddie and Kate, who Jayne says "were both singers".

Jayne has worked hard and consistently to reach the top of her sport and stay there. But she does recognise very much the importance of her parents' support as her career developed: "Freddie and Pat were one million percent behind what we did. They sacrificed for us and our sporting desires. One particular bank holiday, Freddie was driving at Brands Hatch, David was playing golf and I was doing a point to point. Mum went with me because she thought that I was most likely to hurt myself."

At the time of writing, Jayne has just moved to a new yard to plan and produce more Showing success in the future, and to add to her remarkable collection of titles.

Jayne riding The Philanderer, who was Supreme Champion at The Royal International Horse Show twice, in 2008 and 2010. This photo shows him winning it for the second time and being presented with The Winston Churchill Trophy by the actor Martin Clunes. This horse was also Supreme at The Horse of The Year Show in 2009. (Photo: Trevor Meeks)

Jayne by the plaque that marks her inclusion in the British Horse Society's Hall of Fame.
(Courtesy Jayne Ross)

David Williams

It is hard to think of a sport more different from speedway than golf, but Freddie and Pat's son David, who recently turned 60, has spent his whole life since leaving school involved in the sport. Having played on the European tour for 17 years, he retired aged 38 following a training injury to his foot, and moved to the administration side of the sport. He now works as a tournament director for the European Tour.

He did do some motorbike sport when he was young. Freddie made him a little motorbike which he rode as a five year old, and he has a wonderful photo of them together, with David on the bike, outside Wembley Stadium. He also had a scrambling bike, and remembers when he was around 13 or 14 years old, putting the bikes on the car trailer and going with Freddie to a chalk pit deep in the Bedfordshire countryside near Dunstable Downs. He recalls: "It was one of the best days of my life. Dad was like a kid, going around the sides of the quarry, trying to go up a hill and not quite making it, we had so much fun that day." David moved to his current home around 18 months ago, and found the quarry again on a walk in the countryside. Now if he's out walking or cycling, going there brings back memories of that day. For Freddie, maybe it reminded him of similar outings with his father when he was learning to ride a bike on the hills around Port Talbot.

David watched speedway, first at Wimbledon, and then the Wembley Lions when Freddie was team manager. He says that "I loved going to speedway. I knew all the teams and 'everything' about them and used to tell my dad about the riders in the teams Wembley were riding against. I remember going to the away matches, places such as Newport and Belle Vue. With my friends, we would sit in the Royal Box at Wembley, or go down to the pits."

For his secondary education, David got a scholarship to go to Millfield as a cross country runner. Millfield is an unusual school, offering a boarding school education similar to other Public schools, but also offering sports scholarships to talented young athletes. Welsh rugby union legend Gareth Edwards, Olympic swimmer Duncan Goodhew and cricketer David Graveney are some of the famous sports stars who are former students. However, there are also politicians, academics and broadcasters listed on the school's website. The website says that "Millfield is an inspirational school where pupils are celebrated for who they are, and encouraged to reach their personal best." David says that it aimed for people to "excel in what they wanted to do."

David became friendly with a couple of golfers at school, and soon – having never played golf before – it became his main sport. After three years at Millfield, he decided he wanted to be a golfer. This was helped by the family having moved to Delgarth in Hertfordshire in 1967. When he was aged around 14, a golf course was built adjoining their land. It was a nine hole 'par 3' course which was suitable for a youngster learning the game. He does admit that at school he "played and practiced when he shouldn't have been". Once asked by a teacher why he had missed a 10am class, he admitted that he had been hitting golf balls to prepare for a match that afternoon.

His parents supported him, but he does recall bumping into them at Millfield once when he was not expecting a visit. Freddie said that they were there because he was delivering a car, but in fact – as he found out after he had left the school – they had been asked to come because he was neglecting his academic work. "My mind was set on becoming a professional golfer; but they should have told me off! They were always supportive, but academically should have pushed me a bit harder."

David left Millfield with a handicap of three, and was playing off par by the time he was 18. He entered amateur tournaments to get experience, and had a good year in 1979, winning the Berkshire Trophy, which was a stroke play event for amateurs. That helped him into the England amateur team for the home internationals. David recalls: "I wanted to get on with my career. I could have tried to get into the Walker Cup team to play for Great Britain, but I wanted to get out there and play professional golf."

He says that it was "hard going" initially, but he was helped by a change in the qualification rules for the European Tour in 1984. Before then, to play every event, a golfer had to be in the top 60, which was very difficult to break into. But for 1985, it was agreed that the top 125 players would be included in every event. David says that "It was a make or break year for me and a lot of people. I finished 124th and got my card for the tour. I had got married, and missed one event. In the last one, I finished 21st and got my card by £21.50 [in cumulative prize money]. In the last round of the last event I finished one under par. If I had scored par, I would have missed qualification."

That was massive, I went year by year from 124th to 77th, 68th, 62nd and then 31st. The rankings were on prize money then. I got as much as I could out of my game, especially my short game.". David kept his card at this elite level until 1992, missed qualification for one year, and then got back in. He says that he was "always in good shape" and prided himself on keeping fit. But an injury to his foot on a skiing machine while training meant that by the end of 1996, he could barely walk, and had to retire from golf at the age of 38. He does say that while he loved playing the game, it did mean often missing family occasions, because if he made the cut in a tournament, he would be away for the weekend.

He says that he "loved playing" and would have continued, but for his injury, maybe joining the senior tour at the age of 50. He thinks that "It was the best job in the world, doing what you love doing, what people work all week to do at the weekend for fun." However, he says that the European Tour in the early 1980s was very different from today, with the golfers pulling their own trolleys round the course, and having to retrieve balls themselves that they had hit in practice. If he made the cut, he would get a caddy for the last two rounds whose player had missed out on making the cut.

David was attached to a club, Woburn, but never went down the route of becoming a club professional. He was PGA qualified, and had that as a safety net if he had needed it. As well as the European Tour events, he would also play in regional events, and pro-am events. Among the highlights of his years as a professional player were his performance in the Motorola tournament in 1988, and finishing 12th in the Open at Royal Birkdale in 1991. He says he was a "decent player" not a 'great' one, but maybe is being hard on himself, having performed for most of his career at the top level of his chosen sport.

After being forced to retire, he moved into the administration of the sport, initially as a rules official, and now as a tournament director for the European tour, which involves a lot of travel. The players welcomed having a former tour player in the rules official role, which included setting up the course. His role now involves managing a team of officials, aiming to make sure that tournaments run smoothly and keep to time. The latter is very important because so many tournaments are now covered live on television.

He also works as a referee in the Ryder Cup, which he first did in 2002. His first match involved Tiger Woods, but he knew Steve Williams (no relation), then Woods's caddy, from his playing days, and Williams introduced him to Tiger, who he made a connection with straightaway. He also refereed the famous match involving Darren Clarke, who was playing a few weeks after his wife has died. Emotions ran very high, and he says that the crowds and noise in the Ryder Cup are "massive."

David says that he had "fantastic support and positiveness" from his parents. Freddie wondered how he "stayed calm and didn't lose his temper." David says that in golf a player "must be patient and know when to take a risk. It is very different from the guts, determination and drive in speedway. In all sports it is important to know your limitations. Freddie was the 'iceman' very calm and cool, as much as speedway can be. He was comfortable with the big occasion and used to a big stadium with a lot of people."

David's wife Sarah works as a Chartered Accountant, as does their elder daughter Amy. His younger daughter Lucy followed him into playing golf. He says that "She was a relatively late starter, I didn't push it, and at 14 she wanted to have a go. Two years later, she entered the Herts County Championship Ladies event for the first time and won it. It was an incredible performance. She then won the English Mid-Amateur Championship for players aged over 18, and in 2011 won the English Amateur Championship, beating the current number one, Charley Hull. It was a 'gutsy' performance – she was one down with two holes to play, birdied the 17th hole and then eagled the 18th to tie the match. She then birdied the first hole of the 'sudden death' play-off to win the hole and the title."

She then turned professional, and went to university to do a degree in Applied Golf Management Studies, which included full PGA Qualification. At the age of 23 she won the Women's PGA Professional Championship. She got a card for the European Ladies Tour, with David caddying for her when available. In 2014 she qualified for the Women's USA Open, where David was her caddy. He was also her caddy for the Ladies Open at Royal Birkdale the same year.

However, in 2015 she decided to retire from professional golf. David says that she didn't enjoy the travelling, found that the rewards were poor for the amount of time and travel involved and "wanted a normal life". David says he was "ridiculously proud" of her achievements and could see "a bit of Freddie in her – she was a player for the big occasion." She trained as a teacher and now teaches in a local school.

Since Lucy retired, David has played very little, and doesn't miss it. He may play again in the future when he retires, but for now still enjoys his work as a tournament director and has spent his whole career involved in a sport that he loves.

Sarah Williams

Sarah says that she was "born to be involved in equestrian sport" which was always there when she was growing up. She always remembers ponies being around when she was young, and says that "I could ride before I could walk."

The Williams family moved to Delgarth in Hertfordshire when she was one year old. When the family first moved to Delgarth there were just a couple of run down stables that couldn't have been used for horses. Basically, Dad built all the stables and barns and laid the concrete yard himself with help from a few mates. We were always doing something there as when we moved there. It was a lovely big house but everything was overgrown. It was very much work in progress for the first 10 years but everyone got stuck in.

Eventually, there were stables at the new house, with 10 boxes for horses, and 15 acres of ground around the house. She says that Freddie always remembered being invited to stay at Bill Kitchen's big house when he was a young Wembley rider, and always wanted to provide a similar home for his family.

David with the replicas of the World Championship trophies won by Freddie.
(Photo: Peter Lush)

Left: David on his mini-bike with Freddie giving him a push start at Wembley.
Right: David caddying for Lucy in the US Open at Pinehurst in 2014. (Both courtesy David Williams)

Sarah focused on her riding. (Courtesy Sarah Williams)

Freddie, Pat, Harriet and Joanna at the 2012 Olympics. Freddie thought the whole of the Olympics was simply wonderful. (Photo: Jayne Ross)

She thinks that Delgarth, a seven bedroom house, was the realisation of that dream. Sport was very much part of her home environment when growing up – there was a swimming pool and sauna, as well as a tennis court at the house as well. These were "both put in by Dad and used by all the family and hundreds of family friends and their kids."

Apart from equestrian sport, she also played tennis, and enjoyed running. She says that "David and his daughters Lucy and Amy were very good runners, as is my son Freddie and so was I." Freddie, as well as being a talented footballer, is a very good cross country runner and in 2018 won the Oxfordshire Inter-Schools Under 11 title for Cokethorpe School.

Her equestrian career was very much supported by her parents. She recalls that they always believed that in sport she should "Do it properly, not just take part. Always be competitive, be 'in it to win it'." She "always had nice ponies" and was trained by Gill Watson, one of the top three day Eventing trainers. She competed at the Royal International Horse Show and Horse of the Year Show for many years along with competing as a member of the East Hertfordshire Pony Club before moving onto Eventing full-time.

Eventing is a very challenging equestrian sport. A three day event involves dressage, show jumping and cross country. The Olympic website says that it is "the most complete combined competition discipline and demands of the competitor and horse considerable experience in all branches of equitation. It covers every aspect of horsemanship: the harmony between horse and rider that characterise dressage; the contact with nature, stamina and extensive experience essential for the cross country; the precision, agility and technique involved in jumping." She says that she took part in one day events, but the aim was always to compete at a three day event.

It also offers the chance for international recognition and to ride for Great Britain. Sarah was chosen twice to represent Great Britain in the junior European team championships, once in Belgium and then in Rome. She won a Bronze medal in Belgium, and then achieved Gold in Rome on her horse Spiritos.

However, she then stopped competing at the top level. A bad fall, and lack of horses to ride meant that she decided to go travelling for three years, spending time in South Africa, Australia and New Zealand.

She is still involved with horses. She started working for KBIS, an equine insurance company, and is now a director there. And her partner, Charlie Morlock, is a racehorse trainer. In the past he has run his own yard, but now works as a manager for Nicky Henderson, one of the country's top National Hunt trainers.

Another sport that Sarah and in fact the whole of the extended Williams family enjoy is skiing. She recalls that "We went skiing every year. We were all good skiers, Freddie in particular. He used to shout at us if we were not skiing properly. Sometimes he would get frustrated with Mum because she was not fast enough. But he was also very safety conscious."

Sarah now takes her son, Freddie, skiing, although his main sporting interest is football. He plays for Wantage, his local team, and Swindon Town's Elite Under-11s. Freddie was "Dad's world and I wish he was here to give him some of his advice," she says. "He lived for Freddie and he would be so incredibly proud of what he has achieved." She has many photos of them together and believes that her Freddie "certainly has his Grandpa's competitive nature and determination." She says that as a youngster Freddie "did have a pony, but was not keen. Typical boy!"

As Sarah now takes her son to his sporting activities, she looks back at the support that she, Jayne and David got from their parents: "We were not pushed to be academic, although we all were privately educated. The important thing was to be in the sports teams. Every weekend Mum and Dad would be watching Jayne and me at horse shows, or David playing golf. Dad would always drive the lorry to the events, even passing his HGV licence and never complained about leaving at four in the morning and eating yet another picnic lunch. Many a time I remember Mum and Dad swapping drivers in the lorry whilst still on the move on the motorway – never stopping for a break."

She does remember her Dad's ride on Aldaniti, as part of a fundraising event for Bob Champion's cancer charity, and helped him prepare for it, but says that he very rarely rode horses.

She has been to some speedway meetings, but it has never been a regular activity for her. She does feel that the sport failed to involve Freddie after he retired. Despite him being the most eminent Welsh Speedway rider, and (at that time) one of only two British riders to win the World Championship twice, it was not until 2012 that he was asked to present the trophies at the Cardiff Grand Prix, and usually was not even given complimentary tickets and was always far too proud to ask for them. "There should have been more recognition of his achievements" she thinks.

But, overall, the influence of Freddie and Pat on her sporting activities is very clear, and it has carried on to the next generation with her son, albeit on the football pitch rather than on a motorcycle or a pony.

Freddie keeping his grandson Freddie steady on a pony.
(Courtesy Sarah Williams)

Kate and Freddie looking after Freddie at the seaside.

Above: Freddie, Sarah holding Freddie and Pat enjoying
the annual Christmas outing to Harrods.
Left: Freddie in Swindon Town FC kit.
(All courtesy Sarah Williams)

Joanna Anthony

Joanna has recently retired from skating, but can look back on a successful career mainly as a professional skater with *Disney on Ice*. This part of the Disney organisation portrays Disney stories and characters using top class ice skaters.

With her grandmother Pat having been an Olympian ice skater and her parents both top class equestrians, it is no surprise that those were the two sports she considered taking up when she was young. She recalls: "I can't remember the first time I stepped on the ice, but I imagine it was pretty soon after I could walk. My [older] sister Harriet skated and was technically the better skater and very talented. I spent a lot of time at the ice rink while Granny [Pat] took her there. I started taking lessons, but also quit and gave up at least three times saying I didn't want to skate while she progressed. If Granny and my mum had their way, Harriet would have skated and I would have ridden because I had a natural 'seat'. However, I was always a little bit scared of the ponies going too fast and being out of control. Harriet didn't like getting up early to skate and I did, so when she decided to stop skating, I chose to continue and that is when I really was serious about it.

I was also born 'pigeon toed' and skating helped as you have to skate in a straight line or you will fall over. I remember Grandpa [Freddie] telling me that Kristi Yamaguchi had also been pigeon toed and she had started skating to help with her feet. She then went on to win the Olympics so if she could straighten her feet so could I. He would also tell me to walk like Charlie Chaplin to help me turn my feet out."

Joanna says that the biggest highlight of her career was "winning the British Junior Championship in 2004. The whole family was there and winning the same title as Granny won in 1948 and having our names engraved on the same trophy made all the hard work and endless hours in the rink worth it." She had been third in the Championship the previous year. When she was in England, she trained in Swindon with mother and daughter team of coaches, Lesley Norfolk-Pearce and Natasha Larkin.

She has "pretty vivid memories of the day she won the title. Mostly that my family was there. Mum, Dad, Granny, Grandpa, my paternal Grandmother Moccy, Harriet, Sarah and some other friends. I skated a 'clean programme' and then had to wait to see what the other girls did. I couldn't watch. I can remember waiting for the results and when they were posted there were a lot of tears and I remember thinking 'we did it'. It wasn't just me. Everyone had played a part in making it happen, Granny for driving me to the rink and putting me on the ice, Grandpa for getting up in the morning to make tea and make sure the car was warmed up for us, and the rest of the family for the hours of travel and support they had given me. It was a team effort." Joanna also competed for Great Britain, in competitions in Italy and Belgium and at two ISU Junior Grand Prix in Courcheval in France and in Belgrade.

Another highlight of Joanna's career has been "Performing around the world with *Disney on Ice* ... Granny was not very supportive in the beginning, hoping I would keep competing to make it to the Olympics like her. That was not what was in store for me. I joined Disney on Ice in 2007 and was able to play Madison Square Gardens in New York as one of my first performances. Granny, Grandpa, Mum and Harriet were all able to be there. They originally came to see one show and ended up buying tickets to see it again. I think that changed all their minds that this was a good choice for me and the ice show was a good choice. How many people can say they performed at Madison Square Gardens [one of America's top sports venues] with their family in the audience? Pretty amazing!"

Top and bottom left: Joanna Anthony skating at the Bislett Stadium in Oslo where her grandmother Pat competed in the 1952 Olympics. Bottom right: With family friend Jo Powell, Jayne and Sarah. (Courtesy Jayne Ross)

Prior to joining *Disney on Ice*, she "was living and training in Los Angeles. I was at the point of trying to decide if I would keep competing because it was becoming very expensive to keep me in the States with the best coaches. A friend told me about the opportunity to audition. I never thought I would join an ice show because I had always thought I would make it to the Olympics. That dream was becoming very hard to reach so I went to the audition to keep all my options open. They offered me a contract that day and I decided to use all my years of training as a way to make money and still skate, instead of spending money to skate, as it had become with competing. I have never regretted my decision. I have travelled the world and met my best friends and husband, while still doing what I loved and performing on the ice."

The support from Pat was very important. She says that "Granny was never my coach, but was always in the rink with me. She drove to my lessons at 5am and would sit all day watching and giving advice. Sometimes we didn't see eye-to-eye because the sport had progressed a lot since she skated. She was known for being good at figures, drawing patterns in the ice with your blade, very precise and specific. By the time I was at the same level, figures no longer existed and I was performing double and triple jumps. Something that during her time wasn't even thought of."

Joanna's family were also an important influence on her: "Everyone in our family has a drive and passion for what they do. Grandpa always told us that whatever we choose to do we should do well and give it 100 per cent. Second place is the first loser. Winning was always the goal, but Grandpa was always supportive if he knew we had given 100 per cent and tried our best. Unfortunately, most of the family chose sports with judges, so sometimes no matter how well you skated or rode it was down to someone else's opinion whether you win or not, and this didn't always go in our favour.

Grandpa was always a huge part of any thing we did as kids, he would travel to see Harriet sing at school, or to watch her run in her cross-country races and team matches. He wanted to support us all. For me he would get every morning to make tea and warm the car up before Granny and I would leave for the ice rink. If Granny couldn't take me he would. He wanted us to give 100 per cent. Whatever we did we should do it well, whether a sport or school work. A quote he had posted on the door in the kitchen was 'Hide not your talents, they for use were made. What's a sundial in the shade?' – Benjamin Franklin. This has always stuck with me. Show off what you can do, but do it well."

At the time of writing, Joanna is "touring with Roger and Hammerstein's Cinderella Tour. I am the Star dresser for the lead and part of the wardrobe team. When I finished performing with *Disney on Ice* I was able to join the wardrobe team. I now have the opportunity to still be a part of the shows, but now from backstage instead of in front of the curtain. I still have plans to be a skating coach one day. I always want to be a part of the skating community and help young skaters have the opportunities that I have enjoyed."

Her contact with speedway has been limited: "The first time I ever went to speedway was in Costa Mesa, California. Granny and Grandpa used to take me there to train with Granny's friend John Nicks – another Olympian in 1948 and 1952, also coached Sacha Cohen and many other top skaters. We went to speedway on Saturday nights. I remember the smell and how people would come and shake Grandpa's hand when they found out he was there. One of my favourite memories is the 2012 Grand Prix in Cardiff. It was the first time my now husband Nick had been to speedway. Grandpa took him to the track to teach him about the sport. It was amazing to be there as a family and see how many people wanted to meet him. He is a hero to so many, but to us he is the best father and grandfather."

Appendix: Freddie Williams Statistics and Records

The World Championship

1948: (British Riders Championship) First Division round: 5 rides 10 pts @ Wembley (staged at Wimbledon)

1949: Third round: Glasgow Ashfield 5 rides 14 pts. Qualified for next round but withdrew due to injury

1950: Championship Round: Belle Vue 5 rides 8 pts, Wembley 5 rides 13 pts, West Ham 5 rides 14 pts. Qualified for final with 33 pts. Final: 5 rides 14 pts, World Champion.

1951: Championship Round: Wembley 5 rides 11 pts, Birmingham: 5 rides 13 pts. Qualified for final with 24 pts. Final: 5 rides 7 pts. Finished 9th.

1952: Championship Round: Wembley 5 rides 13 pts, Birmingham 5 rides 14 pts. Qualified for final with 27 pts. Final: 5 rides 13 pts. Runner-up.

1953: Championship Round: Wembley 5 rides 13 pts, Norwich: 5 rides 12 pts. Qualified with 25 pts. Final: 5 rides 14 pts. World Champion.

1954: Championship Round: Belle Vue 5 rides 7 pts, Wembley 5 rides 14 pts. Qualified for final as second reserve with 21 pts. Did not ride.

1955: Championship Round: Wembley: 5 rides 12 pts, Belle Vue 5 rides 9 pts. Total of 21 pts, did not qualify for final.

England
(England score first in results column)

Date	Opponents	Venue	Points	Result
26/5/49	Australia	Wembley	9 (+2)	41–67
18/6/49	Australia	Birmingham	7 (+1)	53–55
413/7/9	Australia	New Cross	6 (+2)	62–46
17/12/49	Australia	Sydney	5 (+1)	32–76
6/1/50	Australia	Sydney	6	41–67
21/1/50	Australia	Brisbane	3 (+2)	35–72
28/1/50	Australia	Sydney	3 (+1)	40–68
3/2/50	Australia	Sydney	2 (+2)	40–68
11/2/50	Australia	Melbourne	2 (+1)	38–70
6/6/50	Australia	West Ham	5 (+2)	47–60
31/8/50	Australia	Wembley	8 (+2)	53–55
1/6/51	Australia	Harringay	11	48–60
30/6/51	Australia	Bradford	13	59–49
3/7/51	Scotland	Glasgow A	10	58–50
19/7/51	Australia	Wembley	12	49–58
4/8/51	Australia	Birmingham	2 (+1)	46–62
15/9/51	Scotland	Edinburgh	10	52–56
12/2/52	New Zealand	Hastings	6	17–31
9/6/52	Australia	Wimbledon	7 (+2)	52–56
13/8/52	Australia	Wembley	10 (+1)	52–56
9/7/52	Australia	Belle Vue	1 (+1)	50–58

11/8/52	Scotland	Liverpool	18 (Max)	52–56
20/8/52	Australia	New Cross	8 (+1)	46–62
5/9/52	Scotland	Motherwell	13	52–56
12/9/52	Australia	Harringay	12 (+2)	55–53
20/6/53	Australia	Norwich	3 (+1)	46–62
3/7/53	Scotland	Leicester	6 (+3)	66–42
13/8/53	Australia	Wembley	8	57–51
14/9/53	New Zealand	Wimbledon	14 (+1)	62–45
25/9/53	New Zealand	Bristol	18 (Max)	77–31
29/9/53	New Zealand	West Ham	13	56–52
2/12/53	South Africa	Johannesburg (Wembley)	13	54–54
18/12/53	South Africa	Johannesburg (Wembley)	17	61.5–44.5
22/1/54	South Africa	Johannesburg (Wembley)	18 (Max)	62–45
19/2/54	South Africa	Johannesburg (Wembley)	15	51–56
10/8/54	Australasia	West Ham	5 (+1)	60–48
13/6/55	Australasia	Wimbledon	10 (+1)	39–67
23/6/55	Australasia	Wembley	17	67–41
5/7/55	Australasia	West Ham	4 (+2)	42–66

Summary:

39 matches
22 versus Australia
4 versus Australasia
4 versus New Zealand
5 versus Scotland
4 versus South Africa
Won: 11
Drew: 1
Lost: 27
Scored 293 points and 30 bonus points for a total of 323

NB: The last 2 tests in Australia in 1949–50: Different publications show different team line ups for these matches. I have included Freddie in the Melbourne test rather than the final test in Adelaide because that source gives heat details.

Team Honours:
National League Division One (NLD1) Championship Winners: 1949, 1950, 1951, 1952, 1953; Runners-up: 1954.
National Trophy (NT): Winners 1948, 1954; Runners-up 1951, 1955.
London Cup (LC): Winners 1948, 1949, 1950, 1951, 1954.

Wembley Lions: Freddie Williams averages 1947 to 1956

Year	Club	Division	M	R	P	BP	TP	CMA	FM	PM
1947	Wembley	NL1	1	2	1	0	1	2.00		
		British Speedway Cup	1	3	2	0	2	2.67		
1948	Wembley	NL1 & NT	30	124	155	36	191	6.16		
		Anniversary Cup	12	48	50	15	65	5.42		
		London Cup	4	20	26	2	28	5.60		
1949	Wembley	NL1	35	140	232	27	259	7.40	1	1
		London Cup	2	10	6	1	7	2.80		
1950	Wembley	NL1 & NT	34	139	276	19	295	8.49	4	2
		London Cup	4	23	47	5	52	9.04		
1951	Wembley	NL1 & NT	37	155	340	29	369	9.52	2	7
		London Cup	6	34	70	5	75	8.82		
1952	Wembley	NL1 & NT	40	166	379	15	394	9.49	7	4
		London Cup	2	11	16	4	20	7.27		
1953	Wembley	NL1 & NT	22	95	222.5	6	228.5	9.62	4	2
		Coronation Cup	16	64	138	5	143	8.94	2	
		London Cup	2	12	27	0	27	9.00		
1954	Wembley	NL1 & NT	34	144	295	25	320	8.89		2
		RAC Cup	6	24	43	5	48	8.00		
		London Cup	4	23	54	5	59	10.26		
1955	Wembley	NL1 & NT	30	144	229	14	243	6.75	1	1
1956	Wembley	NL1	10	35	38	7	45	5.14		
		Totals	332	1416	2646.5	225	2871.5			

CMA: Calculated match average, based on four rides.
R: Rides. P: Points BP: Bonus points. TP: Total points. FM: Full maximum. PM: Paid maximum.
NL1/NLD1: National League.
NT: National Trophy. LC: London Cup. Ind: Individual meeting. WC: World Championship.

1947 to 1956 matches for Wembley

1947

				R	P	BP
4 April 1947	Harringay 20	Wembley 16	London Easter Best Pairs Reserves Match @ Harringay including Freddie Williams	3	2	0
21 August 1947	**Wembley 54**	**Wimbledon 41**	**BSC**	**3**	**2**	**0**
11 September 1947	Wembley 44	North of England 39	Ch @ Middlesbrough	4	3	0
23 October 1947	**Wembley 60**	**Bradford 24**	**NLD1**	**2**	**1**	**0**

BSC: British Speedway Cup. Ch: Challenge match.

1948

Note: Part of season Lions based at Wimbledon (matches marked *).

				R	P	BP
25 March 1948	Wimbledon 30	Wembley 52	Ch	2	1	1
26 March 1948	West Ham 49	Wembley 35	Ch	2	4	1
9 April 1948	Harringay 39	Wembley 45	NL Division 1	2	3	1
13 April 1948	West Ham 54	Wembley 30	NLD1	4	1	0
21 April 1948	New Cross 56	Wembley 27	NLD1	4	3	1
24 April 1948	Bradford 38	Wembley 46	NLD1	4	4	1
29 April 1948	***Wembley 52**	**Belle Vue 31**	**NLD1**	4	8	1
1 May 1948	Belle Vue 42	Wembley 42	NLD1	4	6	1
6 May 1948	***Wembley 44**	**Wimbledon 39**	**NLD1**	4	5	1
13 May 1948	***Wembley 51**	**Bradford 33**	**NLD1**	4	5	2
17 May 1948	Wimbledon 27	Wembley 57	NLD1	4	9	1
20 May 1948	***Wembley 40.5**	**New Cross 43.5**	**NLD1**	4	4	0
26 May 1948	New Cross 46	Wembley 38	NLD1	4	5	2
27 May 1948	***Wembley 31**	**Harringay 50**	**NLD1**	4	8	0
29 May 1948	Belle Vue 53	Wembley 43	Anniversary Cup	4	3	0
3 June 1948	***Wembley 40**	**West Ham 44**	**NLD1**	4	3	1
5 June 1948	Bradford 66	Wembley 30	AC	4	2	1
10 June 1948	***Wembley 45**	**Belle Vue 51**	**AC**	4	4	2
15 June 1948	West Ham 49	Wembley 47	AC	4	5	2
17 June 1948	***Wembley 47**	**Harringay 49**	**AC**	4	6	2
18 June 1948	Harringay 59	Wembley 36	AC	4	4	0
23 June 1948	New Cross 49	Wembley 46	AC	4	3	0
24 June 1948	***Wembley 49**	**New Cross 47**	**AC**	4	2	1
28 June 1948	Wimbledon 40	Wembley 56	AC	4	5	1
1 July 1948	***Wembley 60**	**West Ham 36**	**AC**	4	5	2
8 July 1948	***Wembley 60**	**Wimbledon 35**	**AC**	4	7	3
15 July1948	***Wembley 61**	**Bradford 35**	**AC**	4	4	1
22 July 1948	***Wembley 59**	**Belle Vue 25**	**NLD1**	4	7	3
29 July 1948	***Wembley 35**	**Harringay 49**	**NLD1**	4	1	0
30 July 1948	Harringay 53	Wembley 28	NLD1	4	4	0
31 July 1948	The Rest 39	Wembley 45	Ch @ Birmingham	4	4	1
5 August 1948	***Wembley 57**	**Bradford 27**	**NLD1**	4	7	1
12 August 1948	***Wembley 39**	**West Ham 45**	**NLD1**	4	3	2
19 August 1948	***BRCQR**	**W. Lamoreaux 15**	**BRCQR**	5	10	
23 August 1948	Wimbledon 35	Wembley 49	NLD1	4	9	1
26 August 1948	***Wembley 64**	**Belle Vue 42**	**NT**	5	4	2
28 August 1948	Bradford 37	Wembley 47	NLD1	4	6	2
31 August 1948	West Ham 61	Wembley 46	LC SF	5	3	0
2 September 1948	**Wembley 67 [113]**	**West Ham 40 [101]**	**LC SF**	5	11	1
4 September 1948	Belle Vue 64 [106]	Wembley 44 [108]	NT	5	4	1
9 September 1948	**Wembley 73**	**Harringay 35**	**NT SF**	5	10	2
10 September 1948	Harringay 52 [87]	Wembley 56 [133]	NT SF	5	3	3
18 September 1948	Belle Vue 48	Wembley 36	NLD1	4	3	1
23 September 1948	**Wembley 65**	**New Cross 40**	**LC F**	5	4	0
24 September 1948	New Cross 58 [98]	Wembley 50 [115]	LC F	5	8	1
30 September 1948	**Wembley 60**	**Wimbledon 24**	**NLD1**	4	11	0
5 October 1948	West Ham 38	Wembley 46	NLD1	4	7	1
7 October 1948	**Wembley 64**	**New Cross 44**	**NT F**	5	5	2
8 October 1948	New Cross 52 [96]	Wembley 56 [120]	NT F	5	4	1
14 October 1948	**Wembley 41**	**New Cross 43**	**NLD1**	4	4	1
16 October 1948	Wembley 45	West Ham 39	Ch @ Norwich	4	8	1

1949

				R	P	BP
8 April 1949	Harringay 31	Wembley 53	NLD1	4	9	1
15 April 1949	West Ham 44	Wembley 40	NLD1	4	8	0
16 April 1949	Belle Vue 45	Wembley 39	NLD1	4	2	0
18 April 1949	Wimbledon 42	Wembley 42	NLD1	4	4	0
23 April 1949	Birmingham 54.5	Wembley 29.5	NLD1	4	8	0
30 April 1949	Bradford 51	Wembley 32	NLD1	4	2	1
6 May 1949	New Cross 40	Wembley 44	NLD1	4	5	1
12 May 1949	**Wembley 53**	**New Cross 31**	**NLD1**	**4**	**11**	**0**
19 May 1949	**Wembley 54**	**Bradford 30**	**NLD1**	**4**	**6**	**1**
21 May 1949	Birmingham 34	Wembley 49	NLD1	4	4	2
27 May 1949	Harringay 37	Wembley 47	NLD1	4	4	0
2 June 1949	**Wembley 49**	**Wimbledon 35**	**NLD1**	**4**	**8**	**0**
3 June 1949	New Cross 48	Wembley 36	NLD1	4	8	1
6 June 1949	Wimbledon 39	Wembley 45	NLD1	4	9	1
9 June 1949	**Wembley 40**	**Harringay 44**	**NLD1**	**4**	**3**	**1**
16 June 1949	**Wembley 58**	**West Ham 28**	**NLD1**	**4**	**7**	**3**
23 June 1949	**Wembley 53**	**New Cross 31**	**NLD1** First paid max	**4**	**10**	**2**
25 June 1949	Bradford 34	Wembley 50	NLD1	4	5	3
28 June 1949	West Ham 39	Wembley 45	NLD1	4	7	1
30 June 1949	**Wembley 47**	**Belle Vue 37**	**NLD1**	**4**	**7**	**3**
2 July 1949	Belle Vue 52	Wembley 32	NLD1	4	2	0
7 July 1949	**Wembley 62**	**Birmingham 22**	**NLD1**	**4**	**9**	**1**
14 July 1949	**Wembley 58**	**Wimbledon 26**	**NLD1**	**4**	**8**	**2**
15 July 1949	Harringay 30	Wembley 53	NLD1	4	9	0
21 July 1949	**Wembley 65**	**Harringay 19**	**NLD1 First max**	**4**	**12**	**0**
25 July 1949	Wimbledon 40	Wembley 44	NLD1	4	7	1
26 July 1949	**Wembley 45**	**Bradford 39**	**NLD1**	**4**	**10**	**0**
26 July 1949	**Wembley 48**	**Belle Vue 36**	**NLD1**	**4**	**10**	**0**
28 July 1949	**Wembley 49**	**Birmingham 35**	**NLD1**	**4**	**10**	**0**
1 Sept 1949	**Wembley 45**	**Belle Vue 39**	**NLD1**	**4**	**5**	**1**
5 September 1949	Wimbledon 48	Wembley 36	Ch	3	3	0
8 Sept 1949	**Wembley 47**	**Wimbledon 37**	**NLD1**	**4**	**5**	**0**
1 October 1949	Odsal 50	Wembley 33	NLD1	4	2	1
6 October 1949	**Wembley 58**	**West Ham 50**	**LC F**	**5**	**1**	**0**
11 October 1949	West Ham 42 [92]	Wembley 66 [124]	LC F	5	5	1
13 Oct 1949	**Wembley 47**	**West Ham 36**	**NLD1**	**4**	**1**	**0**
15 October 1949	Birmingham 50	Wembley 34	NLD1	4	2	0

140

1950

				R	P	BP
29 March 1950	New Cross 49	Wembley 70	Ch	5	10	0
31 March 1950	Bristol 50	Wembley 70	Ch	5	9	0
7 April 1950	West Ham 38	Wembley 46	Ch	4	8	1
8 April 1950	Wimbledon 44	Wembley 76	Ch	5	11	0
17 April 1950	Edinburgh 38	Wembley 46	Ch	4	10	0
2 May 1950	West Ham 33	Wembley 51	NLD1	4	9	0
5 May 1950	Bristol 43	Wembley 40	NLD1	4	7	1
6 May 1950	Birmingham 35	Wembley 49	Ch	4	10	0
11 May 1950	**Wembley 43**	**New Cross 41**	**NLD1**	**4**	**4**	**1**
12 May 1950	Harringay 29	Wembley 55	Ch	4	5	3
17 May 1950	New Cross 36	Wembley 48	NLD1	4	6	1
18 May 1950	**Wembley 46**	**Wimbledon 38**	**NLD1**	**4**	**7**	**1**
22 May 1950	Cradley Heath 36	Wembley 48	Ch	4	11	0
25 May 1950	**Wembley 48**	**Belle Vue 36**	**NLD1**	**4**	**10**	**1**
27 May 1950	Belle Vue 45	Wembley 39	NLD1	4	3	1
29 May 1950	Harringay 36	Wembley 48	Ch @ Coventry	4	8	0
1 June 1950	**Wembley 58**	**Bristol 26**	**NLD1**	**4**	**7**	**1**
3 June 1950	Bradford 41	Wembley 43	NLD1	4	5	0
8 June 1950	**Wembley 51**	**Harringay 33**	**NLD1**	**4**	**9**	**1**
12 June 1950	Wimbledon 34	Wembley 50	NLD1	4	5	2
15 June 1950	**Wembley 60**	**Birmingham 24**	**NLD1**	**4**	**5**	**2**
22 June 1950	**Wembley 60**	**West Ham 24**	**NLD1** FM	**4**	**12**	**0**
23 June 1950	Harringay 31	Wembley 52	NLD1	4	11	0
29 June 1950	**Wembley 59**	**Bradford 25**	**NLD1** PM	**4**	**11**	**1**
1 July 1950	Birmingham 39	Wembley 45	NLD1	4	9	0
6 July 1950	**Wembley 45**	**New Cross 36**	**NLD1** PM	**4**	**12**	**0**
7 July 1950	Bristol 48	Wembley 35	NLD1	4	11	0
13 July 1950	Wembley 33	Wimbledon 48	NLD1	4	9	0
18 July 1950	West Ham 51	Wembley 32	NLD1	4	6	0
20 July 1950	**Wembley 39**	**Belle Vue 45**	**NLD1**	**4**	**10**	**0**
27 July 1950	**Wembley 54**	**Bristol 29**	**NLD1** FM	**4**	**12**	**0**
29 July 1950	Bradford 52	Wembley 32	NLD1	4	7	0
3 August 1950	**Wembley 59**	**West Ham 25**	**NLD1** PM	**4**	**11**	**1**
5 August 1950	Birmingham 79	Wembley 29	NT	5	4	0
10 August 1950	**Wembley 53 [82]**	**Birmingham 51 [130]**	**NT**	**5**	**9**	**2**
17 August 1950	**Wembley 58**	**Harringay 50**	**LC SF**	**6**	**12**	**2**
18 August 1950	Harringay 56 [106]	Wembley 51 [109]	LC SF	6	14	0
24 August 1950	**WCQR**	**Aub Lawson 15**	**WCQR**	**5**	**13**	**0**
7 Sept 1950	**Wembley 56**	**Wimbledon 51**	**LC F**	**6**	**12**	**1**
11 September 1950	Wimbledon 56 [107]	Wembley 52 [108]	LC F	5	9	2
14 Sept 1950	**Wembley 53**	**Second Div Stars 30**	**Ch**	**4**	**8**	**2**
21 Sept 1950	**WCF**	**Freddie Williams 14**	**WCF**			
27 Sept 1950	New Cross 39	Wembley 45	NLD1	4	4	1
28 Sept 1950	**Wembley 59**	**Birmingham 25**	**NLD1**	**4**	**10**	**0**
30 Sept 1950	Belle Vue 40	Wembley 44	NLD1	4	8	0
5 October 1950	**Wembley 52**	**Bradford 32**	**NLD1**	**4**	**8**	**1**
6 October 1950	Harringay 36	Wembley 48	NLD1	4	9	1
9 October 1950	Wimbledon 41	Wembley 43	NLD1	4	10	0
11 October 1950	Birmingham 47	Wembley 37	NLD1	4	4	0
12 October 1950	**Wembley 54**	**Harringay 30**	**NLD1** FM	**4**	**12**	**0**

FM: Full maximum. PM: Paid maximum. DH: Double header.

141

1951

				R	P	BP
23 March 1951	West Ham 44	Wembley 40	Ch	4	10	0
2 April 1951	Wimbledon 33	Wembley 51	Ch FM	4	12	0
14 April 1951	Belle Vue 43	Wembley 41	NLD1	4	9	1
16 April 1951	Edinburgh 49	Wembley 35	Ch	4	11	0
17 April 1951	West Ham 37	Wembley 47	NLD1	4	7	0
20 April 1951	Bristol 48	Wembley 35	NLD1	4	8	1
21 April 1951	Wembley 40	Harringay 44	Ch@ Norwich	4	5	0
25 April 1951	New Cross 31	Wembley 51	Ch	4	7	1
2 May 1951	Chapelizod 42	Wembley 42	Ch @ Dublin PM	4	11	1
7 May 1951	Walthamstow 45	Wembley 39	Challenge	4	6	0
12 May 1951	Bradford 25	Wembley 59	NLD1 PM	4	11	1
14 May 1951	Wimbledon 47	Wembley 37	NLD1	3	6	0
17 May 1951	**Wembley 49**	**Wimbledon 35**	**NLD1**	**4**	**11**	**1**
24 May 1951	**Wembley 60**	**Bradford 24**	**NLD1**	**4**	**12**	**0**
26 May1951	Birmingham 41	Wembley 43	NLD1	4	6	1
31 May 1951	**Wembley 56**	**Bristol 28**	**NLD1**	**4**	**8**	**1**
7 June 1951	**Wembley 55**	**Harringay 29**	**NLD1**	**4**	**10**	**1**
9 June 1951	Bradford 40	Wembley 44	NLD1	4	9	0
14 June 1951	**Wembley 49**	**Wimbledon 35**	**NLD1**	**4**	**10**	**0**
15 June 1951	Bristol 37	Wembley 47	NLD1 FM	4	12	0
21 June 1951	**Wembley 44**	**West Ham 40**	**NLD1**	**4**	**7**	**0**
26 June 1951	West Ham 39	Wembley 44	NLD1	4	5	1
28 June 1951	**Wembley 57**	**Belle Vue 27**	**NLD1**	**4**	**10**	**1**
4 July 1951	New Cross 29	Wembley 53	NLD1	4	9	1
5 July 1951	**Wembley 43**	**Birmingham 41**	**NLD1** PM	**4**	**11**	**1**
7 July 1951	Belle Vue 45	Wembley 39	NLD1	4	3	0
9 July 1951	Wimbledon & Bristol 37	Wembley 17	Second Half Ch	3	3	1
20 July 1951	Harringay 47	Wembley 36	NLD1	4	7	1
23 July 1951	Wimbledon 55	Wembley 51	LC	6	10	1
26 July 1951	**Wembley 64 [115]**	**Wimbledon 44 [99]**	**LC**	**6**	**15**	**1**
1 August 1951	New Cross 45	Wembley 63	LC SF PM	6	17	1
2 August 1951	**Wembley 70 [133]**	**New Cross 38 [83]**	**LC SF**	**6**	**13**	**1**
3 August 1951	Bristol 42	Wembley 42	Ch	4	8	1
9 August 1951	**Wembley 52**	**Belle Vue 55**	**NT**	6	12	1
16 August 1951	**WCQR**	**Freddie Williams 11**	**WCQR**	**5**	**11**	
23 August 1951	**Wembley 43**	**Harringay 41**	**NLD1 DH**	**4**	**11**	
30 August 1951	**Wembley 53**	**Bristol 31**	**NLD1 DH** PM	**4**	**11**	**1**
30 August 1951	**Wembley 55**	**New Cross 28**	**NLD1 DH** PM	**4**	**11**	**1**
1 September 1951	Birmingham 45	Wembley 39	NLD1	4	11	
5 September 1951	Belle Vue 46 [101]	Wembley 62 [114]	NT	5	11	1
6 Sept 1951	**Wembley 38**	**West Ham 45**	**NLD1**	**4**	**7**	**0**
12 Sept 1951	New Cross 35	Wembley 49	NLD1	4	10	1
13 Sept 1951	**Wembley 59**	**Harringay 49**	**LC F**	**5**	**6**	**1**
14 Sept 1951	Harringay 49 [98]	Wembley 59 [118]	LC F	5	9	0
17 Sept 1951	Wimbledon 36	Wembley 48	NLD1	4	6	2
20 Sept 1951	**WCF**	**Jack Young 12**	**WCF**	**5**	**7**	
21 Sept 1951	Harringay 35	Wembley 49	NLD1 PM	4	10	2
25 Sept 1951	**Wembley 61**	**Belle Vue 23**	**NLD1 DH**	**4**	**10**	**1**
25 Sept 1951	**Wembley 55**	**Birmingham 29**	**NLD1 DH**	**4**	**10**	**1**
26 Sept 1951	New Cross 53	Wembley 55	NT SF	6	13	1
1 October 1951	Wimbledon 61	Wembley 47	Ch	6	12	
4 October 1951	**Wembley 78 [133]**	**New Cross 29 [82]**	**NT SF** PM	**5**	**13**	**2**
8 October 1951	Wimbledon 58	Wembley 50	NT F	5	7	2

11 October 1951	Wembley 41 [91]	Wimbledon 67 [125]	NT F	5	5	1
15 October 1951	Exeter 42	Wembley 42	Ch FM	4	12	0
18 October 1951	Wembley 57	New Cross 27	NLD1	4	11	

1952

				R	P	BP
26 April 1952	Belle Vue 37	Wembley 47	NLD1	4	6	
28 April 1952	Wimbledon 29	Wembley 54	NLD1	4	8	
3 May 1952	Bradford 45	Wembley 38	NLD1	4	7	2
8 May 1952	Wembley 62	Norwich 21	NLD1 PM	4	11	1
10 May 1952	Norwich 37	Wembley 47	NLD1	4	7	0
14 May 1952	New Cross 40	Wembley 42	NLD1	3	3	1
15 May 1952	Wembley 43	Wimbledon 41	NLD1	4	10	1
17 May 1952	Stoke 40	Wembley 42	Ch	4	8	2
20 May 1952	West Ham 48	Wembley 33	NLD1	4	4	0
22 May 1952	Wembley 55	Belle Vue 29	NLD1	4	9	0
23 May 1952	Bristol 44	Wembley 39	NLD1	4	10	0
29 May 1952	Wembley 51	New Cross 33	NLD1 PM	4	10	2
31 May 1952	Birmingham 53	Wembley 31	NLD1	4	2	0
5 June 1952	Wembley 47	Birmingham 37	NLD1	4	7	0
12 June 1952	Wembley 49	Wimbledon 59	LC	5	5	3
14 June 1952	Norwich 48	Wembley 35	NLD1	4	7	0
16 June 1952	Wimbledon 55 [114]	Wembley 53 [102]	LC	6	11	1
19 June 1952	Wembley 52	Bradford 32	NLD1 FM	4	12	0
20 June 1952	Harringay 42	Wembley 42	NLD1	4	10	1
28 June 1952	Belle Vue 41	Wembley 43	NLD1	4	9	0
30 June 1952	Wimbledon 43	Wembley 41	Ch	4	10	0
3 July 1952	Wembley 60	West Ham 24	NLD1	4	11	0
5 July 1952	Edinburgh 36	Wembley 48	Ch	4	8	1
10 July 1952	Wembley 61	Harringay 23	NLD1 FM	4	12	0
16 July 1952	New Cross 41	Wembley 43	NLD1 PM	4	11	1
17 July 1952	Wembley 66	Bradford 41	NT PM	6	17	1
24 July 1952	Wembley 62	Bristol 22	NLD1 FM	4	12	0
26 July 1952	Bradford 58 [99]	Wembley 50 [116]	NT	6	9	1
31 July 1952	Wembley 52	Wimbledon 32	NLD1	4	7	3
2 August 1952	Birmingham 55	Wembley 29	NLD1	4	8	0
7 August 1952	Wembley 53	Birmingham 29	NLD1	4	9	2
14 August 1952	WCQR	Jeff Lloyd 14	WCQR	5	13	0
16 August 1952	Birmingham 69	Wembley 39	NT	5	2	0
19 August 1952	West Ham 21	Wembley 63	NLD1 PM	4	12	0
21 August 1952	Wembley 59 [98]	Birmingham 49 [118]	NT	6	15	1
28 August 1952	Wembley 63	Norwich 21	NLD1 DH PM	4	12	0
28 August 1952	Wembley 45	New Cross 39	NLD1 DH	4	11	0
30 August 1952	Bradford 35	Wembley 49	NLD1	4	11	0
4 September 1952	Wembley 40	Harringay 44	NLD1	4	11	0
11 Sept 1952	Wembley 56	Bristol 28	NLD1 DH	4	12	0
15 September 1952	Wimbledon 35	Wembley 49	NLD1	4	8	0
18 Sept 1952	WCF	Jack Young 14	WCF 2nd	5	13	
20 September 1952	Belle Vue 45	Wembley 39	Ch	4	8	0
25 Sept 1952	Wembley 58	West Ham 25	NLD1 DH	4	11	0
25 Sept 1952	Wembley 62	Bradford 22	NLD1 DH PM	4	11	1
26 September 1952	Bristol 37	Wembley 47	NLD1	4	11	0
2 October 1952	Wembley 50	Belle Vue 34	NLD1 FM	4	12	0
3 October 1952	Harringay 36	Wembley 48	NLD1	4	9	1
9 October 1952	Wembley 33	Second Division Stars 21	Ch	3	4	1

1953

				R	P	BP
3 April 1953	Harringay 52	Wembley 31	MC	4	10	0
6 April 1953	Birmingham 37	Wembley 47	Ch FM	4	12	0
9 April 1953	**Wembley 48**	**Norwich 36**	**CC @ Wimbledon**	4	9	1
16 April 1953	**Wembley 39**	**Bradford 45**	**CC @ Wimbledon**	4	4	0
18 April 1950	Birmingham 34	Wembley 50	CC	4	9	0
22 April 1953	New Cross 49	Wembley 35	CC	4	8	0
23 April 1953	**Wembley 40**	**Belle Vue 44**	**CC @ Wimbledon**	4	9	0
25 April 1953	Bradford 55	Wembley 29	CC	4	5	1
2 May 1953	Norwich 47	Wembley 37	CC	4	8	1
7 May 1953	**Wembley 38**	**Harringay 46**	**CC**	4	9	0
14 May 1953	**Wembley 51**	**Wimbledon 33**	**CC**	4	9	0
21 May 1953	**Wembley 54**	**Birmingham 30**	**CC** FM	4	12	0
25 May 1953	Wimbledon 61	Wembley 46	LC	6	14	0
28 May 1953	**Wembley 52 [98]**	**Wimbledon 56 [117]**	**LC**	6	13	0
30 May 1953	Belle Vue 46	Wembley 38	Ch	4	6	1
4 June 1953	**Wembley 51**	**Belle Vue 33**	**NLD1** FM	4	12	0
6 June 1953	West Ham 40	Wembley 44	CC	4	11	0
8 June 1953	Wimbledon 47	Wembley 37	CC	4	7	2
18 June 1953	**Wembley 49**	**West Ham 35**	**CC**	4	7	0
19 June 1953	Bristol 36	Wembley 48	CC	4	11	0
26 June 1953	**Wembley 59**	**Bristol 25**	**CC** FM	4	12	0
27 June 1953	Belle Vue 38	Wembley 46	CC	4	9	0
2 July 1953	**Wembley 59**	**Norwich 25**	**NLD1**	4	12	0
4 July 1953	Bradford 40	Wembley 43	NLD1	4	9	1
9 July 1953	**Wembley 57**	**Birmingham 27**	**NLD1**	4	10	0
16 July 1953	**Wembley 60**	**Harringay 48**	**NT**	6	14	0
18 July 1953	Harringay 40[88]	Wembley 68 [128]	NT	5	5	1
23 July 1953	**Wembley 39.5**	**West Ham 44.5**	**NLD1**	4	12	0
24 July 1953	Leicester 28	Wembley 56	Ch	4	11	1
30 July 1953	**Wembley 59**	**Bradford 25**	**NLD1 DH**	4	11	0
30 July 1953	**Wembley 51**	**Bristol 33**	**NLD1 DH** FM	4	12	0
1 August 1953	Norwich 44	Wembley 39	NLD1	4	11	0
3 August 1953	Wimbledon 42	Wembley 41	NLD1	4	5	0
6 August 1953	**Wembley 78**	**Birmingham 29**	**NT** FM	6	18	0
8 August 1953	Birmingham 62.5	Wembley 45.5	NT	5	5.5	0
20 August 1953	**WCQR**	**Jack Biggs 14**	**WCQR**	5	13	
22 August 1953	Harringay 52	Wembley 32	CC	4	7	0
27 August 1953	**Wembley 58**	**Wimbledon 26**	**NLD1**	4	10	0
3 Sept 1953	**Wembley 50**	**Harringay 34**	**NLD1**	4	11	0
5 Sept 1953	Harringay 33	Wembley 51	NLD1	4	11	0
7 Sept 1953	Wimbledon 68	Wembley 40	NT	4	2	0
10 Sept 1953	**Wembley 66 [106]**	**Wimbledon 42 [110]**	**NT** PM	6	17	1
12 Sept 1953	Belle Vue 42	Wembley 42	NLD1 PM	4	11	1
15 Sept 1953	West Ham 33	Wembley 51	NLD1	4	8	0
17 Sept 1953	**WCF**	**Freddie Williams 14**	**WCF**	5	14	
18 Sept 1953	Bristol 40	Wembley 43	NLD1	4	10	0
26 Sept 1953	Birmingham 46	Wembley 38	NLD1	4	8	0

CC: Coronation Cup.

1954

				R	P	BP
16 April 1954	West Ham 48	Wembley 36	RAC Cup	4	4	1
19 April 1954	Wimbledon 58	Wembley 50	Ch	6	13	1
24 April 1954	Wembley 46	Norwich 37	RAC Cup @ Norwich	4	8	0
1 May 1954	Birmingham 44	Wembley 40	RAC Cup	4	11	0
5 May 1954	Harringay 27	Wembley 57	NLD1	4	9	0
6 May 1954	**Wembley 45**	**Harringay 39**	**NLD1**	**4**	**10**	**1**
8 May 1954	Norwich 47	Wembley 36	RAC Cup	4	8	2
10 May 1954	Wimbledon 43	Wembley 40	NLD1	4	6	0
11 May 1954	West Ham 48	Wembley 35	RAC Cup	4	6	0
13 May 1954	**Wembley 33**	**Wimbledon 51**	**NLD1**	4	8	0
20 May 1954	**Wembley 53**	**Bradford 31**	**NLD1**	4	7	1
22 May 1954	Birmingham 38	Wembley 46	RAC Cup	4	9	1
27 May 1954	**Wembley 65**	**Birmingham 19**	**NLD1** PM	4	11	1
2 June 1954	Harringay 44	Wembley 63	LC SF	6	15	2
3 June 1954	**Wembley 60 [123]**	**Harringay 48 [92]**	**LC SF**	6	14	1
5 June 1954	Bradford 45	Wembley 39	NLD1	4	8	0
10 June 1954	**Wembley 50**	**Norwich 34**	**NLD1**	4	11	0
12 June 1954	Norwich 33	Wembley 51	NLD1	4	9	1
15 June 1954	West Ham 46	Wembley 38	NLD1	4	10	0
17 June 1954	**Wembley 54**	**West Ham 30**	**NLD1**	4	11	0
24 June 1954	**Wembley 67**	**Belle Vue 17**	**NLD1** PM	4	9	3
24 June 1954	Wembley 22	New Zealand Slct 14	SH Ch	2	5	0
26 June 1954	Belle Vue 37	Wembley 46	NLD1	4	7	0
1 July 1954	**Wembley 44**	**Norwich 40**	**NLD1**	4	4	0
7 July 1954	Harringay 30	Wembley 54	NLD1	4	9	1
8 July 1954	**Wembley 53**	**Harringay 31**	**NLD1**	4	9	0
15 July 1954	**Wembley 64**	**Birmingham 20**	**NLD1**	4	9	2
17 July 1954	Belle Vue 25	Wembley 59	NLD1	4	9	1
20 July 1954	West Ham 50	Wembley 58	NT	5	7	0
22 July 1954	**Wembley 70 [128]**	**West Ham 37 [87]**	**NT**	6	14	2
29 July 1954	**Wembley 36**	**Wimbledon 48**	**NLD1**	4	11	0
31 July 1954	Norwich 47	Wembley 37	NLD1	4	6	0
2 August 1954	Wimbledon 43	Wembley 41	NLD1	4	9	0
5 August 1954	**Wembley 63**	**Bradford 44**	**NT SF**	5	9	2
12 August 1954	**Wembley 49**	**West Ham 35**	**NLD1**	4	6	1
19 August 1954	**Wembley 69**	**Wimbledon 38**	**LC F**	6	17	0
21 August 1954	Birmingham 31	Wembley 52	NLD1	4	8	1
26 August 1954	**WCQR**	**Eddie Rigg 14**	**WCQR**	5	14	
28 August 1954	Bradford 63 [107]	Wembley 45 [108]	NT SF	6	10	1
30 August 1954	Wimbledon 47 [85]	Wembley 61 [130]	LC F	5	8	2
2 Sept 1954	**Wembley 51**	**Bradford 33**	**NLD1 DH**	4	8	2
2 Sept 1954	**Wembley 50**	**Belle Vue 34**	**NLD1 DH**	4	11	0
9 Sept 1954	**Wembley 61**	**Norwich 46**	**NT F**	5	8	1
11 Sept 1954	Norwich 46 [92]	Wembley 62 [123]	NT F	5	10	2
16 Sept 1954	**WCF**	**Ronnie Moore 15**	**WCF**	Res	DNR	
18 Sept 1954	Birmingham 32	Wembley 52	NLD1	4	11	0
21 Sept 1954	West Ham 32	Wembley 51	NLD1	4	9	0
2 October 1954	Bradford 52	Wembley 32	NLD1	4	5	2
4 October 1954	Wimbledon 31	Wembley 39	Ch Abandoned	3	8	0

1955

				R	P	BP
8 April 1955	West Ham 43	Wembley 53	Ch	5	6	1
9 April 1955	Belle Vue 49	Wembley 47	Ch	5	9	1
11 April 1955	Wimbledon 48	Wembley 48	Ch	5	7	1
25 April 1955	Wimbledon 49	Wembley 46	NLD1	5	8	0
7 May 1955	Belle Vue 57	Wembley 39	NLD1	5	5	0
9 May 1955	Wimbledon 32 Bradford 6 West Ham 20	Wembley 17 Birmingham 15	Inter-track	4	7	0
10 May 1955	West Ham 46	Wembley 50	NLD1	5	10	1
14 May 1955	Bradford 46	Wembley 50	NLD1	5	5	0
21 May 1955	Birmingham 50	Wembley 45	NLD1	4	4	0
26 May 1955	**Wembley 49**	**Wimbledon 47**	**NLD1**	5	10	0
30 May 1955	Wimbledon 51	Wembley 45	NLD1	4	9	0
2 June 1955	**Wembley 66**	**Norwich 30**	**NLD1**	5	11	1
4 June 1955	Norwich 46	Wembley 50	NLD1	5	6	0
9 June 1955	**Wembley Open**	Barry Briggs	Ind	5	7	
11 June 1955	Bradford 55	Wembley 41	NLD1*	4	6	0
16 June 1955	**Wembley 66**	**Belle Vue 30**	**NLD1** PM	5	12	3
18 June 1955	Birmingham 55	Wembley 41	NLD1	5	5	1
21 June 1955	West Ham 48	Wembley 48	NLD1 FM	5	15	
30 June 1955	**Wembley 68**	**Birmingham 28**	**NLD1**	5	8	0
2 July 1955	Belle Vue 53	Wembley 43	NLD1	4	2	0
7 July 1955	**All Star Trophy**	**Jack Young**	**Ind**	5	12	0
14 July 1955	**Wembley 67**	**Belle Vue 41**	**NT**	6	17	0
16 July 1955	Belle Vue 61 [102]	Wembley 47 [114]	NT	5	5	0
21 July	**Empire Trophy**	**Ronnie Moore**	**Ind Runner up in final**	4	10	
26 July 1955	West Ham 50	Wembley 46	NLD1*			
28 July 1955	**Wembley 50**	**West Ham 46**	**NLD1**	5	9	0
30 July 1955	Bradford 45	Wembley 51	NLD1	5	11	0
1 August 1955	Wimbledon 49	Wembley 46	NLD1*	5	11	2
4 August 1955	**Wembley 63**	**Wimbledon 45**	**NT SF**	6	13	2
11 August 1955	**WCQR**	**Brian Crutcher 14**	**WC**	5	12	
13 August 1955	Norwich 51	Wembley 45	NLD1	5	6	0
15 August 1955	Wimbledon 61 [106]	Wembley 47 [110]	NT SF	3	0	0
18 August 1955	**Handicap Trophy**	**Gerald Jackson**	**Ind**	2	1	
23 August 1955	West Ham 58	Wembley 38	Ch			
25 August 1955	**Wembley 61**	**Bradford 35**	**NLD1**	5	6	1
1 Sept 1955	**Wembley 67**	**Wimbledon 40**	**Ch**	5	7	1
3 September 1955	Belle Vue 57	Wembley 38	NLD1*	4	4	1
8 September 1955	**Wembley 43**	**Norwich 64**	**NT F**	5	6	0
10 September 1955	Birmingham 53	Wembley 43	NLD1*	2	1	0
12 September 1955	Wimbledon 77	Wembley 31	Ch	4	1	0
17 September 1955	Norwich 45 [109]	Wembley 63 [106]	NT F	4	5	1
24 September 1955	Norwich 42	Wembley 54	NLD1*	5	4	0
1 October 1955	Swindon 29	Wembley 67	Ch	5	10	3

* Wembley home league fixtures moved to opponent's track.

1956

				R	P	BP
Saturday 31 March 1956	Belle Vue 45	Wembley 39	Ch	4	7	1
Monday 2 April 1956	Wimbledon 61.5	Wembley 46.5	Ch	5	6	1
Saturday 14 April 1956	Norwich 42	Wembley 42	NLD1	4	3	1
Saturday 28 April 1956	Odsal 32	Wembley 52	NLD1	4	6	0
Saturday 5 May 1956	Birmingham 33	Wembley 50	NLD1	3	1	1
Monday 15 May 1956	Poole 55	Wembley 29	NLD1	2	0	0
Monday 21 May 1956	Wimbledon 48	Wembley 36	NLD1	4	3	1
Thursday 17 May 1956	**Wembley 38**	**Wimbledon 46**	**NLD1**	4	4	0
Thursday 24 May 1956	**Wembley 50**	**Birmingham 33**	**NLD1**	4	8	1
Thursday 31 May 1956	**Wembley 61**	**Belle Vue 23**	**NLD1**	3	5	1
Thursday 7 June 1956	**Wembley 57**	**Odsal 27**	**NLD1**	4	8	2
Saturday 9 June 1956	Belle Vue 54	Wembley 30	NLD1	2	0	0

South Africa domestic meetings 1953–54

At Wembley	**Pretoria 40**	Springs 38	FW 12 (debut)
13/11/53	Welcome Trophy at Wembley	FW 15	
20/11/53	Springs 44	**Pretoria 40**	FW 11
3/12/53	**Pretoria 42**	Randfontein 41	FW 12
4/12/53	Wembley 46	**Pretoria 38**	FW 10
5/12/53	Randfontein 39	**Pretoria 45**	FW 10
17/12/53	**Pretoria 47**	Wembley 36 at Randfontein	FW 12
19/12/53	Durban 33	**Pretoria 50**	FW 12
2/1/54	Wembley 44	**Pretoria 40**	FW 11
	Springs 45	**Pretoria 39**	FW 11
	Springs 42	**Pretoria 42**	FW 12
13/2/54	British Empire Best Pairs	FW 12 & IW 8 =20 (runners up)	

South Africa domestic meetings 1955

Springs 45	**Durban 36**	FW 8
Wembley 42	**Durban 40**	FW 7
Randfontein 39	**Durban 41**	FW 9
100 Guineas Trophy:	R Genz 15	FW 11 (third)
Randfontein 40	**Durban 38**	FW 10
SA Open Championship @ Wembley	Trevor Redmond won	FW 12 (joint 4th)
League Play-off		
Springs 54	**Durban 53**	FW 14
Durban 56 [109]	Springs 51 [105]	

Ireland meetings 1951 at Chapelizod

Freddie Williams team 50	Split Waterman team 34	FW 11
Dublin Eagles 42	Bristol 41	FW 7
Dublin Eagles 44	Odsal 39	FW 6
Dublin Eagles 38	Bill Kitchen team 40	FW 10
Dublin Eagles 44	Walthamstow 40	FW 11
Dublin Eagles 42	Abernethy Select 30	FW 11

Bibliography

Books
75 Years of Speedway in South Africa by Christian Weber (published on the internet)
A History of the Speedway Ashes by Peter Foster (Tempus Publishing Ltd 2005)
A History of the Speedway World Championship by Robert Bamford & Glynn Shailes (Tempus Publishing Ltd 2002)
And God Created Richard by Tom Rubython (The Myrtle Press, 2014)
Coming Speedway Stars 1949 (Speedway World)
Heathens – Cradley Heath Speedway 1947–1976 by Peter Foster (Tempus Publishing Ltd 2002)
Speedway in Wales by Andrew Weltch (Tempus Publishing Ltd 2002)
Speedway Star Digest 1961, 1962, 1963
Stenner's Speedway Annual 1948, 1949, 1950, 1951, 1952, 1953, 1954.
Stenner's Speedway Journal Autumn & Winter 1948
Swindon Speedway by Robert Bamford (Tempus Publishing Ltd 2005)
The Actors' Crucible by Angela V. John (Parthian Books 2015)
The Eric Williams Stories (various) by Eric Williams and Ross Garrigan (published on the internet)
Wales 1880 to 1980 by Kenneth O. Morgan
When the Lions roared by Peter Lush & John Chaplin (London League Publications Ltd 2016)

Magazines
Classic Speedway
South African Speedway Monthly
Speedway Gazette
Speedway News
Speedway Star
Speedway World
The Broadsider
Vintage Speedway Magazine

Newspapers
Daily Express
Daily Mail
Daily Mirror
Evening Standard
Port Talbot Guardian
Sunday Dispatch
Wembley News
Western Mail

Websites
International Speedway
Speedway Researcher

Various speedway match programmes.

"Here we are folks, after many months of being stuck to my computer keyboard, I finally finished my autobiography having bashed out every word, dot and comma along the way. It covers my early days growing up in Glasgow, to cycle speedway, road racing, speedway and life after I had hung up my white boots and tartan leathers. This is the story of a wandering Speedway Scotsman and I hope that you enjoy it."

Bert Harkins

Published in February 2018 @ £14.95

Order direct from the publishers: London League Publications Ltd, for just £14.50 post free in the UK. Visit www.llpshop.co.uk for credit card orders or write to (cheques payable to London League Publications Ltd): PO Box 65784, London NW2 9NS. Also available on Amazon and Abe Books, and as an E-Book on Amazon for Kindle.
Or order from any bookshop. ISBN: 9781909885165. 252 pages with lots of photos.